The True Face of Jehadis

Amir Mir, former editor of the *Weekly Independent*, is among Pakistan's foremost investigative journalists. His writings on Islamic militant groups, and their links with the country's military and intelligence establishment, have repeatedly drawn the ire of the Musharraf government in Pakistan.

Amir Mir did his MA in Political Science from the University of the Punjab, Lahore. He began his career in 1988 with the *Frontier Post*, and has since written for many newspapers and magazines in Pakistan as well as abroad, including *The News, The Nation, The Friday Times, Monthly Herald, Newsline, Gulf News, Arab News, Outlook, Tehelka* and the *Asia Intelligence Service*. He is currently affiliated with *Newsline* and the Spanish News Agency EFE, and is also the bureau chief of *Gulf News* in Lahore.

Other Lotus Titles:

Aitzaz Ahsan	*The Indus Saga: The Making of Pakistan*
Alam Srinivas	*Storms in the Sea Wind: Ambani vs Ambani*
Chaman Nahal	*Silent Life: Memoirs of a Writer*
Duff Hart-Davis	*Honorary Tiger: The Life of Billy Arjan Singh*
Namita Bhandare (ed.)	*India and the World: A Blueprint for Partnership and Growth*
Frank Simoes	*Frank Unedited*
Frank Simoes	*Frank Simoes' Goa*
M.G. Devasahayam	*J.P. in Jail: An Uncensored Account*
M.J. Akbar	*India: The Siege Within*
M.J. Akbar	*Kashmir: Behind the Vale*
M.J. Akbar	*Nehru: The Making of India*
M.J. Akbar	*Riot after Riot*
M.J. Akbar	*The Shade of Swords*
M.J. Akbar	*Byline*
Meghnad Desai	*Nehru's Hero: Dilip Kumar In the Life of India*
Nayantara Sahgal (ed.)	*Before Freedom: Nehru's Letters to His Sister*
Rohan Gunaratna	*Inside Al Qaeda*
Maj. Gen. Ian Cardozo	*Param Vir: Our Heroes in Battle*
Maj. R.P. Singh, Kanwar Rajpal Singh	*Sawai Man Singh II of Jaipur: Life and Legend*
Mushirul Hasan	*India Partitioned. 2 Vols*
Mushirul Hasan	*John Company to the Republic*
Mushirul Hasan	*Knowledge Power and Politics*
Neesha Mirchandani	*Wisdom Song: The Life of Baba Amte*
Rachel Dwyer	*Yash Chopra: Fifty Years of Indian Cinema*
Satish Jacob	*From Hotel Palestine Baghdad*
Shrabani Basu	*Spy Princess: The Life of Noor Inayat Khan*
Veena Sharma	*Kailash Mansarovar: A Sacred Journey*
Verghese Kurien as told to Gouri Salvi	*I Too Had a Dream*
Vijaypat Singhania	*An Angel in the Cockpit*

Forthcoming Titles:

Bhawana Somayya	*Hema Malini: An Authorised Biography*
Salma Ahmed	*Cutting Free: An Autobiography*

The True Face of Jehadis

Inside Pakistan's Network of Terror

Amir Mir

LOTUS COLLECTION
ROLI BOOKS

Lotus Collection

© Amir Mir 2006
All rights reserved. No part of this publication may be reproduced or transmitted, in any form or by any means, without the prior permission of the publisher.

First published in Pakistan by Mashal Books in 2004
First published in India by Roli Books in 2006
Second impression 2006
The Lotus Collection
An imprint of
Roli Books Pvt. Ltd.
M-75, G.K. II Market
New Delhi 110 048
Phones: ++91 (011) 2921 2271, 2921 2782
2921 0886, Fax: ++91 (011) 2921 7185
E-mail: roli@vsnl.com; Website: rolibooks.com
Also at
Bangalore, Varanasi, Mumbai and Jaipur

Cover design: Arati Subramanyam
Layout: Kumar Raman

ISBN: 81-7436-430-7
Rs 395/-

Typeset in Minion by Roli Books Pvt. Ltd. and printed at Syndicate Binders, Noida (U.P.)

In memory of my father
Professor Waris Mir

Contents

	Foreword	ix
1	The Rise of Militant Islam in Pakistan	1
2	Jehadis vs the General: Friends Turned Foes	11
3	Pakistan Army: Islamists vs Reformists	23
4	Daniel Pearl's Murder: A Major Blow to Jehadis	37
5	Jaish-e-Mohammad in Disarray	45
6	Who Masterminded the December 1999 Indian Airlines Hijacking?	55
7	Lashkar-e-Toiba: Optimism Over the Future of Jehad	61
8	Harkatul Mujahideen: Its New Face of Terror	73
9	Hizbul Mujahideen: Determined to Defy	85
10	Jamaat-e-Islami: On the FBI watchlist	97
11	Tableeghi Jamaat: Nurturing Jehadis?	101
12	Dawood Ibrahim: Financing Militants?	105
13	Sectarian Monster Haunts Pakistan	113
14	Sipah-e-Sahaba: The Sectarian Soldiers	119

15	Lashkar-e-Jhangvi: The Group of Choice for Hard-core Militants	127
16	The Mullah–Military Alliance	135
17	Musharraf's Half-hearted Madrassa Reforms	141
18	Injecting Jehad Via Textbooks	151
19	Is al-Qaeda Becoming Stronger?	157
20	Taliban: Still Alive and Robust	177
21	Osama bin Laden: A CIA Creation	187
22	Ayman al-Zawahiri: The Brain Behind bin Laden	201
23	Mullah Mohammad Omar: One-eyed Commander	207
24	Khalid Sheikh Mohammad: The 9/11 Mastermind	215
25	Was the Pakistan Air Force Chief Murdered?	223
26	WTC Bombing, Ramzi Yusuf and Pakistan	229
27	Lt. Gen. Mahmood Ahmad and the 9/11 Attacks	233
28	The 9/11 Commission and Pakistan	243
29	Fugitives vs the Federal Bureau of Investigation	251
30	The 7/7 London Attacks, Suicide Bombers, and the Pakistani Connection	257
31	The Terror Charities	271
32	Waziristan Operation: Osama Still at Large	279
33	Is General Musharraf a Liberal or a Jehadi?	293

Bibliography   299
Index   301

Foreword

PAKISTAN'S TWO BLOWBACKS

Mercenaries and auxiliaries are useless and dangerous. For mercenaries are disunited, thirsty for power, undisciplined and disloyal; they are brave among their friends and cowards before the enemy. In peacetime you are despoiled by them and in wartime by the enemy. Mercenary commanders [cannot be trusted] because they are anxious to advance their own greatness, either by coercing you, or by coercing others against your wishes. Experience has shown that only armed princes and republics achieve solid success, and that mercenaries bring nothing but loss.

Machiavelli in *The Prince*

Pakistan has become what it has because of the consequences of two covert wars it took part in. The first war, under General Zia ul Haq, was against the Soviet Union in Afghanistan from 1980 to 1988; and the second was the civil war in Afghanistan and the jehad in Kashmir from 1990 to approximately 2001. The first blowback (or rebound) from the Afghan war brought about a change in the internal situation in Pakistan, in the form of the creation of new centres of power: certain sections of the Pakistan Army, which handled the Afghan war, became more influential because of the spread of their power within civilian institutions.[1] Because of the instrumentalization of Islam, the state began to lose a larger measure of internal sovereignty than was justified by the prosecution of Afghan jehad through non-state actors. The political process in Pakistan suffered the consequences of this blowback when it recommenced after the death of General Zia in 1988.

The chaos that characterized the decade of the 1990s can only be understood in the context of the first blowback. The disorder of the post-2001 period, however, can be understood in the context of the second blowback: the consequence of the Afghan civil war and the jehad in Kashmir. The decade of the 1990s saw the weakening of the political process because the Pakistani state's internal sovereignty was compromised in favour of the non-state actors, which were training in Afghanistan and fighting in Kashmir. Ironically, the decade also saw the weakening of the military leadership in Pakistan because army chiefs began to be selected on the basis of promotions, which were meant to sideline officers with a zeal for jehad or holy war. Although the army was not directly involved in the fighting, a large number of its officers were 'contaminated' by the 'Islamic warrior' image of the Afghan mujahideen. At least two chiefs of Inter Services Intelligence (ISI) were reverse-indoctrinated into the paranoid world-view of, first, Gulbaddin Hekmatyar, and then the Taliban leadership in Kandahar.

The jehad in Afghanistan and in Kashmir were both covert, and, by and large, their effect on Pakistan's civil society went unrecorded. Because of the weakness of the political process in the face of jehad, the massive public indoctrination in favour of the jehadis went on unchallenged. The immunity from prosecution under the penal code, offered to the jehadi organizations by the ISI, added the element of fear in the public mind in addition to the ongoing indoctrination. This led to what can only be described as a massive brainwash of the Pakistani public that merged with the jehadi propaganda, the mission statement of Pakistani nationalism as it had evolved after 1947.

Surrender of internal sovereignty to the private warriors led to a steep fall in the quality of law and order in the country, even as Islam was used as a force to undermine the state in national politics. Youth from all strata of society joined the jehad, took guerrilla training in the camps run by the jehadi organizations funded with Arab money, and swelled the ranks of those that challenged the state's credentials. Society fell back to the tribalism it had partially grown out of in the years when the state still enjoyed internal sovereignty and was able to enforce the municipal law uniformly.

General Pervez Musharraf was elevated to his rank as the army chief by a prime minister (Nawaz Sharif) who had in the past supported the Islamist officers in the army but who had grown to fear the de-legitimizing nature of their faith. Musharraf was like the past chiefs who had suffered because of the mismatch between their world-view and the Islamist mindset nurtured in the Pakistan Army, especially under General Zia ul Haq. When time came to change the jehad (read foreign policy) paradigm, Musharraf's job of 'the great repudiator' was rendered difficult by the Islamist officers who flanked him and by a society, which was by now deeply influenced by the rhetoric of jehad.

General Musharraf's rule coincides with the era of Pakistan's second blowback. In other words, Pakistan is facing the consequences of its actions in the decade of the 1990s: repudiation of the Durand Line through the doctrine of 'strategic depth' and the alienation it engendered in the region to the west of Pakistan, including China in the north; surrender of internal sovereignty to the jehadi organizations that proliferated under the dominant Deobandi and Ahle Hadith confessions; culmination of the policy of 'highlighting' Kashmir in the 1999 Kargil Operation fiasco; and the international perception of jehad as terrorism.

Pakistan has not studied the events of the second blowback. Its intelligence agencies, now required to investigate the very phenomenon that they have helped create, have proved remarkably incapable of understanding it. The national press had developed the habit of not investigating the jehadi militias in the 1990s because of the surrender of internal sovereignty to them by the state (which included safeguarding the right of journalists to report freely and fairly on jehadi activities). The ISI was supposed to have interacted with intelligence agencies of other states, but very little evidence of this kind of activity came to the fore after 2000.

The foreign terrorists were able to hide in Pakistan easily because information about them from their Arab home states was not available. This information became public when some of the intelligence agents of the West published material gained by them from the Arab intelligence agencies.[2] Even after the publication of this information, the element of 'surprise' remained constant in Pakistan, indicating that the ISI was not collating and interpreting this information. The Pakistani press had internalized the gag regime of the mujahideen and now reacted negatively to the revelations. Together with the intelligence agencies, it simply ignored the in-house publications of the various militias engaged in Pakistan's covert wars.

Amir Mir is perhaps the only Pakistani journalist who has made an effort to bring together the published and unpublished information about the jehadi personalities in Pakistan linked to al-Qaeda. He has also juxtaposed the information published abroad and the data available in Pakistan from the heretofore-ignored jehadi publications. In *The True Face of Jehadis*, Amir Mir has produced a mosaic of information based on what has come to light from sources in the Arab world, as communicated by the journalists and intelligence agents of the West; and what has appeared as deadpan news in the Pakistani press.

This kind of work was needed in Pakistan, not so much for the benefit of the common reader as for intelligence agencies now charged with apprehending the terrorists trying to kill President General Pervez Musharraf at the behest of al-Qaeda's Dr Aiman al-Zawahiri. Sadly, the common (Pakistani) reader will be offended by this information because he too, like the Pakistani press, has internalized the surrender of internal sovereignty to the jehadi militias during the 1990s. There is evidence that the Pakistani intelligence agencies, especially the ISI, after the initial shock, have not reconciled to the revelations made in the writings of journalists like Amir Mir. He has not been treated very nicely after he reported certain unpleasant facts, but this book will clarify the nature of the role he is actually playing.

The most lethal aspect of the second blowback has been the effect it has had on the mindset of the Pakistani people. They are in a state of denial about what actually transpired in the decade of the 1990s. Deep alienation, with the West in general and the United States in particular, has made the task of disabusing the collective consciousness of the fantasy of jehad difficult and dangerous. Yet there is a crying need to examine all the sources of information available on what may be called Pakistan's twenty years of meta-history. Amir Mir's inclusion of such authors as Gerald Posner and Bernard Henri-Lévy (BHL) in his book highlights the risk he is running by studying sources that Pakistan has already rejected without reading.

The first author calls into question the conclusion reached by an official inquiry into the death of Pakistan Air Force chief, Air Marshall Mushaf Ali Mir, in 2003. Because of the clash between what is official in Pakistan and what Posner claims he found out from the interrogation of Abu Zubaydah in the United States, his version is still taboo in Pakistan. Yet the reality is that Posner's story is available to the world and there is nothing Pakistan can do about it. Bernard Henri-Lévy's case is even worse because he has been found to be careless and partisan in his confessedly 'novelized' investigation of Daniel Pearl's murder in Karachi.[3] But there is much in Henri-Lévy's book that may be useful, especially in his treatment of the Indian plane hijack that freed Pakistan's arch-jehadi Maulana Masood Azhar. Pakistan has seen translations of another bestselling French author challenging the fact of the 9/11 attacks.[4] Compared to it, Henri-Lévy reads like a laundry list.

The chapter based on Pepe Escobar's piece in Asia Times online, *9/11 and the Smoking Gun* carries details that will not be received well by the official circles in Pakistan. Amir Mir is not judgmental in his discussion: he simply introduces the investigative report and puts together the story of General Mahmood Ahmad's acceptance of American Deputy Secretary of State, Richard Armitage's, offer of 'conditions' to Pakistan when he was stuck in Washington after 11 September 2001. The details concerning the relationship between the convicted terrorist Sheikh Ahmed Omar Saeed and the ISI chief General Mahmood Ahmad has been mentioned by many reports emanating from the West, which are present in this book too.

The conclusion drawn by Pepe Escobar that the ISI got the Tajik-Afghan leader Ahmad Shah Masood killed has been challenged by other sources, but Amir Mir's task has been simply to record all that has been said and written outside Pakistan.[5] Nor is there anything wrong in laying out the details of General Musharraf's conversations with the US ambassador in Pakistan and others, as revealed by interviews given by the general himself to various news channels and magazines.

The ISI–al Qaeda connections highlighted in the book are likewise mined by the author from the thirty-two vital documents declassified by the US State Department on the second anniversary of 9/11. This material seems to support the position taken by General Pervez Musharraf that Pakistan had limited influence among the Taliban and could not persuade the Taliban's supreme commander, Mullah Mohammad Omar, to help capture Osama bin Laden.

As if to balance the earlier sources, Amir Mir takes account of Steve Coll's indictment of the American policy of supporting the Afghan fundamentalists against the Soviet Union in his book *Ghost Wars: The Secret History of CIA, Afghanistan and Bin Laden: From Soviet Invasion to September 10, 2001*. The chapter substantiates his belief that Osama bin Laden emerged from the jehad created by the United States with the help of its two allies, Saudi Arabia and Pakistan. He ends with the June 2004 report of the 9/11 National Commission, which says that Pakistan benefited from the Osama-Taliban relationship because of the trained warriors it provided for its covert low-intensity Kashmir war. The bipartisan commission's praise of Pakistan as an ally against terrorism is in fact a proof of General Pervez Musharraf's successful stewardship of Pakistan's post-9/11 strategy.

The True Face of Jehadis gives us important details of Pakistan's second blowback confronting the government of General Pervez Musharraf. The first one we have more or less refused to analyse, saying the Americans were responsible for it; but the second one is difficult to pin on the Americans. This is not a book of analysis or opinion; it simply puts together the mosaic of reportage in such a way that it creates a narrative that might yield grounds for analysis. This should offend no one.

Khaled Ahmed
Lahore

---

[1] Although the Inter-Services Intelligence (ISI) officers were drawn from the army, their role at the battlefront and their financial autonomy delinked them from the army. Their ability to 'get things done' in the enemy territory as well as within Pakistan changed their view of the army. Under General Zia, the ISI virtually ran the country internally as well as its foreign policy. In 1990, the ISI officers were caught trying to overthrow their own prime minister. After being sacked from the army, they were inducted into the civilian Intelligence Bureau (IB). COAS General Asif Nawaz had to confront the IB as his rival. He complained to the President that he was being threatened by the IB. Similar confrontation was at one time reported between the Military Intelligence (MI) and the ISI. It was in fact a confrontation between the 'warrior' officers in the ISI and the 'professional' COAS. The IB was able to induct a 'religious warrior' general into the ISI

as its chief. A retired ISI chief, who had missed becoming COAS, dared the army chief to take action against him for making statements against the 'secularization' of the army. The most symbolic incident was the sabotage of a decision taken during the Afghan war by the COAS, together with the president and the PM, by a retired ISI chief.

[2] Jason Burke, *Al Qaeda: Casting a Shadow of Terror*, I.B. Tauris (2003): Agencies in Pakistan seemed clueless about a very important al Qaeda personality, Abu Zubaydah. When he was caught in Faisalabad after a shootout, no one in Pakistan knew how important the catch was. Another capture in Karachi of Ramzi bin al-Shibh, an important member of the Hamburg Cell, also drew a blank. If the government in Islamabad knew about him it pretended not to know. It is quite clear that Pakistan remains blocked from information gained by Western writers from Arab intelligence agencies and al Qaeda members being questioned in custody in the United States. In his book *Sleeping with the Devil*, the ex-CIA operative, Robert Baer, links the Saudi ruling family to the activities of the al Qaeda. A decorated officer, Baer revealed some of his findings in an article *The Fall of the House of Saud* published in *The Atlantic Monthly* of May 2003. The man who blew up the Egyptian embassy in 1995 in Pakistan was Ayman al-Zawahiri, whom Lawrence Wright has profiled in *The New Yorker* (16 September 2002) under the title *The Man Behind bin Laden*. There is little information available in the Pakistani media about the terrorists – from Muhammad Atta to Hambali – and Pakistani writers have to find their leads in the books and articles of Western writers. The denial and the trauma among Pakistani citizens springs from this deficit of information about terrorism, which then becomes a great obstacle in the way of a Pakistani government trying to get rid of terrorist cells in the country. Most of the information on which anti-terrorist operations are based comes from outside Pakistan.

[3] William Dalrymple, *Murder in Karachi*, review in *The New York Review of Books*, 4 December 2003: Talking about Bernard Henri-Lévy's book he says, 'The book's principal problem is the amateurish quality of much of Lévy's research. The section on the English childhood of Omar Sheikh begins raising one's doubts about the author's veracity: Omar Sheikh's family live, we are told, on Colvin Street, which does not exist on the London A–Z street atlas. Once we arrive in Pakistan the factual underpinnings of the book fall away. BHL's grasp of South Asian geography is especially shaky: he thinks Muzaffarabad, the capital of Pakistani-held Kashmir (and the major jehadi centre on Pakistani soil), is in India. The madrassa, or religious school, of Akora Khattack, not far from the Indus, he thinks is in Peshawar (it is more than eighty miles outside), while the town of Saharanpur, four hours' drive from the Indian capital, is said to be a remote part of Delhi ... Contrary to what Lévy attempts to prove, it is most improbable that the ISI had a direct hand in Pearl's abduction and murder; but equally it is highly unlikely that Omar Sheikh, widely known to be a violent extremist, was living in Pakistan without the knowledge and support of Pakistani intelligence. Sheikh may well have had links with the ISI since his student days in London; he was certainly connected with its officials after he joined the militant Islamist group Harkatul Mujahideen, which was active in Kashmir and almost certainly backed by the ISI.'

[4] Thierry Meyssan, *L'Effroyable Imposture* (*The Frightening Fraud*): French left-wing

activist Thierry Meyssan comes to the conclusion that the Pentagon was *not* hit by American Airlines Flight 77.

[5] Jason Burke (as above) notes that in 2001 it was Osama's deputy, Ayman al Zawahiri, who wrote out a request to Ahmad Shah Massoud to grant an interview to a Moroccan journalist. The French-speaking Arab journalists were in fact both Tunisian and one of them had explosives tied to his stomach. These suicide bombers blew up Massoud two days before the attack on the World Trade Center.

[6] Although the Inter-Services Intelligence (ISI) officers were drawn from the army, their role at the battlefront and their financial autonomy de-linked them from the army. Their ability to 'get things done' in the enemy territory as well as within Pakistan changed their view of the army. Under General Zia, the ISI virtually ran the country internally as well as its foreign policy. In 1990, the ISI officers were caught trying to overthrow their own prime minister. After being sacked from the army, they were inducted into the civilian Intelligence Bureau (IB). COAS General Asif Nawaz had to confront the IB as his rival. He complained to the President that he was being threatened by the IB. Similar confrontation was at one time reported between the Military Intelligence (MI) and the ISI. It was in fact a confrontation between the 'warrior' officers in the ISI and the 'professional' COAS. The IB was able to induct a 'religious warrior' general into the ISI as its chief. A retired ISI chief, who had missed becoming COAS, dared the army chief to take action against him for making statements against the 'secularization' of the army. The most symbolic incident was the sabotage of a decision taken during the Afghan war by the COAS, together with the president and the PM, by a retired ISI chief.

1
The Rise of Militant Islam in Pakistan

After the end of the Cold War, militant Islam – with its emphasis on jehad or holy war against the infidels (non-Muslims) – came to be seen as the single most important security threat in the West. This version of Islam also posed serious challenges to the authority of the state in many Muslim countries. This was specially so in Pakistan which had emerged as a major breeding ground of Islamic militants during the war against the Soviet occupation of Afghanistan.

In the closing years of the 1980s, these militant and extremist groups – whose violent outlook and philosophy have little to do with the actual teachings of Islam – emerged as among the most virulent international terrorist organizations. Till the 1980s religion in Pakistan was, largely, confined to an individual's private realm. While deeply ingrained in the national psyche, it was kept separate from the day-to-day functioning of the state and the life of the general public. However, with the promulgation of martial law by General Zia ul Haq in 1977 the clergy became increasingly powerful, and in the years that followed, Pakistan became the chief patron and promoter of Islamic militancy.

Islamabad's open and official association with Islamist politics began with General Zia ul Haq's coup against Zulfiqar Ali Bhutto's government in 1977, and it was during his rule that narrow and bigoted religiosity became Pakistan's state policy. In order to gain legitimacy for his rule and to develop close relations with Muslim countries, especially oil-rich Saudi Arabia, Zia ul Haq projected himself as a champion of Islam and his country as the citadel of Islam. The Soviet military intervention in Afghanistan provided him with an opportunity to declare that Islam was in danger in Kabul and jehad should be waged to expel the 'infidel' troops from Afghanistan.

On the domestic front, Zia ul Haq sought the political support of the mullahs for his illegitimate dictatorial regime as he had no other political base. Meanwhile, in the United States, the Central Intelligence Agency (CIA) was ordered to organize and finance Islamic resistance groups against the Soviet occupation troops in Afghanistan. Soon the CIA, in cooperation with the Pakistani state, began organizing armed religious groups there. Under the CIA's supervision, thousands of volunteers from various parts of the world were sent across the Pak-Afghan border to fight the Soviet troops.

China, Saudi Arabia and many other Muslim countries also poured in huge resources in the form of men, material and money to organize resistance to the Soviet forces. Thousands of the Afghan refugees who had taken shelter in Pakistan were recruited as mujahideen (guerilla soldiers engaged in a jehad). By the 1980s, a sophisticated, well-equipped infrastructure to train militant Islamists was available to the Zia regime. The CIA then asked the Inter Services Intelligence (ISI), Pakistan's premier intelligence agency, to oversee the mujahideen operations and provide them with advice and support.

The Zia ul Haq regime was so deeply committed to the Afghan jehad that it even used commandos from the Pakistani army's Special Services Group (SSG) to guide the guerilla operations in Afghanistan. According to careful estimates, the

ISI trained about 85,000 Afghan mujahideen during the Afghan war. As a result, its expertise and capability to conduct covert action improved significantly. A number of officers from the ISI's Covert Action Division received training in the US and many covert action experts of the CIA were attached to the ISI to guide it in its guerilla operations against the Soviet troops, using the Afghan mujahideen and Islamic fundamentalists from Pakistan. The Afghan war soon brought together militants from all over the Muslim world and Afghanistan was turned into a training ground for these fighters. While acting as the frontline state in the Afghan war, Pakistan assumed a supervisory role in training mujahideen. These included a large number of Muslim youth from countries in the Middle East who were desirous of participating in the jehad.

This was bound to revive the idea of Pan-Islamism that lay buried under the debris of the Khilafat movement (the movement from 1919-1924 amongst the Muslims of British India to ensure that the British did not abolish the Caliphate, then claimed by the Ottoman emperor of Turkey) and Gen. Zia ul Haq was there to patronize the idea as he increasingly relied on obscurantist elements for political support. The Pakistani religious parties did not lag far behind in providing volunteers for the Afghan civil war. A large number of training camps were set up along the Pak-Afghan border to impart religious indoctrination and military training to these volunteers.

Following the withdrawal of the Soviet occupation forces from Afghanistan in 1989, the CIA also withdrew from the region. What remained was a huge force of highly motivated, militarily trained, Islamic militants who were now looking for new pastures. As there was no dearth of funds from domestic as well as foreign sources, Pakistan had at its disposal all the means required for the promotion and sustenance of Islamic militancy and, in the process, realize its aim of becoming one of the leaders of the Islamic world.

During the Afghan war, the ISI had especially favoured the Hizb-e-Islami which is led by the Pushtun leader Gulbuddin Hekmatyar, hoping that once in power Hekmatyar would protect and promote Islamabad's strategic interests. However, following the withdrawal of the Soviet troops, and later, even after the fall of the pro-soviet Mohammad Najibullah government in 1992, Hekmatyar was unable to seize power in Kabul. The ISI then devised a plan to raise the Taliban militia as an alternative to Hekmatyar's Hizb-e-Islami. Initially, a majority of the Afghan youth constituting the Taliban militia came from Maulana Fazlur Rahman's Jamiat Ulema-e-Islam-run *deeni madrassas* (religious seminaries) in the Frontier and Baluchistan provinces of Pakistan (both of which border Afghanistan). A major chunk of the Taliban leadership as well as its soldiers actually came from two schools – Darul Uloom set up by Maulana Abdul Haq at Akora Khattak and the Binori chain of madrassa established by Maulana Mohammad Yousaf Binori, with its headquarters in Binori town in Karachi.

At least three of the Taliban's six-member governing council and some of its top military commanders were products of either the Binori town madrassa or one of its affiliated schools scattered all over Pakistan. Sunni fundamentalists to the core and highly motivated, many militiamen of the Taliban had taken part in the Afghan war and, after the withdrawal of the Soviet forces, had returned to their seminaries. It was from among them that Pakistan's former interior minister Maj. Gen. (retd) Naseerullah Khan Babar, acting in unison with the ISI, recruited and raised the Taliban militia in the Spin Boldak area of Kandahar in Afghanistan. Six months before the emergence of the Taliban, camps were set up by Pakistan's Frontier Corps to train them. They were then sent to fight against the local Afghan warlords.

In 1994, the Taliban forces gained control over the Kandahar and Herat regions in Afghanistan. Their drive culminated in the occupation of Kabul in September 1996 after they forced

Burhanuddin Rabbani's government and his supporters to flee to the north, thus bringing nearly two-thirds of Afghanistan under their control. Thus was the Taliban militia of hardline Sunni Muslims catapulted to power in Afghanistan. This highly motivated force of young Afghan fighters was trained, armed, funded, equipped and guided by Pakistan's ISI.

After the Soviet withdrawal from Afghanistan, the new agenda for thousands of Pakistani militants became the 'liberation' of Indian administered Kashmir (Jammu & Kashmir or J&K). By the end of 1989, most of the Pakistan-based jehadi groups and veterans of the Afghan war were joining the jehad in Kashmir. What had begun as an indigenous and secular movement for liberation, soon became an increasingly Islamist crusade to bring all of Kashmir under Pakistani control. Within a couple of years many Pakistan-based militant groups, especially the Hizbul Mujahideen (HM), gained greater prominence and significance as compared to the Jammu & Kashmir Liberation Front and other secular Kashmiri groups that believed in achieving their goals through political means.

By 1992, the ISI was said to be operating thirteen permanent, eighteen temporary and eight joint military training camps for the Kashmiri youth, and some 3,800 Kashmiri militants were being trained in those camps. By the beginning of 1993 an estimated 20,000 young Kashmiris had been trained and armed by Pakistan to fight the Indian forces in J&K. In early 1995 Pakistani officials reportedly estimated that at least 10,000 Islamic militants (besides those of Kashmiri origin) had been trained on the Pak–Afghan border since the end of the Afghan war in 1989. At the end of 1995, it was reported that the ISI, in collaboration with the Jamaat-e-Islami – Pakistan's oldest religio-political party, which subscribes to a fundamentalist Islamic ideology – was raising a Taliban-type force comprising young students from Pakistan with the sole purpose of fighting Indian forces in J&K.

In the process, however, Pakistan became a base and a transit point for many militant groups active in various parts of the world. The fallout of Pakistani military establishment's policy of nursing, promoting and sponsoring Islamic militancy is patently evident. Even after a lapse of fifteen years since the end of the Afghan war, Islamabad is struggling hard to control the jehadi monster it has created. Analysts, therefore, see the General Pervez Musharraf–led government's anti-jehadi drive as a sign of its growing nervousness at the threats posed by the radical Islamists to Pakistan's 'vital national interests'.

Some strict anti-jehadi measures taken by General Musharraf coupled with his efforts towards making peace with India, have infuriated thousands of Islamic militants who spent the past decade and a half in waging a so-called jehad against 'enemy troops' in Jammu & Kashmir. Even before the Islamabad agreement was signed by Musharraf and Atal Bihari Vajpayee in January 2004, most of the Pakistani militant groups had discounted Musharraf's offer to New Delhi of Islamabad's readiness to drop its demand for a plebiscite in the disputed territory of J&K and to resolve the issue by 'meeting somewhere halfway'.

To them, the only solution to the lingering Kashmir dispute is its immediate handover to Pakistan. Thousands of militants belonging to various guerrilla groups, including the Syed Salahuddin led Hizbul Mujahideen, Hafiz Saeed led Lashkar-e-Toiba, Masood Azhar led Jaish-e-Mohammad and the Fazlur Rahman Khalil led Harkatul Mujahideen (HuM), had been waging an armed struggle against the Indian forces within J&K. Prior to the September 11 terror attacks in the United States, Islamabad insisted that it only provided moral support to the militant groups operating in Jammu & Kashmir. But New Delhi had consistently maintained that the ISI fully backed these militant groups with logistical and financial support.

However, after the 9/11 attacks, Washington and New Delhi's interest in curbing the jehadi groups fighting the Indian security forces in J&K dovetailed neatly, compelling Musharraf to roll back his establishment's policy of nurturing jehad and jehadis. Since 9/11, a visibly concerned and perturbed US leadership seems keen on evolving safeguards in some form against the ever-increasing threat of terrorism emanating from Afghanistan and neighbouring Pakistan. As Islamabad moved swiftly to address American concerns by distancing itself from militancy in Kashmir, the militant groups that had long depended on ISI support for their guerrilla activities described the policy change as a betrayal of their struggle for independence.

After throwing in his lot with the US, Musharraf has been trying to gain control over the ISI and its 10,000-strong cadre. Transforming the agency from one that abetted Islamic militancy to one that combats it is a key goal for both Musharraf and the US. However, it is a daunting task. Commonly branded 'a state within the state' or an 'invisible government', the ISI has been sponsoring the Kashmiri militants in J&K for the past decade. After joining hands with the US in late 2001, the Musharraf administration began to disband two major units of the ISI that had close links with Islamic militants in Afghanistan and J&K.

Though the policy change was not publicly announced, the fact is that it was one of the most significant shifts that emerged from Pakistan's decision to align itself with the West after 9/11 and to reduce ties with Islamic militants in Afghanistan and in Kashmir. However, despite the Pakistani government taking tough measures against the jehadis, the supporting structures continue to breed more jehadis – both due to the weaknesses in the state structure and the state's active connivance. This is primarily because the unholy alliance between Pakistan's security agencies and jehadi groups is quite old and has ideological roots. With changed circumstances all over the world, there has been a change in mindsets. What is needed though is a change of heart towards the jehadis by sympathizers in Pakistan's defence and intelligence establishments.

In the current environment, the apparent failure of the Musharraf-led regime to counter Islamist militancy and religious extremism is all the more inexplicable given that the country claims to have handed over more than 500 al-Qaeda operatives to the US authorities since the war on terror began. The will to contain Islamist extremist groups that are not on America's priority list appears to be absent and a significant number of such groups continue to operate within Pakistan, many of them with apparent immunity from the government. The leadership of several such groups, most visibly the Jaish-e-Mohammad, Lashkar-e-Toiba, Harkatul Mujahideen and Hizbul Mujahideen continue to enjoy full freedom of movement and speech despite an official ban.

On the other hand however, despite the fall of the BJP government in India, peace efforts between New Delhi and Islamabad are still on. What has become a major source of concern for the proponents of peace however is India's allegation that the ISI has reopened militant training camps in large numbers in Azad Kashmir (the part of Kashmir that is under the control of Pakistan) and the Northern Areas in Pakistan. An Indian home ministry report issued in June 2004 alleged that the largest militant training camp was located in the Jungle-Mangal area where nearly 300 militants, mostly foreign mercenaries, were being trained for terrorist activities. On 15 July 2004, Richard Armitage, the American deputy secretary of state reiterated that Pakistan had not yet dismantled militant camps in Azad Kashmir. 'I was correctly quoted [in India on 14 July 2004] when I noted that all the terrorist camps [in Azad Kashmir] have not been dismantled,' Armitage told reporters after talks with Pakistan's foreign secretary Riaz Khokhar. The perception in India was that Musharraf was playing a double game as usual – sending his emissaries to meet their Indian counterparts on the one hand, and keeping his jehadis in good mood on the other.

Analysts however believe that it is still too early to predict the precise course of Musharraf's future handling of the Kashmir issue, and that it will not be easy for him to torpedo the Indo-Pak peace process, primarily because of US pressure. The major problem for Musharraf is that he cannot back off from the peace process because not only would that allow India to tighten its grip over the Valley but also leave it under no compulsion to engage in dialogue with Pakistan and resolve the festering Kashmir issue. Though much will depend on the progress of the Indo-Pak peace initiative, there are clear signs that Musharraf's U-turn on Kashmir has driven a wedge between the jehadi leaders and their once all-powerful spy-masters, primarily because of the changing nature and interpretation of the military establishment's 'national interests'.

As the interests of the military establishment and those of the Islamists are no longer fully compatible with each other in the wake of the 9/11 attacks, General Musharraf and the jehadis are clearly on a collision course. The twin suicide attempts on Musharraf's life in Rawalpindi on 25 December 2003 and a similar attempt on his right-hand man Shaukat Aziz in Fateh Jang in July 2004, can be described as classic examples of Frankenstein rising to consume its creator. These deadly attempts clearly demonstrated that the ISI-nurtured jehadi groups have closed ranks and are acting in unison to physically eliminate some of the key US allies in its war on terror.

Interestingly, those who want Musharraf dead the most have traditionally been the closest allies of the general and his all-powerful military establishment. In Afghanistan as well as in Kashmir, Pakistan's intelligence agencies hit a jackpot when they first realized the efficacy of covert warfare as a way of bleeding a stronger adversary while maintaining the option of plausible deniability. In Afghanistan, a majority of the resistance cadres came from within the ranks of motivated Islamic militants who were prepared to die for the cause as well as to kill the communists.

The same policy was used in J&K, creating, in the process, a nexus between groups fighting in Afghanistan and those operating in the Kashmir Valley. However, the military establishment's policy had a flip side to it. The Islamic militants cooperated with the state so long as it suited them, i.e. till they were being given space for their jehadi activities and for the propagation of their ideology. Pan-Islamism is their creed and they do not believe in the nation state. Their ideology runs counter to Musharraf's changed policy of 'Pakistan-first'. It also militates against the state policy of non-interference in other countries' internal affairs. Thus, having changed tack, General Musharraf now faces a dilemma. There are those in the establishment who believe that he will not be able to change the nature of the relationship between the militants and the military overnight, even if he sincerely desires this.

2

Jehadis vs the General: Friends Turned Foes

General Pervez Musharraf's revelation in a television interview in June 2004, that some junior officials of the Pakistan Army and the Pakistan Air Force had been arrested for their suspected involvement in one of the two assassination attempts on him in Rawalpindi in December 2003 only served to confirm what had long been suspected: Islamist extremists and their ideological partners in the garrison are acting in unison to eradicate the general, a key American ally in the US led war against terror.

On 25 December 2003 General Musharraf had a providential escape after two suicide bombers rammed his motorcade with their bomb-laden cars at a petrol station two kilometres from his army residence in Rawalpindi, killing sixteen people and injuring fifty-four others. This was arguably the deadliest of at least six abortive attempts on his life from the time he deposed Mian Nawaz Sharif as the prime minister in October 1999. According to the report on the investigation – which was the most extensive ever conducted for a crime in Pakistan – a Pakistani national believed to be the key contact person for the top al-Qaeda leadership, coordinated with the Pakistan-based jehadi groups, and elements in the Pakistan Army, Air Force and the Rawalpindi police to carry out the two assassination attempts on Musharraf. The military investigation of the two successive attempts in December 2003 was headed by Lt. Gen. Ashfaq Kiyani, Commander 10 Corps, Rawalpindi. A team comprising dozens of military investigators worked for about four months and Gen. Musharraf was informed about the completion of the investigation and identification of the suspects in May 2004.

A few days after the suicide attacks, the ISI arrested Mohammad Naeem of the Special Branch, Capital Police, Islamabad. Mohammad Naeem had received a call on his cell phone a few minutes before the suicide attacks which made him a suspect. The call was tracked to the cellphone of Mohammad Jameel Suddhan, one of the two suicide attackers and a Jaish-e-Mohammad activist from Balakot in Azad Kashmir. The other suicide bomber was identified as Khaliq Ahmed alias Hazir Sultan, a Harkat al-Jehad al-Islami (HuJI) operative who hailed from the Panjsher valley of Afghanistan. It is now known that the two suicide car bombers, who narrowly missed the president's vehicle, were receiving live information on his motorcade's movement through another police official assigned to Rawalpindi's Civil Lines police station. Mohammad Naeem was deployed at the Convention Centre in Islamabad where Musharraf had gone to preside over a function. Investigators believe that Naeem contacted Jameel on his cellphone and conveyed to him the precise location of the presidential convoy.

Naeem's possible role showed that the assassination attempts could not have been just the handiwork of the al-Qaeda but probably also involved those in Musharraf's inner circle who have turned against him for reversing Pakistan's Afghan and Kashmir policies. The two suicide bombers had links with Pakistani intelligence agencies before they went to fight in Afghanistan against the Northern Alliance a few years ago. 33-year-old Jameel, was a resident of Torarh, in Poonch district, Azad Kashmir. His identity was established when detectives rummaging through the debris of the explosion recovered his torso and national identity card. Post 9/11, Jameel and Khalique had been captured by the Northern Alliance troops. They were among the several hundred Pakistani jehadis who were released by Kabul after negotiations with Islamabad. On their return to Pakistan, they were set free by their intelligence minders who could subsequently have instigated them to launch the attacks.

On 25 December 2003, in the half-hour before Mohammed Jameel ended his life, he was a busy man. As he sat in a pickup truck loaded with deadly explosives, he made and received no fewer than 109 calls on his cellphone, talking, at least in some cases, to accomplices in the plot to kill the president of Pakistan. Jameel may have assumed that the trail of evidence he was leaving behind would be destroyed in the blast. If he thought so he was wrong. Not only did he and a second car bomber fail to kill Musharraf but the memory card of Jameel's cellphone, which investigators found intact amid the detritus of the blasts, led the authorities to dozens of suspected collaborators.

Interestingly, during his days of captivity in Baharak Jail, in Panjshir Valley in Afghanistan, where he was held by the Northern Alliance, Mohammad Jameel had claimed that he was a captain in the Pakistan Army. The Pakistani authorities dispute Jameel's claim, saying that he must have done so to minimize the volume of the humiliation being meted out to the Pakistani prisoners by the Northern Alliance troops. The official version as provided by an intelligence agency holds:

> As a matter of fact, after his defeat on several war fronts at the hands of the Taliban troops which were now marching towards the Punjsher Valley, the commander of the Northern Alliance forces Ahmed Shah Masood released a fabricated list of the Pakistan Army prisoners to mislead the international community. Projecting the jehadi prisoners from Pakistan as members of the Pakistan Army was a ploy by Masood to give a false

impression to the world that it was the Pakistani army which was helping the Taliban move forward at various war fronts, especially in those areas which were once considered to be the power pockets of Masood.

In order to get confessional statements of their liking, the Northern Alliance forces severely tortured the Pakistani prisoners and warned them that if they want to save their lives, they should make confessions in accordance with the wishes of Ahmed Shah Masood. Mohammad Jameel, who was apprehended while taking shelter in a mosque of Chareaka, south of Kabul, was the first one who surrendered his will at the mercy of his captors by falsely admitting that he was a member of the Pakistan Army with the rank of Captain. Audio films and photographic sessions were held in which these prisoners were shown to the foreign media people. Having detained them for over seven months, the prisoners, including Jameel, were shifted to Siraj Jail for their onward journey from Baghram airport to an underground jail in Tehran (Iran) where they were kept for next five months.

They were once again asked the same question – whether they were members of Pakistan's armed forces. The prisoners pleaded to have nothing to do with the Pakistan Army and that they were the members of mujahideen groups, which were aiding the Taliban forces against the Northern Alliance troops. In Tehran jail, two persons who spoke fluent Urdu interrogated them. During their five-month detention period, they were never allowed to see daylight.

Notwithstanding the Pakistan government's denials that Mohammad Jameel had anything to do with the Pakistan Army, according to a US defence intelligence source: 'The man who tried to kill General Pervez Musharraf in December was a spy in Pakistan's Inter Services Intelligence agency (ISI).'[1] Moreover, a news analysis carried by the South Asia Analysis Group website, claimed that 'the Pakistan government had played down the fact that one of the two suicide bombers – Mohammad Jameel, resident of Androot, Police Station Torarh, in Poonch district, Azad Kashmir – belonged to the Suddhan tribe of Azad Kashmir, the same tribe to which Gen. Mohammad Aziz Khan, the

Chairman of the Joint Chiefs of Staff Committee, and Maj. Gen. (retd) Mohammad Anwar Khan, the President of AJK, belong.'[2]

The 25 December suicide attacks on Gen. Pervez Musharraf were preceded by another incident on 14 December 2003. Then Musharraf had escaped an assassination bid as a powerful remote-controlled bomb planted under a bridge in Rawalpindi exploded fifty-five seconds after his convoy passed over it. The blast could have proved deadly had the signal jammer system in his bullet-proof car not jammed the remote-controlled device for fifty-five crucial seconds while the presidential convoy crossed the bridge near the 10 Corp HQ (headquarters). According to government sources, two consecutive attempts on General Musharraf's life in a highly protected military area close to the Army House and the corps headquarters could not have been possible without the attackers having regular access to top-secret information about the general's movement. In the two previous attempts on his life in Karachi in 2002, the suspects included an officer of the rangers and a naval dockyard worker. This means the investigators cannot rule out similar involvement of low-level government officials in the 2003 attacks.

The government sources went on to say that a 'source report' that had spoken of the possibility of a suicide attack on Gen. Pervez Musharraf had reached senior levels of the intelligence hierarchy, but the information had not received the attention it deserved. That oversight on the part of the Military Intelligence (MI) chief, Maj. Gen. Tariq Majid, who was privy to that intelligence tip but failed to react appropriately, led to his immediate transfer. He was replaced by General Musharraf's military secretary, Maj. Gen. Nadeem Taj. The investigators had highlighted some specific areas where the security lapse was particularly appalling. In the bridge blast case for instance, according to the investigators it would have taken the terrorists hours to lay 550 pounds of explosives under the culvert and wire them up with remote-controlled triggers.

The bridge was blown up using C4 explosive, the best quality military plastic explosive available. The C4 plastic explosive, largely manufactured in the US but widely supplied to military forces around the world, resembles white, uncooked pastry or dough, and can be kneaded and moulded into any shape in total safety. The explosive had been expertly tied to each of the five horizontal bars on the sliding side of the bridge that had no load-bearing pillars. There can also be little doubt about the accuracy of the estimate of the quantity of explosives used in the attempt: the blast was so powerful that a thick layer of reinforced concrete was literally ripped off the bridge. It is astonishing that the terrorists managed to do all this without being noticed in a military neighbourhood.

According to the investigative agencies, five of Pakistan's leading militant groups which have supporters in the military establishment, have been working in tandem to physically eliminate General Musharraf. The 25 December twin suicide attacks confirmed the involvement of at least two of these jehadi groups – Jaish-e-Mohammad (JeM) and Harkat al-Jehad al-Islami. As stated earlier, the suicide bombers were identified as Muhammad Jameel, a Jaish-e-Mohammad activist from Azad Kashmir and Khalique Ahmed, a Harkat al-Jehad al-Islami operative from Afghanistan. JeM, led by Maulana Masood Azhar and the HaJ, headed by Qari Saifullah Akhtar, are components of the five-member Brigade 313, launched in 2001 after the US-led allied forces attacked Afghanistan. The three other brigade components included Lashkar-e-Toiba (LeT), Lashkar-e-Jhangvi (LeJ) and Harkatul Mujahideen al-Alami. The leadership of this group had pledged to target key Pakistani leaders who in their opinion were damaging the cause of jehad to further the American agenda in Pakistan.

That the two assassination attempts on Musharraf were carried out by the Brigade 313 was confirmed by an arrested leader of Lashkar-e-Jhangvi, Akram Lahori, who revealed during interrogation that in May 2002, over 100 members of the group had sworn on the Holy Koran in Karachi to physically eliminate Musharraf at all cost. Lahori was arrested along with his accomplice Attaur Rehman alias Naeem Bukhari for crimes which include the bombing of the US consulate in Karachi, the Mominpura massacre in Lahore and several other sectarian killings. Lahori's confessions led to the arrest of three hardcore activists of Harkatul Mujahideen al-Alami – Muhammad Imran, Mohammad Hanif and Sheikh Mohammad Ahmed – for making an abortive attempt on Musharraf's life in Karachi by blowing up an explosive-laden car.

In light of the revelations made by Akram Lahori and other arrested jehadi leaders, information is being collected about the potential suicide bombers belonging to the five components of Brigade 313 who are still at large. The security agencies have intensified their hunt for at least five members of the JeM and Jamaat-ul-Furqa suicide squads. Another five of their associates had died in 2000 while carrying out three suicide missions in Islamabad, Murree and Taxila. Mohammad Sarfraz, a resident of Attock lost his life while conducting the 17 March 2002 suicide attack on the Protestant International Church in Islamabad's diplomatic enclave which killed half a dozen people.

Three other suicide bombers from the JeM, (now renamed Khudam-ul-Islam) – Rehan Babar, a resident of Muzaffargarh, Qari Zarrin, a resident of Mansehra and Nawaz Gujjar, a resident of Gujranwala – blew themselves up less than 24 hours after killing six people inside the Christian School at Gharial in Jhika Gali near Murree on 5 August 2002. Having fled the scene, the terrorists were trapped by the security agencies near Kohala Bridge, where they blew themselves up to evade arrest. In addition, Kamran Butt, a resident of Rawalpindi, lost his life while carrying out the 9 August 2002 grenade attack on Christian Hospital in Taxila, in which four female nurses died.

The intelligence agencies failed to identify the suicide bombers in May 2002 suicide attack in front of Sheraton Hotel,

Karachi where the bomber rammed his explosive-packed car into a bus which was carrying French engineers, killing eleven of them besides three others. In June 2002, an unidentified suicide bomber exploded his car outside the US consulate in Karachi killing twelve Pakistanis. Subsequent raids carried out by the authorities led to the arrest of over a dozen suspected suicide bombers and recovery of a huge quantity of explosives. All those arrested belonged to the JeM and admitted during interrogations that the suicide bombing was an intrinsic part of their strategy.

The arrested JeM members revealed that the suicide bombings were planned in November 2001 in the wake of the US-led allied forces' attack on Afghanistan when the operational commander of the group, Maulana Abdul Jabbar, alias Maulana Umar Farooq, returned to Pakistan and called a meeting at the Balakot training camp. The participants in the meeting decided to resist the increasing US influence in Pakistan through any means possible, including suicide bombings. The suicide missions were launched in March 2002 and continued for the next six months, successfully hitting six targets in Islamabad, Karachi, Murree, Taxila and Bahawalpur. When the intelligence agencies directed Masood Azhar to put an end to these operations, Maulana Abdul Jabbar dissented and was expelled from the group. He subsequently launched his own group, called Jamaat-ul-Furqa, but was arrested by the intelligence agencies in connection with the 2002 suicide bombings.

Sheikh Rashid Ahmed, the Pakistani Information Minister, stated on three occasions after the 25 December Rawalpindi attacks that the suicide-bombers, who nearly killed Musharraf were a mix of jehadis from within and outside Pakistan. 'Kashmiri and Afghan militant groups were behind the latest assassination attempt on General Pervez Musharraf. Both the suicide bombers have been identified. One of them belonged to Kashmir and the other was from the North West Frontier Province. It's a huge network of terrorists having tentacles from

Kashmir to Afghanistan and has international ties,' Rashid said. Information acquired by intelligence sources substantiates Sheikh Rashid's claim.

During the investigation into the two assasination attempts in December 2003, the military investigators questioned about 150 suspects, including four dozen Pakistan Air Force (PAF) and Pakistan Army non-commissioned personnel. The investigation showed glaring administrative loopholes in the Pakistan Air Force's security apparatus. Prior to the latest investigation, it had maintained no record of the movement of its personnel to and from their official residential facilities after office hours. The Air Intelligence, the intelligence wing of the PAF, surprisingly had no idea that about two dozen of its personnel at the Chaklala airbase had been attending meetings with religious extremists, and that in the first week of December 2003, they were making active preparations at the PAF base to bomb the presidential motorcade.

The military investigation also led to the arrest of the civilian religious extremists, including three clerics, involved in the indoctrination of PAF technicians and in planning the attacks. A small group of religious extremists who had stored and supplied the C4 explosives to the air force technicians and the suicide bombers were also arrested. The military investigation headed by Lieutenant General Kiyani also cited lapses in the presidential security codes and arrangements. The police is responsible for General Musharraf's security in his capacity as the president of Pakistan. Presidential security codes are governed on the basis of elaborately detailed procedure in the 'Blue Book', but a special detachment of the Military Intelligence is responsible for his security as the chief of army staff.

The investigation discovered glaring loopholes in the presidential security plan on 14 and 25 December 2003. The investigators were surprised to learn that the air force technicians had spent two days making several trips beneath Lai Bridge to strap large quantities of the C4 explosive to its pillars without being noticed either by the police or the Military Intelligence, which was supposed to keep an eye on the presidential route. The military investigation also focused on the leakage of information about the jamming device in Musharraf's car that had delayed the remote-controlled trigger for the bomb blast at Lai Bridge on 14 December. The investigators believed that this piece of information had prompted the terrorists to use the suicide bombers for the 25 December attack.

The military investigation concluded that on 14 December 2003, attackers identified as low-level technicians of the PAF, had blasted Lai Bridge seconds after Musharraf's car passed over it in Rawalpindi on its way from the airport to Army House. The investigators describe the first attempt as the exclusive handiwork of over a dozen brainwashed technicians of the PAF who lived nearby in an air force residential facility. The air force technicians were reportedly directed, motivated, and armed by the Pakistani contact person of al-Qaeda. On 25 December 2003, the two suicide bombers who rammed two cars laden with explosives into the presidential motorcade were motivated by the same al-Qaeda operative aided by his contacts in the Rawalpindi police.

In a television interview in June 2004, Gen. Musharraf identified Amjad Farooqui, the man who had also allegedly masterminded the kidnapping and murder of the *Wall Street Journal* reporter Daniel Pearl, as the chief plotter of the two attempts on his life in Rawalpindi. On 26 September 2004, the Pakistani security agencies also caught up with the elusive Amjad Hussain Farooqui, and killed him in an encounter in Nawabshah, Sindh. Amjad Farooqui alias Imtiaz Siddiqui, the lynchpin of the al-Qaeda network in Pakistan, had been indicted for the murder of the *Wall Street Journal* reporter Daniel Pearl in Pakistan. But he had proved elusive till then. According to Pakistani intelligence sources, the arrest and extradition of the Harkat al-Jehad al-Islami chief Qari Saifullah Akhtar from Dubai in August 2004, and the information he provided to his interrogators, led to the raid at Amjad Farooqi's Nawabshah hideout.

The panic that seized Musharraf's security staff after the latest assassination attempts on him revolves around the problem of creating a watertight security regime. Already, the general is surrounded by a security protocol that can be ranked amongst the most stringent in the world.

Following the two suicide attempts on his life, the Musharraf-led administration has accelerated its ongoing anti-jehadi drive. However, the task appears to be long and dangerous because the jehadi tentacles have spread far and wide. On the run after coming under suspicion, these groups appear more dangerous and desperate than ever as they are not ready to accept the harsh fact that, at least for the time being, the days of jehad are over.

---

1. News report by the United Press International, Washington, 26 February 2004.
2. Raman, B., *Army Plot to Kill Musharraf: Today's News Four Months Ago*, 28 May 2004, www.saag.org/papers11/paper1010.html.

3
Pakistan Army: Islamists vs Reformists

Since the 9/11 terror attacks in the US and Gen. Pervez Musharraf's subsequent decision to make Pakistan a frontline state in the US-led war on terror, conflicting ideologies have caused fissures in the Pakistan Army, pitting the so-called Islamists and Reformists against each other.

These fissures had, however, rarely spilled out into the open, merely articulated, as they were, as whispers in the corridors of power or innuendos in newspaper articles. All this changed in August 2003 following the arrest of a group of officers from the Pakistan Army for their alleged links to al-Qaeda and other extremist militant organizations. These arrests were followed by the release of a letter in October 2003, allegedly by renegades within the force, written on a General Headquarters (GHQ) letterhead and sporting the monogram of the Pakistan Army. The letter launched a scathing attack against Gen. Musharraf and his pro-US policies, bringing to the fore the raging ideological conflict and internecine rivalry within the Pakistani army.

The Pakistan Army became a politicized army in the very first decade of the creation of Pakistan. It literally was the power behind the throne in Pakistani politics and soon seized political control. Thereafter, it has frequently intervened to seize political power by imposing military rule for protracted periods. General Zia ul Haq seized power in 1977 and his dictatorial regime lasted for twelve years. General Musharraf seems to be headed for an equally long stint as the dictator of Pakistan. Having enjoyed prolonged periods of political power, the Pakistan Army has been subject to the corrosive influences of corruption and influence-peddling which are usually the bane of politicians. At the same time, the top military leadership, despite claiming to pursue a liberal political agenda, continues to rely on Islamic fundamentalists as political allies.

The politicization of the Pakistan Army has led to further spread of Islamic fundamentalism – a phenomenon that has found fertile ground in Pakistan primarily due to socio-economic reasons. Large masses of the urban and rural poor, with no avenues for economic advancement, are being drawn to fundamentalism. As the soldiery of the army is largely drawn from the rural and urban masses, it would be well nigh impossible for it not to be infected with the virus of Islamic fundamentalism being propagated by thousands of *deeni* madrassas across Pakistan. During the Zia ul Haq regime, the composition of the Pakistan Army cadre was changed at the expense of the urbanized, Westernized looking middle-class and upper-class élite, and preference in officers' commissions was given to the emerging rural-educated generation with strong leanings towards conservative Islam. This large body of Islamist officers, commissioned during the Zia ul Haq regime, forms the backbone of the present day Pakistan Army, and its members have since moved up the ranks.

The resentment within the Army is believed to be at two levels: among junior officers who view with contempt General Musharraf's attempts at getting the army to combat rather than abet Islamist militancy, and amongst the upper echelons where Musharraf finds himself pitted against a few of his senior generals. Musharraf himself admitted on 27 May 2004 that personnel at a junior level within the army and the air force were involved in attempts on his life in December 2003.

'Well, there are some people in uniform, junior level . . . Air Force and Army . . . but they are very small,' Musharraf said, while responding to queries on TV.[1] He added that most of the armed forces personnel who were involved were now in custody and would be tried by a military court, but did not disclose the category (commissioned officers or others) and ranks of the personnel accused of being involved in the plot.

Musharraf, however, claimed that the accused were motivated by greed. 'Some of them are (in it) not even for religious motivation, some of them are (in it) for money,' he said. Musharraf added that he was very sure that none of the senior people of the armed forces were involved in the attempts on his life. 'We have unearthed everything, we know exactly who is involved, we know the entire picture of both the actions and exactly the names, we know their faces, we know their identities, we know their families, we know everything,' he said.

Yet, this was not the first instance of involvement of army personnel in activities motivated by Islamic militancy in contravention of military professionalism. A Hong Kong–based web newspaper reported in August 2003 the arrest of several army officers, claiming that they were conspiring to stage a coup against General Musharraf.[2] As other Pakistani newspapers began to speculate on the number of the officers arrested, and the conspiracy they were involved in, the normally reticent Inter-Services Public Relations Department issued a brief statement on 31 August 2003: 'Three to four army officers of the rank of lieutenant colonel and below are under investigation by the agencies for possible links with some extremist organizations.'

The director general of Inter Services Public Relations (ISPR), Maj. Gen. Shaukat Sultan, however said that there were no senior officers among them. Two lines of investigation were pursued in the post-arrest scenario: one, the connection between the incarcerated officials and extremist organizations; two, and quite incredibly, a possible link between some of them and India's external intelligence agency, the Research and Analysis Wing (RAW). According to defence sources, those investigated for their RAW connections belonged to the ranks of non-commissioned officers. A dozen junior commissioner officers were arrested in Islamabad, Karachi and Hyderabad (in Sindh, Pakistan), primarily on charges of spying for India.

The investigations had actually begun in July 2003 and came as a shock to intelligence authorities when it was revealed that the concerned officers, all of whom are from the non-commissioned ranks, were in fact trained RAW agents. According to the intelligence sources, the whole episode was kicked off with an anonymous call made to Mumbai from a public call office in Hyderabad in December 2002. Though the caller, who provided sensitive army information to the Indian side, could not be traced, he did give a lead to the intelligence agencies by mentioning an address during the phone call. The Pakistani intelligence got its first break a few months later when a non-commissioned officer was arrested in Hyderabad. During the interrogation, he repeated the same address mentioned in the phone call. Subsequently, a few more army officers were taken into custody from Karachi and Hyderabad. During interrogations, the arrested officers conceded that they were trained RAW agents of Indian origin planted in the Pakistan Army.

However, it was the group allegedly connected to al-Qaeda that posed an ideological challenge to General Musharraf. On 15 March 2003, top al-Qaeda leader Khalid Sheikh Mohammad was arrested from the Rawalpindi residence of a Jamaat-e-Islami office bearer, Ahmed Quddus. Subsequently, the Pakistani authorities arrested Quddus's uncle, Maj. Adil Quddus, from Kohat in the NWFP on 16 March.

The next round of arrests was made in August 2003, with the arrest of five more middle-ranking Pakistan Army officers. This was apparently the first instance within the army when someone at colonel level had been arrested. Two colonels, two majors and one captain were picked up by the agencies over a period of two weeks in August 2003. Those arrested included Col. Abdul Khalid Abbasi (General Headquarters), Lt. Col. Abdul Ghaffar (Headquarters Army Aviation Command), Major Muhammad Rohail (2nd Corps), Major Attaullah (2nd Corps) and Capt. Dr Usman Zafar (Mujahid Battalion).

In September 2005, a military court in Panu Aqil Cantonment imprisoned three of arrested army officers and dismissed three others from service for having links with al-Qaeda. The military court sentenced Major Quddus and Colonel Abdul Ghaffar to ten years and three years in prison respectively while Major Attaullah, Major Faraz and Captain Zafar were dismissed from the Army service. Another accused, Colonel Khalid Abbasi, was sentenced to six months in prison besides dismissal from the service.

Lt. Col. Abdul Khalid Abbasi was considered to be a religious-minded individual who used to conduct daily lessons on the Holy Koran for junior officers of the Pakistan Army. He was eventually charged with giving asylum to al-Qaeda operatives, one of whom was a foreigner. Khalid Abbasi was suspected when an alleged terrorist made telephonic contact with him and sought his consent for two people to stay with him for a few days. This call was intercepted by American agents who had set up a state-of-the-art espionage system in Pakistan to monitor communications conducted across the airwaves.

However, the interrogators failed to ascertain whether or not Lt. Col. Khalid Abbasi was working with Maj. Adil Quddus. Quddus's house in Kohat cantonment was thoroughly searched by army officials before his arrest, in a rapid sequence of events set in train following the capture of the FBI's most wanted, Khalid Sheikh Mohammad. Those who interrogated Khalid believe that he might have moved from his Karachi hideout to Rawalpindi in order to facilitate an assassination attempt on

Musharraf. The assassination theory, however, received a fresh impetus through an audiotape that the al-Qaeda released on 11 September 2003, the second anniversary of 9/11.

In it, Ayman al-Zawahiri, Osama bin Laden's deputy, said: 'We ask our Muslim brethren in Pakistan: till when will you put up with the traitor Musharraf, who sold Muslims' blood in Afghanistan and handed over the Arab mujahideen to crusader America? The officers and soldiers of the Pakistani army should realize that General Musharraf will hand them over as prisoners to the Indians ...' He then went on to add, 'Act, O Muslims in Pakistan before you wake up from your slumber to find Hindu soldiers raiding your homes in complicity with the Americans.'

Zawahiri's tape predictably fanned suspicions in the Pakistan Army, prompting Musharraf to comment live on TV the same day. 'I have the full support of the armed forces of Pakistan and I must be the poorest commander if none of my generals are with me... Every man down to the sepoy is with me and behind me – let me assure you that. There should be no such misperception that anyone is against me.'[3]

Musharraf's assertions apart, political analysts believe that the divide between the Islamic fundamentalists and those who are relatively liberal in the army has sharpened because of the General's half-hearted attempts to give the army a liberal outlook acceptable to the West. His efforts are being resisted by some rogue elements that are the product of Zia ul Haq era when public display of Islamic orthodoxy and conservatism was considered to be an asset. At the same time, the army officers were taught during the days of Zia ul Haq that Islam was integral to the ideology of the army. Prior to that, the Pakistan Army used to project a moderate and liberal face of Islam. Whether a person strictly observed Islamic teachings and rituals or not was viewed as a matter of personal choice.

The place of Islam in the army underwent a change in the 1980s due to domestic and external factors. The chief of army staff, Gen. Zia ul Haq, who seized power in July 1977 by overthrowing an elected government, used Islam and conservative Islamic groups to legitimize his military rule and to undercut opposition to his rule. He pampered conservative and orthodox Islamic groups in the political and cultural domains and encouraged Islamic orthodoxy and conservatism in the army. Zia ul Haq was the first army chief and head of state to attend the annual congregation of the Tableeghi Jamaat or TJ (an organization that propogates Islam worldwide) at Raiwind, encouraging many officers to openly associate with the organization and publicly demonstrate their religiosity, something which army personnel had avoided in the past.

Other religious groups too cultivated links with army personnel. This fitted with the Zia ul Haq regime's identification with conservative and orthodox Islamic values and the rise of Islamic conservatism in the society. Zia ul Haq used to encourage his officers to say their prayers five times a day, and those who did so were favourably considered for promotion. Indeed, with the passage of time, it became essential that anyone seeking a high position in the army or the ISI display appropriate religious fervour. Even more favoured were officers with a background in the Islami Jamiat Talaba (the student wing of the Jamaat-e-Islami). Such connections led to the emergence of individuals like Lt. Gen. Hameed Gul, Brig. Imtiaz Ahmed Billah and dozens of others who made their names in political operations in favour of Islamic parties or in conspiracies to unseat leaders of secular parties from power, such as the Pakistan People's Party's twice-elected prime minister Benazir Bhutto.

Even after Zia ul Haq's death in an airplane crash in August 1988, people were careful to at least pay lip service to his legacy. Musharraf demonstrated his affection for Zia ul Haq by inducting the latter's elder son, Ejazul Haq in the federal cabinet in 2004 as minister for religious affairs. The fact remains that the Pakistan Army, largely through the ISI, actively supported and promoted the Taliban during its formation and ultimate seizure of power in Afghanistan in 1996. The external factor contributing to this was Pakistan's active involvement with the Afghan resistance against Soviet military intervention in Afghanistan from 1979 to 1989 and the subsequent activism of the Afghan mujahideen. The struggle against Soviet troops in Afghanistan enabled conservative Islamic groups to acquire acceptability, not to mention the material resources that they were provided with during that period.

The ISI's active role in support of the Afghan resistance brought Pakistan Army personnel into contact with conservative Islamic groups who were engaged in armed struggle against the Soviet occupation. After the withdrawal of Soviet troops, the ISI maintained contacts with some Afghan mujahideen groups. This adversely affected the delicate balance the Pakistan Army had traditionally maintained vis-a-vis Islam. Many officers and men were attracted to radical Islamic ideology. They talked of jehad as a legitimate political strategy for the state of Pakistan. In line with Islamabad's official policy, the ISI was allowed to encourage the militant Islamic groups operating from Pakistan to actively support insurgency in Jammu & Kashmir.

The decade-long ISI-sponsored Islamic militancy was bound to have implications for the army, whose personnel were directly exposed to the militancy and propaganda by Islamic groups. The Pakistani state openly identified with Islamic orthodoxy and militancy, and it became fashionable to publicly support the militant Islamic groups engaged in insurgency in J&K.

Having realized that the Islam-oriented activism adopted by the Pakistani army officers was affecting the organization's professionalism and discipline, the military hierarchy is now attempting to rein back the politicized Islamic elements in the army and to reassert the army's tradition of keeping Islam and professionalism in their appropriate places. Under General

Musharraf, the selection process for the higher echelons of the army has been made rigorous with a stronger emphasis on service record and professionalism. This minimizes the prospects of an officer with a record of political activism or having links with extremist groups reaching the senior command level. The army pays greater attention to the material interests of its senior officers, both in service and after retirement, in a bid to dissuade them from giving in to extraneous religious or political influences.

Unfortunately, however, some religious-minded pro-jehad officers already occupy the top echelons of the Pakistan Army. The alleged release of an unsigned letter on the GHQ letterhead in October 2003 had hinted at the prevalent resentment among the second-ranking leadership of the Pakistan Army. The letter, written in Urdu in the form of a petition, had been circulating among army officers for quite some time before being made public on 20 October 2003, when Makhdoom Javed Hashmi, president of the Alliance for Restoration of Democracy released it at a press conference in Islamabad. Hashmi's decision to make it public was construed as sedition and he was subsequently sentenced to twenty-three years in prison for inciting mutiny in the army.

Among other things, the letter demanded that the army high command permit the Pakistan parliament to debate the Kargil operation, determine the motives behind it and the causes of its failure. It also contained a scathing attack against General Musharraf and his pro-US policies. Addressed to the 'national leadership', the letter states, 'We, on behalf of the Pakistan Army, assure the nation that it is your army – the army of Islam and Pakistan, and we expect every member of the parliament, from whichever party he belongs, to work for the sovereignty of the parliament.' It goes on to describe Musharraf and his cabal as 'national criminals' who have not only plundered the national wealth with impunity but have also helped the Americans, Jews and Christians to kill 'our Afghan brothers'. 'Pervez Musharraf has turned Pakistan – the fort of Islam – into a slaughterhouse of the Muslims,' it says. The letter applauds the parliament, claiming that had it not been constituted, the Pakistan Army would have been dispatched to Iraq to kill 'our brothers'. The letter asks the parliament to discuss a range of issues: 'What were the objectives behind the Kargil venture? Why did Pakistan suffer massive losses, even higher than what it sustained in the 1965 and 1971 wars? Why has not Pakistan, like India, instituted an inquiry commission into Kargil?' The letter then goes on to make a sensational claim: the commander of the Kargil war, Maj. Gen. Javed-ul-Hasan, had worked under the CIA's supervision when he was a military attaché in the US for four years. 'The Kargil war was waged at the behest of the US. He (Major General Hasan) was even attacked by the officers and jawans for his poor planning of the (Kargil) war. But his mentors got him promoted as Lieutenant General, though he should have been sacked.'

The letter brings under the scanner the coup Musharraf had staged against the then prime minister Nawaz Sharif in October 1999 and then turns the spotlight on corruption in the army, questioning the allotment of prime plots of land in Lahore to brigadiers and generals.

Finally, the letter demands that the parliament institute a national judicial inquiry comprising those chief justices of the Supreme Court and provincial high courts who were in office at the time of the 1999 coup. 'The patriotic elements in the Pakistan Army will reveal these national secrets before the national judicial commission so that the culprits are brought to task in accordance with Article 6 (awarding death penalty to anyone who overturns the Constitution) of the 1973 Constitution.' Lest anyone be in any doubt about the agenda of those who wrote the unsigned letter, it concludes: 'Our aim – a free army and a sovereign Pakistan.' Such damning information and prickly demands infuriated the military top brass, especially Musharraf.

Inter-Services Public Relations director general, Major General Shaukat Sultan felt that the letter Hashmi had released was forged and was meant to harm the unity of the armed forces. Federal Information Minister Sheikh Rashid Ahmed dismissed the letter as a ploy by RAW to damage Pakistan's armed forces.

However, there are those in the military circles who believe that the letter Javed Hashmi had released was not fabricated because many other members of parliament too had received copies of it. Disgruntled officers now seem to be waging their battle through anonymous missives. For instance, in the recent past, one such letter divulged information about the arrest of Pakistan Army officers (Col. Khalid Abbasi and others), which was being kept secret by the military authorities. Though its contents were dismissed outright, the Inter Services Public Relations Department subsequently announced the arrest of army officers for their links with al-Qaeda and other militant groups.

According to military sources, army intelligence agencies have been reporting about the discontent brewing in the army. For one, some sections are not pleased with the talk about striking a compromise with India on Kashmir. Second, they are opposed to Pakistan reducing its role in the region on US insistence. In an attempt to mount pressure on Musharraf, the Islamist dissidents allegedly distributed an audiocassette entitled *Crush India* among the border villages and the army camps, units and forward posts.

The cassettes contained provocative songs, speeches and apocryphal stories about martyrs, all intended to imbue the soldiers with the spirit of jehad. The cassette reportedly stated: 'Since Independence, our army has been fighting with the enemy which is five times larger and equipped with latest weapons. But our army is equipped with a special weapon the enemy doesn't have—the spirit of jehad. Every Pakistani soldier is a soldier of Islam. He will be rewarded by Allah.'

The renegades had also circulated a booklet among junior officers underlining the benefits of waging jehad against India. It stated, 'One who kills a kafir will not go to Hell ever and there will be no shortcoming in his prosperity as regards to wealth and good food. The soldiers of Islam should know that winning or losing is in the hands of the Almighty and defeat can only be provided by God ...,' and that even if soldiers die during a jehad, 'their pain would be equivalent to that of a mosquito bite.'

Currently, hundreds of Pakistan Army and Air Force personnel as well as many civilians are being held by the military authorities at the Attock Fort. The civilians were arrested across the country – from the port city of Karachi in the south to the South Waziristan tribal area on the Afghan border. They are being detained for their direct or indirect involvement in the December 2003 assassination attempts on Musharraf. The detainees include members of militant organizations such as Harkatul Ansar and its associate body, the Shuhada Foundation which was created by the ISI to support bereaved families of those killed by Indian troops in Kashmir. The detainees have been divided into those who lured the military personnel to act against their chief in the name of Islam, those who hatched the conspiracies, those who financed them and those who knew the conspirators.

Between October and December 2004, the military courts in Pakistan sentenced to death several officers of the Pakistan Army and Pakistan Air Force for plotting to assassinate General Pervez Musharraf. The first death sentence was handed down to a soldier, Muhammed Islam Siddiqi, after he was court-martialled. Among the number of charges against him, the most significant one related to abetting a mutiny against General Musharraf. Siddiqi was also charged with receiving training in Bhimber, Azad Kashmir, at a terrorist training camp run by Jaish-e-Mohammed.

Sepoy Islam Siddiqi was sent to the gallows on 20 August 2005 in New Central Jail Multan, after General Musharraf turned down his mercy petition. The court documents identify the executed soldier as Abdul Islam Siddiqui of the Defence Services Guard Company attached to the Punjab regiment.

In December 2004, the military courts sentenced at least three Pakistan Air Force (PAF) servicemen to prison terms ranging from two to nine years for alleged links with an outlawed militant group. Though the trials were not announced, according to the relatives of the convicted they were tried in two southern PAF bases between October and December 2004. According to Aslam Khattak, a former Air Force officer and the father of one of the defendants, Nasruminallah Khattak, the three airmen were charged with giving donations to the banned Sunni extremist group Jaish-e-Muhammad, and of receiving small-arms training at the group's camp in Balakot. 18-year-old Khattak, was sentenced to two years in prison, as was 19-year-old Saeed Alam. Another young airman, Munir Ahmed, was given a nine-year sentence, according to his brother. Well-placed military sources say that as many as thirty personnel of the Pakistan Army, its Special Services Groups and the Air Force are facing the death penalty in several court-martial proceedings underway in military courts in the Kharian Army Cantonment, about 60 miles from Islamabad. All of them were arrested for their involvement in the December 2003 suicide attacks on General Musharraf.

The convicted include Havaldar Mohammad Younis, of 98 Air Defence Regiment of the Pakistan Army, who was awarded with ten years hard labour, two low-ranking officials of the army's Special Services Group, Naik Arshad Mahmood and Lance Naik Zafar Iqbal Dogar. On 8 March 2005, the trial court handed down death sentence (in absentia) to one of the accused, Naik Arshad Mahmood, while the other eight (all civilian) were given different jail terms. Other members of the group that conspired to kill Musharraf and have been sentenced included Ghulam Sarwar Bhatti, Ameer Suhail, Rana Muhammad Naveed, Ikhlas Ahmed and Abdul Basit.

Given all these developments, it seems unlikely that Musharraf's efforts to transform the Pakistan Army from a fundamentalist force into a moderate and liberal one will succeed in the near future. The general however remains upbeat, 'Let me tell you, all my commanders are with me totally – each and every general is with me,' he said on TV in September 2003.[4] One can only hope the general is right.

---

1. *Follow up with Fahd,* Geo TV, 27 May 2004.
2. *Asia Times,* www.atimes.com, 30 August 2003.
3. *Talking Point,* BBC TV, 11 September 2003
4. Ibid.

4

Daniel Pearl's Murder: A Major Blow to Jehadis

No other single factor forced the Pakistani military establishment to undo its decades-old pro-jehad policy in Jammu & Kashmir and Afghanistan than the ghastly murder of the American journalist Daniel Pearl, who was killed in Karachi in January 2002.

Three years after the murder, the American intelligence sleuths involved in the investigations believe that Pearl was kidnapped and killed because he had uncovered some vital links between the Pakistani intelligence establishment and al-Qaeda. At the same time, they are convinced that Sheikh Ahmed Omar Saeed, already convicted for the murder, was actually a double agent of the Pakistani intelligence as well as al-Qaeda.

Sheikh Omar was a key operative of the Jaish-e-Mohammad, the jehadi outfit founded and led by Maulana Masood Azhar. He was also an ISI agent and his involvement in Pearl's murder generated enormous American pressure, forcing General Musharraf to take on the jehadi groups in Pakistan, besides disbanding (for the time being) the Kashmir and Afghanistan desks of the ISI, which had close links with Islamic militants.

On 22 March 2002, General Musharraf said in Islamabad that Daniel Pearl had been over intrusive. Musharraf said,

'Daniel Pearl had come from Mumbai and made intrusion into the areas which are dangerous and he should have avoided it. Perhaps he was over-intrusive. A media person should be aware of the dangers of getting into dangerous areas. But unfortunately he got over-involved.' Yet the million dollar question remains: what exactly had Pearl got himself 'over-involved' in?

The *Wall Street Journal* reporter came to Pakistan in the aftermath of the 9/11 attacks to cover the US-led war on terror. But unlike most western journalists who, after coming to Pakistan, sought official help for reporting and got hooked up with local journalists, Pearl decided to steer clear of any official patronage. Besides visiting Islamabad and Karachi, he was spotted in cities like Bahawalpur, Peshawar and Quetta, where foreign journalists did not usually venture, given the desperation of the extremist jehadis at the time who were fuming because of the US-led attack on Afghanistan.

Pearl's movements made the Pakistani intelligence agencies suspicious and they were keeping a close watch on him. Some say he was working on the so-called shoe bomber, Richard Reid's story, exploring the latter's alleged links with Pakistani jehadi groups. (Richard Reid was the British al-Qaeda operative, sentenced to prison in the US after admitting to trying to blow up a plane using bombs hidden in his shoes.) Some say he was trying to explore possible links between the Pakistani intelligence agencies and the al-Qaeda network.

Whatever the truth may be, the fact remains that Pearl had become very interested in stories involving the Inter Services Intelligence, which is often referred to as a state within the state. On 24 December 2001, he reported on the alleged ties between the ISI and a Pakistani NGO, Ummah Tameer-e-Nau (Islamic Reconstruction), which is led by a Pakistani nuclear scientist Bashiruddin Mahmood, and which was working on giving Osama nuclear secrets before 9/11. He then reported that Masood Azhar-led Jaish-e-Mohammad still had a functioning headquarter in Bahawalpur and working bank accounts, even after General Musharraf claimed to have banned the group. He was also investigating the alleged links between the shoe bomber Richard Reid, some Pakistani militants connected to the ISI, and the infamous Indian mafia don Dawood Ibrahim.

Subsequently, a plan was chalked out by his abductors to lure Pearl into a position where he could be kidnapped. He was abducted from Karachi on 23 January 2002. The day Pearl was kidnapped he had left his Karachi rest house to meet British-born Islamic militant Sheikh Ahmed Omar Saeed at the Metropol Hotel. Pearl hoped Omar would arrange a subsequent meeting with Pir Mubarak Shah Gilani, head of a small extremist group called Tanzeem-ul-Furqa. Having initially met Omar along with his colleague, a local journalist, Pearl chose to venture out alone. According to a taxi driver who drove Pearl to the hotel, he asked him to stop near the hotel and got out. He then went to a car parked nearby in which four persons were waiting. One of them got out, introduced himself and invited Pearl to get in. He willingly did so. The car then departed.

In an e-mail to the US authorities four days later, an unknown group, The National Movement for the Restoration of Pakistani Sovereignty, sent ransom demands along with pictures of the 38-year old reporter in chains. The list of demands raised by the abductors included freedom for the Taliban prisoners, specifically of Mullah Zaeef, Taliban's former ambassador to Pakistan, and the release of F-16 fighter planes to Pakistan. The Pakistani authorities subsequently launched a drive for Pearl's recovery. They started looking for Omar Sheikh after finding out that it was he who, under an assumed name, had laid the trap for Pearl. They took into custody Omar Sheikh's father, wife and young child in order to force him to surrender.

On 5 February 2002, Omar Sheikh surrendered to Brigadier Ejaz Hussain Shah, the home secretary of Punjab, who had previously served in the ISI as its Punjab chief and is now holding the coveted slot of Director General Intelligence Bureau in Islamabad. Ejaz kept Omar in custody for a whole week and then handed him over to the Karachi police authorities for interrogation. The public announcement about his arrest said he was captured on 12 February 2002 and did not refer to the fact that he had been in ISI's custody since 5 February 2002. He then confessed to the kidnapping of Daniel Pearl.

During interrogations, Omar told the members of a joint team of American and Pakistan officials that he was an ISI agent who had been operating from Lahore since his December 1999 release from prison in India. The then Vajpayee government was compelled to release Omar Sheikh, Mushtaq Ahmed and their jehadi mentor, Maulana Masood Azhar, from prison after the hijackers of an Indian airliner demanded the same. During interrogations, Omar reportedly named two officers of Pakistan Army's Special Services Group – Subedar Mohammad Saleem and Subedar Abdul Hafeez – as his trainers in the use of guns, rocket launchers, grenades and other explosives. Omar is said to have volunteered to describe his role in the explosion outside the Jammu & Kashmir state assembly building in October 2001, the attack on Indian Parliament in December 2001 and the January 2002 American Centre hit in Calcutta.

However, the most disturbing revelation Omar made was that his captors might have killed Daniel Pearl by then. On 20 February 2002, three men approached a Karachi-based journalist, offering to sell a compact disk depicting Pearl's death for US$ 200,000 as well as a promise of global coverage. These men had been seen previously distributing press releases for an unknown militant group. Lacking the apparatus needed to play the CD-ROM, the three men returned the next day with the footage converted to videotape. With a player arranged from a local video store, the journalist was able to view and confirm the tape's gruesome images.

The video was titled, 'The Slaughter of the Spy-Journalist, the Jew Daniel Pearl'. The tape made its way to the Pakistani government and the US government, and eventually it leaked onto the Internet through a jehadi site. The film consisted of a Pearl monologue describing his Jewish upbringing, his family's involvement in the creation of Israel, and his feelings regarding the current controversy. His monologue was presented in edited sound bites; at times he appeared relaxed and his speech was natural, but during other parts he was tense and his speech sounded forced. Most of what he said was not terribly controversial, and notably he did not claim to be a spy for the US or Israel.

According to the FBI investigations, when Daniel Pearl's throat was first slashed, a technical error caused it not to be captured on film, thus it had to be re-filmed. In the video, Daniel Pearl's corpse is shown naked from the waist up, laying on a blanket; a man's arm is holding his head forward so that his cut neck cannot be seen. With the knife in his other hand, the man proceeds to cut deeper into Pearl's neck, from the back to the front. There is little blood. The man holding the knife is now strongly believed to be Khalid Sheikh Mohammad, the then chief operational commander for al-Qaeda, who was arrested from Rawalpindi in March 2003.

On 17 May 2002, three held activists of banned militant group, Lashkar-e-Jhangvi, helped the Karachi police recover a chopped-up body of Daniel Pearl from a vacant plot in the Gadap Town, owned by Al-Rashid Trust. The trust was founded in the 1980s by Mufti Ahmed as one of the several ostensibly humanitarian relief organizations, which used to finance numerous jehadi outfits like Jaish-e-Mohammad. The three detained suspects were among the six alleged associates of Omar Sheikh and had revealed during interrogation that the US journalist had been kept in a house in Orangi Town when he was alive. But after his murder his remains were buried at a desolate spot in Gadap Town. Acting upon this information the Karachi police dug the plot and recovered Pearl's body parts.

The million-dollar question pops up once again – why was Pearl kidnapped in the first place and then killed? The *Wall*

Street Journal quoted Omar Sheikh in a March 2002 report telling his investigators that, 'he was falling into my trap so easily, so I thought, I might as well do it.' Omar's aim, wrote the *Journal*, was to, 'strike a blow against the US and embarrass the pro-US Pakistan government.' The fact, however, remained that, while helping the Karachi police in the investigations, the FBI investigators stationed in Pakistan just exposed the continued level of interaction between the ISI and Omar before and after the Pearl kidnapping. Alarmed at the interrogation results, the ISI high-ups had to intervene to obstruct these investigations. In fact, in the beginning of March 2002, the Karachi police bosses were ordered to stop Omar's interrogations.

According to American intelligence findings, in the days right before 11 September, a flurry of money transfers occurred between the 11 September paymaster in the United Arab Emirates, presumably Omar Sheikh, and Mohammad Atta, one of the 9/11 hijackers. Between 6 and 10 September 2001, $26,315 was wired from the hijackers back to the UAE – left over money from the 11 September plot. On 11 September the investigations reveal, in the hours before the attacks, the paymaster transferred $40,871 from Omar's UAE bank accounts to his Visa card, and caught a flight from the UAE to Pakistan. There are records of him making six ATM withdrawals in Karachi on 13 September 2001 and then his trail goes cold. Afterwards, Omar visited Afghanistan to meet Osama bin Laden. The American intelligence sleuths suspect that after the 11 September attacks, Omar acted as a go-between for Osama bin Laden and the ISI, which makes perfect sense given his involvement with both groups.

Omar Sheikh's trial began on 22 April 2002 at an anti-terrorism court and he was convicted three months later and sentenced to death for the murder. Sheikh, for his part, has already challenged the verdict to execute him and his appeal has been pending for the past two years. Omar is presently detained in an isolation ward in Hyderabad Jail, where he is being guarded round-the-clock. Meanwhile, Islamabad has already turned down Washington's request to extradite Omar to the United States. In fact this was the second instance when British-born Omar was charged with kidnapping an American citizen.

In November 2002, Omar was secretly indicted in the United States for the 1994 kidnapping of four Westerners in India, including Bela Nuss of California. Then, Omar had organized the abduction of one American and three British tourists from a hotel in New Delhi to press for Maulana Masood Azhar's release from Indian custody. The hostages were driven to a safe house near Saharanpur in Uttar Pradesh, where police officers located them on October 31 1994. Omar and his accomplice, a Pakistani national ISI agent, Abdul Rahim, were arrested after a brief shootout, in which an Uttar Pradesh Police commando was killed. The four hostages were rescued unharmed.

Analysts believe Omar Sheikh epitomizes the links between Osama bin Laden, Pakistan's military and intelligence establishments, the 9/11 hijackers, British jehadis and Kashmiri militants. And putting him on the death row, and holding him in an isolation cell helps Musharraf keep a key witness out of American, British and Indian hands. But that isolation seems to be one-sided, as Omar seems rather effective in communicating with the outside world. While using the protection of his jail cell, he reportedly keeps in touch with his friends and cohorts and advises them on the future course of action.

In April 2005, Omar Sheikh gave an exclusive interview to the Karachi-based monthly *Newsline* from his Hyderabad prison cell, in which he conceded having met Osama bin Laden twice in Afghanistan. Omar further admitted involvement in the kidnapping of foreigners in India in 1994 for which he served time there, and the abduction of Daniel Pearl, but added that he didn't physically take part in the actual events. This claim ties in with new evidence unearthed by the American authorities in which it was revealed that while Omar was part of the conspiracy to kidnap Pearl – which included luring the reporter to the site of the abduction by e-mail, he was not physically present either at the time of the kidnapping, or his murder. However, Omar is believed to have played the role of adviser to the kidnappers, orchestrating from the background how best to get maximum mileage from the scheme.

The American intelligence sleuths stationed in Pakistan believe that the mystery surrounding the dastardly murder of Daniel Pearl may never be fully solved if Sheikh Ahmed Omar Saeed remains in Pakistan, dead or alive, and is not handed over to the United States. Here, too, there is an anomaly: While Pakistan has helped the US capture around 500 al-Qaeda fighters and operatives including Pakistani nationals and send them to Guantanamo Bay, Sheikh Ahmed Omar Saeed remains an exception.

5
Jaish-e-Mohammad in Disarray

Jaish-e-Mohammad (JeM), led by Maulana Masood Azhar, seems to be in disarray after losing the support of the Inter Services Intelligence. The ISI had to tighten the noose around its own creation, once the outfit was found involved in the 25 December 2003 twin suicide attacks on General Musharraf's life in Rawalpindi. Renamed Khudam-ul-Islam after being banned in January 2002, JeM has already split into two groups.

The reasons for the once blue-eyed cleric of the establishment falling from grace are manifold. For one, the Musharraf-led establishment has become wary of the maulana in the wake of Washington's allegations that his group was linked to the al-Qaeda. The Interpol has also requested Islamabad for his custody for the December 1999 hijacking of an Indian aircraft. Before that, Maulana Masood Azhar had been among the establishment's most trusted jehadi leaders who gingerly trod the credibility tightrope. One season the Maulana would be mouthing impassioned anti-India rhetoric, sending his militants across the Line of Control and the next would see him lying low. In return, the JeM chief received the patronage of the Pakistani intelligence apparatus. All this however seemed to be changing towards the end of 2003, and not entirely because of the diplomatic pressure New Delhi and Washington had exerted over the years.

To begin with, a glimpse of the clout Masood Azhar formerly enjoyed: nothing illustrates this more vividly than the Pakistani government's decision to decline a request by Interpol that Masood Azhar be taken into custody. Interpol had been prompted to act at the behest of the US Department of Justice which wanted charges filed against the maulana from Bahawalpur and Ahmed Omar Saeed Sheikh for their involvement in at least two crimes committed against American citizens – the 2002 murder of journalist Daniel Pearl and the 1999 hijacking of Indian Airlines flight IC-814 (with a US citizen Jeanne Moore aboard). The Americans claimed that under their law they had the right to investigate crimes against their citizens committed anywhere in the world.

According to a senior interior ministry official, many requests had already been turned down by Islamabad prior to the one made by Interpol: the Musharraf regime had rejected in September 2002 the FBI's request to interrogate Azhar for his alleged links with the al-Qaeda, which was accused of plotting US journalist Daniel Pearl's gruesome murder in Karachi. Islamabad had argued that Maulana Masood Azhar did not have a role in the murder and that the principal culprit: Omar Sheikh and his three accomplices had already been tried and sentenced to life imprisonment by a Pakistani court. Though the presence of US national Jeanne Moore aboard IC-814 could have led to trouble for Masood Azhar, the government of Pakistan had rejected the Interpol request for his custody on the grounds that he was not a hijacker and his incarceration in India had been illegal. In other words, Masood Azhar could not be accused of any crime.

Ordinarily, the reprieve should have emboldened Maulana Masood Azhar to brazenly espouse the jehadi cause. Instead, since the beginning of 2004 he finds himself, at least temporarily, out of favour with the establishment. This is because Washington appears convinced of his al-Qaeda links and because of the belief that he, along with other jehadi leaders, had been providing logistical support to fugitive al-Qaeda and Taliban leaders. However, the ongoing tussle between Maulana Masood Azhar and the Musharraf-led government took a new turn on 15 November 2003 when his jehadi group was banned for the second time since January 2002. While the government outlawed Khudam-ul-Islam, Jamaat-ul-Dawa, the political offshoot of the already outlawed militant group, Lashkar-e-Toiba, was placed on the interior ministry's watch-list. Five days later on 20 November, the federal government banned three more jehadi groups: Jamiat-ul-Ansar (formerly known as Harkatul Mujahideen), Jamaat-ul-Furqa (a splinter group of JeM) and Hizbul Tehrir.

The leadership of the outlawed group says the government action of banning the groups had emanated from the US. Significantly, the move came a day after the then US ambassador to Pakistan, Nancy Powell, said while speaking in Karachi that Washington was concerned about the re-emergence of several banned Islamic militant organizations in Pakistan. 'These groups pose a serious threat to Pakistan, to the United States and to the region. We are particularly concerned that these groups are re-establishing themselves with new names,' said Powell. She noted that Hafiz Mohammad Saeed, founder of the outlawed LeT, was also addressing rallies across the country as the leader of a new group, Jamaat-ul-Dawa. 'He is up to his old habits of urging holy war against Indian forces in the disputed Kashmir region,' she said. Jamaat-ul-Furqa, Powell had added, was one of the groups blamed for the December 2001 attack on the Indian parliament. The ambassador then urged Pakistan to enhance its efforts to stop these groups from infiltrating into the Indian-controlled part of Kashmir.

Interestingly, however, it seems that after Maulana Masood Azhar it is Hafiz Mohammad Saeed who is now in the establishment's good books. He is the leader of Jamaat-ul-

Dawa, generally considered to be the most effective jehadi group operating in Kashmir, and has apparently managed to elude the government's wrath. Instead of being banned along with Khudam-ul-Islam, Jamiat-ul-Ansar and Jamaat-ul-Furqa in December 2003, Jamaat-ul-Dawa was only cautioned and placed on the watch-list. Of the six militant groups outlawed in December 2003, Khudam-ul-Islam seems to be the hardest hit. When Masood walked to freedom in Kandahar on 31 December 1999, as a result of the hijacking of the Indian plane, few people in Pakistan had any clue of what the maulana was up to or how events would unfold when he returned to Pakistan.

Within a few weeks of his return, Masood announced on 31 January 2000 the formation of his own militant group, Jaish-e-Mohammad to fight against the Indian occupation forces in Kashmir. The organization was widely supported by the country's top Islamic scholars, especially Mufti Nizamuddin Shamzai of Binori Town Mosque, who was later killed in Karachi in May 2004. The dramatic emergence of the new jehadi group was seen by many in Pakistan as an ISI ploy to keep the network of jehadi organizations divided so that they could be easily controlled. The formation of JeM eventually caused the first serious split within Harkatul Mujahideen, formerly Harkatul Ansar, which had been banned by the US in 1997 due to its association with bin Laden. Unable to comprehend Masood's decision to launch his own group, the leadership of HuM unanimously decided to distance itself from their former secretary general.

Hostility developed between the two groups when a large number of the former HuM activists now associated with Jaish managed to wrest control of over a dozen HuM offices in Punjab. The HuM group's leadership reacted sharply and accused Masood of being 'a greedy Indian agent who was out to damage the Kashmiri jehad'. On the other hand, Masood received an unprecedented response from the former HuM cadres, primarily because of his oratorical skills, recognition as a scholar and the four-year jail term he had served in India. Masood's image was greatly enhanced by his spymasters in Punjab when he was allowed to travel to Lahore with scores of Kalashnikov-bearing guards. The ISI restrained him only when his anti-Musharraf statements became too aggressive.

JeM had largely confined its operations within J&K and the only recorded instance of its operations outside Kashmir had been the 13 December 2001 attack on the Indian parliament in New Delhi. Earlier, on 10 October 2001, a month after the terror attacks on the US, Masood Azhar had renamed JeM. The move was also motivated by reports that the US was considering the option of declaring it a foreign terrorist group because of its involvement in the explosion outside the Jammu & Kashmir legislative assembly on 1 October 2001. Despite the renaming, the US State Department designated JeM as a foreign terrorist organization in December 2001. General Musharraf too banned the group in January 2002. However, in no time, Masood got his group registered under the new name of Khudam-ul-Islam.

Lt. Gen. (retd) Javed Ashraf Qazi, former director general, ISI, was quoted as saying in March 2004: 'We must not be afraid of admitting that the Jaish-e-Mohammad was involved in the deaths of thousands of innocent Kashmiris, in the bombing of the Indian parliament, in Daniel Pearl's murder and in attempts on General Pervez Musharraf's life.'[1] The current education minister in the Musharraf government and a senator of the ruling Pakistan Muslim League (Quaid-e-Azam), Qazi went on to say that both the JeM and LeT had harmed the Kashmir struggle the most.

As things stand today, Jaish-e-Mohammad seems to be in disarray, especially after the swoop in 2003 in which hundreds of Azhar's followers were arrested and the Khudam offices sealed across Pakistan in connection with the December 2003 suicide attacks on Gen. Musharraf. One of the suicide bombers, Muhammad Jamil, was identified as a JeM activist from Azad Kashmir. Many other activists belonging to the group had been arrested earlier for carrying out suicide attacks on churches and missionary institutes in Islamabad, Murree and Taxila. However, those close to Masood insist that those involved in these attacks were in fact dissidents who had been expelled from their group for violating party discipline. 'The expulsions of Maulana Abdul Jabbar and other leaders eventually led to a split in our group,' claimed Khudam-ul-Islam, spokesman, Maulana Yousaf Hussain Naqshbandi. 'The dissidents were adamant to carry out suicide missions against the US interests in Pakistan to avenge the fall of the Taliban regime in Afghanistan,' he added.

The ameer (leader) of JeM, Sindh chapter, Maulana Abdullah Shah Mazhar, was the first to leave Masood Azhar. He launched his own outfit, Jamaat-ul-Furqa, in October 2001. He was soon joined by Maulana Abdul Jabbar alias Maulana Umer Farooq, *nazim*, military affairs and by twelve other commanders, all of whom decided to quit their parent group. Maulana Abdul Jabbar became the chief of Furqa while Mazhar was nominated as the *nazim-e-aala* (chief organizer) and secretary general of the splinter group. Unnerved by the development, Masood informed the ISI top brass in writing that his group had nothing to do with Jamaat-ul-Furqa and that he was no longer responsible for their actions. He wrote that the expelled members were sectarian terrorists who should be arrested instead of being allowed to regroup.

According to Abdullah Shah Mazhar, as quoted in the *Friday Times* in December 2003, Masood Azhar was appointed JeM chief by religious scholars Mufti Nizamuddin Shamzai, Maulana Shabbir Ali Shah and Maulana Waliullah, who were the moving spirits behind the group's creation. 'And these scholars have already deprived Masood of that position. Seven out of ten members of the Jaish Supreme Council, which Maulana Azhar claimed to have favoured him, had dissociated from him. I am one of them.'

He was further quoted as having said: 'We are all united and running the party for the very cause for which it was actually launched. Masood Azhar has nothing to do with the cause of jehad now. Our main difference with Azhar was that he deviated from the cause of jehad while the organization was ostensibly created for waging jehad to liberate Occupied Kashmir. Unlike Azhar and his masters in the Pakistani intelligence agencies, we are not ready to compromise jehad for the sake of funds.' On the other hand, Masood Azhar's younger brother and the deputy chief of Khudam-ul-Islam, Maulana Abdul Rauf, says that Jabbar and Mazhar had no interest in jehad and just sought to grab the group's assets. 'We have taken up the grabbing of several mosques owned by the Jaish at the higher level and will get their possession sooner or later,' says Rauf, who was released by the security agencies after being questioned in connection with the Rawalpindi suicide bombings against Musharraf.

Though Masood Azhar has bowed to the agencies' warning by directing his followers not to harm American interests in Pakistan, strong fears prevail in the intelligence circles that dissident members of JeM, who were unknown and had gone underground, were the ones who posed the real threat. They are spread throughout Pakistan, and are desperate to avenge the Taliban's fall and the arrest of al-Qaeda agents in Pakistan. Both the JeM factions, Khudam-ul-Islam and Jamaat-ul-Furqa, already banned by the government, are now openly in conflict – the former led by Masood and the latter by his former right hand man, Abdul Jabbar. Jabbar had been declared a proclaimed offender in connection with two deadly terrorist attacks: one on a Taxila church and the other on a missionary school in Murree. Interestingly, however, Maulana Abdul Jabbar was released by the security agencies in August 2004.

Although Maulana Masood Azhar is trying to conceal his diminishing clout over his cadre, the reality is that Abdul Jabbar's group largely controls the dominant faction of JeM, renamed Jamaat-ul-Furqa. The need for a new name arose after the US State Department placed JeM on its terrorist watch-list. The decision to float Khudam was Masood's ruse to demonstrate that he had not lost control over the group and had instead chosen to establish a new one. Apart from these two factions, according to militant and intelligence circles, JeM has broken into many splinter groups which have chosen to defy the military establishment's diktat of not attacking US interests in Pakistan.

The present split in JeM is however also a story of bitter wrangling over the organization's finances. Some of the group's insiders accused Masood and his cohorts of misusing these to enrich themselves. They said that besides having developed differences over jehad, distribution of finances was another major cause of conflict between Abdul Jabbar and Masood Azhar. Insiders relate a story of vested interests, corruption, greed and deep differences over strategy behind the split. JeM and Al-Rashid Trust, both blacklisted by the US State Department, are considered quite close. When the former was founded, Al-Rasheed Trust donated Rs 20 million ($360,000) as seed money. Later, thousands of people joined JeM and helped raise funds to the tune of an estimated one million rupees a day.

A substantial amount of this money was spent on establishing training camps and paying those families whose members had been killed in J&K. But, simultaneously, the lifestyle of many JeM leaders had become incredibly lavish. For instance, Masood Azhar, who comes from a lower-class family that resided in a slum area of Bahawalpur, moved to the city's posh Model Colony. He and his confidants began driving around in Land Cruisers and Land Rovers, escorted by a retinue of gunmen. The Jabbar faction alleges that Masood also appointed his relatives and friends to oversee JeM's mushrooming assets: seminaries, publications, offices and bungalows. His blatant favouritism and lavish lifestyle irked those who had spent grim years in Afghanistan and Kashmir. As the funds kept pouring in and Masood was giving mesmerizing speeches, JeM kept flourishing.

Murmurs of dissent in the group first surfaced when Masood Azhar opted to keep quiet about Musharraf's U-turn on Afghanistan post-9/11. Several prominent JeM members favoured retaliatory attacks against US interests to pressurize the military ruler against supporting Bush. However, under pressure from the security agencies, Masood refused to relent. Subsequently, many of the groups members quietly went over to Afghanistan to fight with the Taliban; some even brought back Arab fighters to Pakistan and provided them shelter. Though these members did not leave JeM, insiders said that differences in approach inaugurated a period of cold war within the organization.

Not willing to wait any longer for Masood's approval, the dissidents launched a spate of attacks on what they described as 'US interests'. The more violent of these were on a Taxila church and a missionary school in Murree. The police subsequently arrested Saifur Rehman Saifi who was responsible for JeM's upper-Punjab operations. During interrogation, Saifi revealed that he had been asked by Jabbar to launch attacks, including suicide missions, on US interests. This disclosure prompted Masood Azhar to begin a purge within the group to avoid the wrath of the security agencies. Meanwhile, many of those who were reportedly involved in carrying out anti-US terror operations in various parts of the Pakistan were arrested, allegedly at the behest of Masood loyalists.

The internecine squabbles erupted into a gunfight between the contending JeM factions on 22 June 2003 when Masood Azhar had wanted to deliver a Friday sermon at Masjid-e-Batha in Sakhi Hassan, Karachi. His arrival sparked a veritable battle between the two factions, each keen to gain control over the mosque and the adjoining seminary. Eventually the police intervened, but not before several militants were injured. Two weeks prior to the incident, the two groups had clashed in a bid to capture another mosque. Then Masood tried to deliver a Friday sermon at Binori Town mosque in Karachi, but the mosque's administrator did not permit him the use of the premises. Another scuffle between the two rival factions was reported at a mosque in the Korangi area in Karachi.

As things stand there are fears that ongoing disputes over possession of the various JeM offices, mosques and other material assets could lead to more serious clashes between the two banned groups: Khudam-ul-Islam and Jamaat-ul-Furqa. However, no one can say with any certainty at this point in time which one of them will eventually survives.

Masood Azhar is an alumnus of the Binori madrassa in Karachi. The Darul Uloom Islamia Binori Town mosque has one of the largest seminaries in Pakistan and it is one of the most influential centres of Deobandi Sunni ideology. It has led the anti-Ahamdiya and the anti-Shia movements in Pakistan over the last fifty years, churning out religious extremists since 1951. The top leadership of the Taliban has come out of Binori, as have leaders of extremist and terrorist organizations like the Harkat ul Mujahideen and Sipah-e-Sahaba Pakistan (SSP). After the Indian government released Azhar he went to the Binori mosque to announce the formation of JeM. It is here that he had learnt his anti-Americanism and rabid anti-Shia philosophy at the feet of men like Haq Nawaz Jhangvi, the founder of the anti-Iran, anti-Shia Sipah-e-Sahaba, who was killed in 1990.

6

Who Masterminded the December 1999 Indian Airlines Hijacking?

In the post-Taliban period, the war-torn, impoverished landscape of Afghanistan has become the new playground for India and Pakistan to score strategic points over each other. Having expanded its presence and influence in post-Taliban Kabul, India has also made substantial progress in its efforts to lead the international community to believe that Islamabad has been using terrorism as an instrument of foreign policy to pressurize Delhi to engage in negotiations over the Kashmir dispute.

Having established its consulates in the Afghan cities of Herat in the west, Kandahar in the south and Jalalabad in the east, the Indian government is making renewed attempts to get hold of any evidence that could prove the involvement of Pakistani intelligence agencies in the 24 December 1999 hijacking of an Indian Airlines plane.

Two officials from the Central Bureau of Investigation (CBI) in India and a couple of FBI officials visited Kandahar in the second week of October in 2003 to interrogate the Taliban masterminds of the operation that saw the Indian Airlines plane seized by hijackers immediately after it took off from the

Kathmandu airport. Before proceeding to Kandahar, the Indian officials obtained the prior permission of the Northern Alliance government to question several Taliban operatives including Mullah Wakil Ahmad Muttawakil who was Afghanistan's foreign minister during the Taliban rule and a key witness in the hijacking.

The Indian Airlines flight IC 814 was on its way to Delhi from Kathmandu when five armed men hijacked it over Varanasi. They first took it to Amritsar and from there to Lahore. After refuelling in Lahore, the plane took off for Dubai where the hijackers allowed twenty-one passengers to disembark before they flew it to Kandahar. Although an Indian national, Rupin Katyal, was murdered by the hijackers, the rest of the passengers returned home safely after spending a week in captivity. They were freed in exchange for the release of three top militants: Maulana Masood Azhar, Ahmed Omar Saeed Sheikh and Mushtaq Ahmed Zargar. Ahmed Omar Saeed Sheikh has subsequently been indicted and sentenced in Pakistan for his involvement in the murder of the American journalist Daniel Pearl. Both Indian and American authorities had subsequently registered separate cases against the hijackers.

The Pakistani intelligence agents in Kabul are learnt to have provided highly disturbing information to their bosses back home, to the effect that after invading Afghanistan the FBI sleuths had seized exceptionally revealing tape-recorded conversations between the hijackers of IC 814 and the air traffic control in Kandahar. Some of the information contained in those tapes was recently shared with the Indian intelligence, following which an FBI team went to India and a CBI team visited Kandahar. The FBI extended full cooperation to the CBI because an American national, Jeanne Moore, was amongst the passengers of the ill-fated flight. A criminal case was subsequently registered in the US against the hijackers. Having recorded Moore's testimony, the FBI teams visited New Delhi thrice to discuss her abduction and progress in the case. The FBI has also set up an office in New Delhi to cooperate with India to curb growing terrorism. The CBI, on the other hand, claims to have acquired the record of the incoming calls at the Air Traffic Control of Kandahar airport.

French writer Bernard Henri-Lévy writes in his book, *Who Killed Daniel Pearl* : 'Two high-ranking officers of the ISI were present on the tarmac in Kandahar when the Indian negotiating team landed there. They were later joined by colleagues from the special operations wing of the ISI's Quetta station. Negotiations were being conducted over wireless sets. The five hijackers got careless and inadvertently allowed Indian negotiators to overhear them taking instructions from Urdu-speaking men.'[1]

During and after the hijack drama, Islamabad vehemently denied having any role in it and went to the extent of offering to negotiate on New Delhi's behalf. The fact, however, remains that Mufti Abdul Rauf (the younger brother of JeM founder, Maulana Masood Azhar) and his brother-in-law, Yusuf Azhar, were among the hijackers who secured Masood Azhar's release by the Indian government from a Srinagar jail.

According to well-placed intelligence sources, the CBI has informed the FBI that Wakil Ahmed Muttawakil had played a double role during the plane hijack, leaving the then Foreign Minister Jaswant Singh red-faced by going back on several commitments made during the negotiations with the hijackers. The Indian side says that Muttawakil, who acted as an interlocutor at Kandahar after the IC-814 plane landed there, was also hostile during the negotiations. When Jaswant Singh landed in Kandahar with the three terrorists, Wakil Ahmed had made it a point to assure him that the hijackers and the terrorists would be held in Afghan custody until all the Indians left Kandahar. However, as soon as the three Pakistani militants were handed over to the hijackers, they were provided with a jeep in which they victoriously drove away.

The CBI believed that Muttawakil would be able to divulge more details about the intricacies of the hijack, such as the contacts that hijackers had with the outside world and the instructions and logistical support they had received from Pakistan. Therefore, in July 2003, India requested the Bush administration to permit the CBI to grill Muttawakil. After being denied access for almost two years, Indian investigators finally succeeded in debriefing Mullah Wakil Ahmad Muttawakil along with a few other Taliban leaders.

The FBI investigators are convinced that on several occasions Mullah Muttawakil had used the air traffic control (ATC) channel to speak to the hijackers and to some Pakistani officials. Therefore, he, more than any other Taliban official, had the total picture of how the hijack was facilitated by Pakistan and where the five hijackers were headed after the dramatic events came to an end. India insists that Pakistan's role in the hijacking should be seen within the context of the Taliban's then official spokesman, Abdul Haj Mutmaen's statement that the hijackers and terrorists who had been released from Indian jails were left on the Pak–Afghan border near Quetta, Baluchistan.

From India's point of view, any evidence that could establish the role of Pakistani intelligence officials in the hijack could exert enormous pressure on Islamabad to take custody of the IC-814 hijackers. Under the South Asian Association for Regional Cooperation convention on extradition and mutual assistance in tackling criminal activities, the Indian government made two formal requests for the extradition of the five hijackers and their accomplices. However, the government of Pakistan refused to oblige, maintaining that if any person suspected of being involved in the hijacking was to be found on its territory or in Pakistan-occupied Kashmir, Islamabad would undertake to apprehend and prosecute the suspect.

Soon afterwards, the Interpol authorities issued a red corner alert (look-out notice) to Pakistan, the UK, the UAE, Nepal and Bangladesh against the five hijackers and two accomplices who are believed to be the key conspirators in the hijacking.

However, the Indian side is not very hopeful about getting their custody.

The CBI, in addition, has already filed a chargesheet against ten people in the hijacking case, including three Indians. The other seven accused are all Pakistani nationals. Two Pakistanis, Yusuf Azhar and Abdul Rauf, are believed to be the key conspirators. The CBI chargesheet alleges that the hijackers possessed a very sophisticated satellite telephone to communicate with their mastermind in Rawalpindi. 'And when the Taliban authorities in Kabul refused to allow the hijacked aircraft to land, which was communicated by the hijackers to the authorities in Rawalpindi, they were asked to proceed to Kandahar,' the chargesheet states. Islamabad has, however, repeatedly denied these charges.

---

1. Lévy, Bernard Henry, *Who Killed Daniel Pearl?*, Melville Publishing House, Hoboken, 2004.

7
Lashkar-e-Toiba: Optimism Over the Future of Jehad

The Islamabad agreement between India and Pakistan in January 2004 came as a blow to even the most optimistic among the Pakistan-based militant groups waging an armed struggle against India in Jammu & Kashmir. But the leaders of the most feared among these, Lashkar-e-Toiba (LeT), and its parent organization, Jamaat-ul-Dawa, are still hopeful about the future of jehad and are keeping their fingers crossed.

LeT happens to be an Ahle Hadith (Wahhabi) jehadi group that was formed in 1986 by Hafiz Mohammad Saeed and his associates as the military wing of the Markaz Dawa Wal Irshad or Centre for Religious Learning and Social Welfare. LeT and Markaz soon set up military training camps in the eastern Afghanistan provinces of Kantar and Paktia, both of which had a sizable number of Ahle Hadith (Wahhabi) followers of Islam, with the aim of participating in the jehad against the Soviet occupation of Afghanistan. Because the LeT joined the Afghan jehad at a period when it was winding down (the Soviets invaded in 1979), the group did not play a major part in the fight against the Soviet forces, which pulled out in 1989. However, the Afghan campaign helped the LeT leadership to gain the trust of the ISI. During 1989–90, however, the LeT leaders turned their attention from the internecine squabbles in Afghanistan to Kashmir, which is where the outfit was to gain fame.

As the world applauded the sagacity of the two nuclear-armed neighbours in signing the Islamabad accord in January 2004, most of the jehadi groups bristled with rage at Gen. Pervez Musharraf's agreeing not to permit any territory under Pakistan's control to be used for carrying out acts of terrorism of any kind. Interestingly, however, unlike other militant leaders, Saeed, the most vocal proponent of the Kashmir jehad, decided to abstain from issuing any further statements criticizing the Islamabad accord.

According to those close to Hafiz Saeed he was asked by the establishment to remain silent in order to avoid possible action against the Jamaat-ul-Dawa and the LeT. He was also promised that there would be no restrictions on the activities of the two groups, be it the collection of funds and organizing public rallies or the recruitment of jehadi cadres and their training. In other words, despite having restricted the activities of the other jehadi groups, the establishment continues to extend its support to Jamaat-ul-Dawa and LeT.

According to Hafiz Saeed's close aides, the Islamabad agreement between India and Pakistan would not greatly affect their activities in the Kashmir valley as they had sufficient arms and ammunition in the valley to resist the Indian security forces for at least the next six months. They further claimed that young jehadis from various parts of Pakistan continue to throng to their training camps in Azad Kashmir before being pushed across the Line of Control into Jammu & Kashmir. LeT is the only jehadi group operating from Azad Kashmir, which still keeps a comparatively larger number of activists at its Muaskar-e-Toiba and Muaskar-e-Aqsa camps in Muzaffarabad where young jehadis are reportedly sent after having been trained at Jamaat-ul-Dawa's Muridke headquarters.

Unlike the earlier strategy of sending out large groups comprising thirty to sixty militants each on regular basis from the training camps located on the LoC, LeT decided to keep training militants in limited numbers and send out smaller groups of not more than five to fifteen people separated by long intervals. With over 2,200 unit offices across Pakistan and over two-dozen launching camps along the Line of Control, LeT boasts of being the largest jehadi outfit in the country. The Muridke camp is the first stop for recruits who are vetted for their suitability to wage jehad. In the next phase they are given a two-step military training course. The first comprises a 21-day basic course called Daura Aam followed by a three-month advanced course called Daura Khaas. The advanced course is oriented towards guerilla warfare, with training in the use of arms and ammunition, and in ambush and survival techniques.

After lying low for over a year under government pressure, Hafiz Saeed became active once again, making fiery speeches across Punjab. In one of his Friday sermons in March 2004 in Lahore, he declared that recruitment for the LeT cadres had again begun and over 7,000 young men had already been recruited in the past six months to conduct jehad-e-Kashmir. He was further quoted as saying that around 800 youngsters were killed while fighting the Indian army in 2003.

Even before the Islamabad agreement, the activists of Dawa and LeT had never been obliged to observe the ban imposed by General Musharraf himself, which prevented the jehadi groups from collecting funds and holding public rallies. While banning LeT and a few other militant groups in January 2002, General Musharraf had declared he would remain firm in his stand against terrorism and extremism. However, in practical terms, no step had ever been taken to dismantle or even disarm LeT which carried out the infamous 22 December 2000 attack at the Red Fort in New Delhi.

Nowhere is General Musharraf's unfinished business more visible than at the sprawling 200-acre headquarters of Jamaat-ul-Dawa and the LeT at Muridke, 45 km from Lahore, protected by barbed wire and bearded Kalashinkov-toting men. From here these outfits continue to pursue their jehadi agenda uninterrupted. This campus has already been transformed into a mini-Islamic state that prohibits music, television and smoking in its premises. According to rough estimates, over Rs 50 million have so far been spent on Markaz Dawa Wal Irshad, as this place is called. Markaz runs a network of social services, including sixteen Islamic institutions, 135 secondary schools, five madrassas, and a $300,000-plus medical mission that includes mobile clinics, an ambulance service and blood banks.

As to where exactly the money came from for the establishment of the Markaz, those close to Hafiz Saeed say that the Palestinian jehadi scholar, Abdullah Azzam, bought it for the organization. Azzam was also one of the inspirations behind the creation of the Palestinian militant group Hamas, and was once considered the religious and political mentor of Osama bin Laden. To this day, Jamaat-ul-Dawa uses Azzam's speeches and publications to train and motivate its cadres. Also noteworthy is the fact that LeT, before it renamed itself Jamaat-ul-Dawa in 2002, had links on its website to the official Hamas website and the then English mouthpiece of al Qaeda, www.Azzam.com.

US-based Pakistani writer, Hassan Abbas, notes in his book *Pakistan's Drift into Extremism, Allah, the Army and America's War on Terror*, that Azzam had studied Islamic jurisprudence at Egypt's Al-Azhar University, and worked as a professor in University of Jordan in Amman and later in Saudi Arabia. He goes on to say:

> As soon as the Afghan crisis erupted in 1979–80, he rushed to Pakistan where a teaching position at Islamic University in Islamabad was waiting for him. This assignment, however, proved to be temporary and he shifted to Peshawar shortly thereafter, where he established an organization named Mekhtab al-Khadamat (Service Bureau) for Afghan mujahideen. With generous Saudi funds this group managed travel and training for

volunteers coming to participate in Afghan jehad from across the Arab world...

In a short span of time, Azzam proved to be a valuable asset for both the ISI and the CIA, though he largely operated independently and was more loyal to his Saudi financiers than anyone else. His real long lasting contribution though was the inspiration that he provided to Osama bin Laden in the mid 1980s through his speeches in Saudi Arabia. Laden's Peshawar based Bayt-ul-Ansar (House of the Helpers), involved in work similar to that of Azzam's group provided an opportunity to both Abdullah Azzam and Osama bin Laden to work together, though Azzam was already a prominent figure then and Osama was not.[1]

During these times, Abdullah Azzam reportedly came into contact with Hafiz Saeed and the two discussed the idea of establishing Markaz Dawa Wal Irshad. Hafiz Saeed was then tasked to draw up a plan to raise the centre at Muridke near Lahore. However, before if could become fully functional, Abdullah Azzam was assassinated along with his two sons in a powerful bomb blast in Peshawar on 24 November 1989. The ISI believed it to be the work of the Israeli intelligence agency Mossad. Others blame Osama bin Laden and the ISI for the killing. Peter Bergen, a renowned journalist and the world's leading expert on al-Qaeda, believes that there is a strong possibility that the Soviets and/or Afghan communists killed Abdullah Azzam. The mystery has never been resolved.

In December 2001, a year after the Red Fort attack in New Delhi (on 22 December 2000), the US State Department had included LeT in the list of its officially designated terrorist groups. Apparently this move had been in the offing as the US administration had blocked the financial assets of LeT following the armed attack on the Indian parliament in New Delhi in December 2001. Some days later Hafiz Mohammad Saeed, addressed a press conference in Lahore and announced that Maulana Abdul Wahid would now head the organization. While stepping down as LeT chief, Saeed said he would now lead

Jamaat-ul-Dawa, the new name for Markaz Dawa Wal Irshad. Maulana Abdul Wahid Kashmiri, who belongs to Poonch district in Jammu, was appointed the new head of Lashkar.

At the press conference, Hafiz Saeed said these changes were meant to counter intense Indian propaganda that Pakistan had been sponsoring the jehad in the Valley, adding however that his withdrawal from the high office of ameer of LeT was not due to any internal or external pressure, from Islamabad or Washington. A week later Hafiz Saeed was detained on the flimsy charges of making inflammatory speeches and inciting people to violate law and order. According to *Jehad Times*, the LeT mouthpiece, Hafiz knew that he was to be arrested and had reorganized the group in anticipation. Subsequent news reports in the US media had alleged that Saeed was closely associated with bin Laden's 'International Islamic Front for Jehad against the US and Israel'. The government of Pakistan strongly refuted these reports. The Lahore High Court finally let off Hafiz Mohammad Saeed in November 2002.

Having stepped down as LeT chief, he had to look for a role for Jamaat-ul-Dawa which was more acceptable to the world at large. Dawa survived a number of restrictions and threats from the authorities over the next couple of years primarily because it had dissociated itself from LeT. In a bid to prove that the Kashmir insurgency was an indigenous freedom struggle, LeT had to announce in 2002 that it was formally shifting its base to 'Indian Held Kashmir'. Dawa on its part chose to camouflage its jehadi agenda and to concentrate on its prime objective of spreading the teachings of Islam. According to Hafiz Saeed's associates, the caution exercised by him helped their organization survive a fresh ban imposed by Musharraf on several extremist groups in November 2003.

According to intelligence sources the Dawa chief is more amenable to the ISI control than the leader of any other jehadi group. He is agreeable to waging a 'controlled jehad' in the Valley whenever asked to do so. The LeT is also perceived to be more dedicated to the cause of Kashmir liberation and hence more useful, given the fact that it has a larger Pakistani component than most other jehadi cadres. Its Punjabi base also works in its favour as it makes it easy for Lashkar militants to blend with the local population of Jammu, which is linguistically allied to Punjab.

LeT is an extremely secretive organization that takes great care to conceal the real identities of its office-bearers, except the ameer and the fighters. Over 2,500 students are currently enrolled at the Muridke complex and the teachers insist that all of them are Pakistanis. The education, Islamic and Western, is from the primary to the university level for both men and women and the students are brainwashed into propagating Islam and waging jehad against infidels.

Apart from the fact that its recruits have the best weapons and state-of-the-art communication technology, LeT is also reported to have a propaganda arsenal. It publishes magazines in many languages, has a website, and also plans to set up its radio station. Apart from its schools, many volunteers from other educational institutions, some even from the UK and US, join LeT. Fighters from over seventeen countries, including Algeria, Sudan, Yemen, Iran, Chechnya and the UK, have either been killed or detained in Kashmir. LeT also took part in the Kargil conflict. According to its magazine *Majallah Al-Daawa*, the first group of infiltrators who fought pitched battles with the Indian army in upper Drass and Batalik were Lashkar volunteers. It was only subsequently that the Pakistani army took over

Despite a government interdiction, banners can easily be seen in the urban and rural areas of Punjab urging young boys to enroll themselves for jehad with Jamaat-ul-Dawa and LeT. The banners usually carry the telephone numbers of the area offices. Similarly, LeT and Dawa activists can be seen outside mosques distributing pamphlets and periodicals preaching the virtues of jehad in Kashmir, Palestine, Chechnya, Kosovo and

Eritrea, besides vowing to plant the flag of Islam in Washington, Tel Aviv and New Delhi. The LeT leadership describes the Hindus and Jews as the principal enemies of Islam and claims the India and Israel are the main enemies of Pakistan.

The donation boxes of LeT and Jamaat that had disappeared after the militant groups were banned reappeared in public places as well as in mosques all over the Punjab. However, most Jamaat funds still came in the form of anonymous donations sent directly to its bank accounts from various parts of the world. Some insiders believe that Jamaat had raised so much money, mostly from sympathetic Wahhabis in Saudi Arabia that it planned to open its own bank.

The Markaz Yarmuk in Pattoki is emerging as the second important base for Jamaat-ul-Dawa after Markaz Dawa in Muridke. In 2003, for the second consecutive year, Jamaat held its annual congregation in Pattoki.

Those close to Hafiz Saeed are convinced that General Musharraf will neither abandon the militants nor the military option until there is a formal resolution of the lingering Kashmir dispute. They pointed out that the last time General Musharraf had promised to put an end to cross-border infiltration to the visiting US deputy secretary of state, Richard Armitage, in May 2003 the militants were held back for only a couple of months before being allowed to resume infiltration across the LoC. Indeed, should the Indo-Pak peace initiative fail; there are those in the military establishment who believe LeT could once again be the frontline jehadi group in Jammu & Kashmir and Hafiz Mohammad Saeed the new public face of the Kashmir militancy.

HAFIZ SAEED'S EMPIRE CRUMBLING

Currently though, Prof Hafiz Mohammad Saeed appears to be fighting for his political survival after a group of disgruntled Jamatul Dawa leaders have revolted against his leadership.

According to well-placed Jamaat insiders, some of the rebel members of the newly formed splinter group, largely consisting of Lashkar-e-Toiba cadres have even taken an oath to assassinate Hafiz Saeed, who they accuse of nepotism, diverting the party from its original objectives and misuse of resources. The new group includes some top leaders of Jamatul Dawa and Zakiur Rehman Lakhvi, the ameer of the now defunct LeT.

The differences between the two groups are serious and are likely to become more so when the question of division of assets arises. This is why some press reports insist Hafiz Saeed is fighting for more than just political survival.

Hafiz Mohammad Saeed came under fire from his close associates in December 2001, when he renamed Markaz Dawa Wal Irshad as Jamaat-ul-Dawa and separated the LeT's infrastructure from Jamaat. Many of his colleagues, including the LeT chief Zakiur Rehman Lakhvi, disapproved of the decision, which was meant to put the Jamaat in control of all funds collected locally and abroad. According to a 18 July 2004 report of *Daily Times*, the dissenters within Jamaat-ul-Dawa and LeT felt that as donations were collected in the name of jehad and the mujahideen, the leadership of Jamaat-ul-Dawa had no right to the money as it was only a preaching organization.

As Hafiz Saeed failed to satisfy Zakiur Rehman Lakhvi and his other associates, they subsequently decided to launch Khairun Naas, principally comprising LeT commanders and fighters. According to a close associate of Zakiur Rehman Lakhvi, Khairun Naas and the LeT are basically the same, but as LeT has been banned in Pakistan, the new group was named Khairun Naas. He claimed that the Jamaat-ul-Dawa headquarters in Muridke and the group's assets in Azad Kashmir were under the control of Khairun Naas. 'All the Al-Dawa model schools, seminaries, hospitals, health centres, and other such assets in the Sindh province are also under Khairun Naas's control because the heads of these institutions are siding with us,' he added. Khairun Naas leaders were also annoyed at Hafiz Saeed's second marriage to a fallen comrade's 28-year old widow. On the other hand, however, Saeed's associates say he still enjoys the support of some leading Jamaat-ul-Dawa leaders including Maulana Abdul Rehman Makki and Maulana Saifullah Qasoori. They insist that Khairun Naas has been established by the intelligence agencies to weaken the jehadis in Kashmir. 'Hafiz Saeed was under tremendous pressure from the agencies not to preach jehad any more and to limit his activities,' said one of his close comrades.

Some in the Pakistani intelligence community though believe that the ISI has orchestrated the split because of mounting pressure from the US to ban Jamaat-ul Dawa. While re-banning the various jehadi organizations associated with al-Qaeda in 2003 under their new names, General Pervez Musharraf refrained from re-banning Jamaat and LeT. Instead, he put them on a so-called watch list, despite the fact that the US State Department has already designated the LeT as a foreign terrorist group along with HuM and JeM, and it has been banned in the UK, Australia and some other countries.

According to analysts, as LeT has been in the forefront of militancy in Kashmir and has been close to the ISI, the Musharraf administration is avoiding any action against it under the pretext that the organization, which is active in the Indian territory, had no links with Jamaat-ul Dawa in Pakistan. The US pressure on Musharraf to ban Jamaat and LeT has intensified after its sleeper cells in the US were identified. The counter-terrorism agencies of many countries of the world have been increasingly concerned over the activities of LeT because of its role in the training of a number of Indonesians and Malaysians, including the brother of Hambali of Jemaah Islamiyah, in one of its madrassas in Karachi.

On the other hand, in a bid to counter the newly launched Khairun Naas, Hafiz Saeed and a coterie of his trusted aides are spending much of their time in Dewal Sharif near Muzaffarabad to recruit an increasing number of militants. Hafiz Saeed's topmost priority now is to form a new cadre of highly trained militants, not only for militancy in Jammu & Kashmir, but also to counter the might of his former comrades from Lashkar-e-Toiba.

LeT Militants Fighting in Iraq

The arrest of a senior LeT operative from Baghdad in April 2004 reinforced the perception that Pakistan continues to be a springboard for cross-border terrorism. Danish Ahmed from Bahawalpur area of Punjab and a close associate of the high-ranking LeT leader, Zakiur Rahman, was arrested in Baghdad by the allied forces and identified as a former commander of the organization's forward camps across the LoC, who had visited Jammu & Kashmir at least six times between 1997 and 2001.

According to international media reports, Danish played a central role in the organization's operations in Jammu & Kashmir from at least 1999, operating under the nom de guerre Abdul Rehman al-Dakhil. The media reports quoted Danish's interrogators as saying that he had trained many of the Pakistani militants in the use of arms and explosives at LeT's Muaskar Abu Bashir camp.

The international media reports went to the extent of alleging that up to 2,000 militants between the ages of 18 and 25 have set up a full-scale unit for suicide squad operations against the allied troops in Iraq. Most of these come from towns of Punjab province, where LeT's political patron Jamaat-ul-Dawa, wields considerable influence.

According to analysts, among all the Pakistani jehadi groups, there are many reasons why LeT is the most suited to operate in Iraq. First, unlike the Deobandi jehadi groups such as JeM and HuM, LeT does not have any political ambitions within Pakistan. The Deobandis have built a powerful political movement within Pakistan, but their political participation has also resulted in periodic tussles with the Pakistani army, which although highly supportive of jehad in Afghanistan and India, nevertheless brooks no challenge to its vice-like grip on political power within the nation. By contrast, the LeT-led Pakistani Wahhabi movement has traditionally stayed apolitical, and instead focused on global jehad outside Pakistan. Given this, LeT has had a free hand to operate within Pakistan.

On April 20, 2005, the Treasury Department of the United States spotted new organizations working on behalf of the banned LeT and declared them as terror-financer or terror-finance receiver. The Treasury announcement, channeled through the Office of Foreign Assets Control (OFAC), said that new names of LeT have been added as operating in contravention to terror-finance prevention rules. These names will now figure on the list of specially designated persons and organizations against which alerts have been communicated worldwide.

According to an 20 April 2005 press release of the US Treasury Department, the primary entry change appears below: Lashkar-e-Toiba (a.k.a. Al Mansooreen; a.k.a. Al Mansoorian; a.k.a.; Army of the Pure; a.k.a. Army of the Pure and Righteous; a.k.a. Army of the Righteous; a.k.a. Lashkar e-Toiba; a.k.a. Lashkar-i-Taiba; a.k.a. Paasban-e-Ahle-Hadis; a.k.a. Paasban-e-Kashmir; a.k.a. Paasban-i-Ahle-Hadith; a.k.a. Pasban-e-Ahle-Hadith; a.k.a. Pasban-e-Kashmir), Pakistan.

---

1. Abbas, Hassan, *Pakistan's Drift into Extremism: Allah, the Army, and America's War on Terror*, M.E. Sharpe, New York, 2004.

8

Harkatul Mujahideen: Its New Face of Terror

The drive against extremists being conducted by the Musharraf administration has brought into sharp focus Harkatul Mujahideen's alleged al-Qaeda links, amidst reports that the Federal Bureau of Investigation is seeking the custody of Maulana Fazlur Rahman Khalil, the Harkat chief and the only jehadi leader from Pakistan with a record of being close to Osama bin Laden.

Harkatul Mujahideen Al-alami, an offshoot of Harkatul Mujahideen has been accused since 2002 of mounting two abortive attempts on General Pervez Musharraf's life and a number of suicide bombings in the port city of Karachi. On 29 September 2001, weeks after the 9/11 terror attacks, the Pakistan government had banned Harkatul Mujahideen in compliance with the UN Security Council order to all its member states to crack down on terrorist outfits. The order was motivated by the Bush administration's decision on 24 September 2001 to freeze Harkatul Mujahideen assets along with those of twenty-six other organizations and individuals in connection with a worldwide campaign against the possible sources of terrorism.

The US ban is said to have led to the formation of Harkatul Mujahideen Al-alami which first came into prominence in June 2002 when the Karachi Rangers arrested five extremists in connection with the suicide bomb blast outside the American Consulate in Karachi. In July the same year, three persons involved in the bombing were arrested. The three accused confessed their involvement in the act that had left twelve people dead, and also admitted that they had planned to blow up General Musharraf's car in Karachi in April 2002.

They told their interrogators that they had parked a Suzuki high-roof vehicle full of explosives but the remote-controlled device developed a technical fault at the eleventh hour and failed to work. The same Suzuki vehicle was later used for the suicide bombing attack on the US consulate in Karachi. Two of a three persons arrested were produced at the press conference in Karachi. They included Muhammad Imran, ameer of Harkatul Mujahideen Al-alami and Mohammad Hanif, *naib* ameer of the group and in charge of its *askari* (military) wing.

Muhammad Imran was produced before a Karachi court a few days later where he told the reporters present in the courtroom: 'I am a member of the Harkatul Mujahideen. The Harkatul Mujahideen Al-alami is the product of the rangers and the security agencies. And let me tell you there is no split in the Harkatul Mujahideen.' Although the authorities identified Imran and Hanif as Al-alami leaders, they were unable to produce any thing on the group in terms of literature or any other propaganda material. The intelligence community therefore concluded that Harkatul Mujahideen Al-alami was nothing but Harkatul Mujahideen under a different name.

In May 2004, the Karachi police arrested Al-alami's third ranking leader after a shootout and seized a huge quantity of arms and ammunition. Carrying a reward of Rs 3 million on his head, Kamran alias Atif alias Khalid alias Uncle alias Bhaijan, was wanted in the June 2002 US Consulate bombing and in the failed attempt on Gen. Pervez Musharraf's life in Karachi.

According to investigations carried out by the security and intelligence agencies, about fifty highly trained operatives of Harkatul Mujahideen, using Al-alami as a cover, are bent upon targeting Gen. Pervez Musharraf, American interests in Pakistan and law enforcement officials. Harkat adheres to the Deobandi school of Islamic thought and its members are fanatic Sunni Muslims. Subscribing to a pan-Islamic ideology, the group aims to achieve the secession of J&K from India through violent means and its eventual merger with Pakistan. About 60 per cent of its estimated 1000-strong initial cadre were from Pakistan and Afghanistan.

The group was born out of Harkat al-Jehad al-Islami, which was launched as a part of the Pakistan-based jehadi network fighting the Russian troops in Afghanistan. Two Pakistani Deobandi religious bodies, Jamiat Ulema-e-Islam (JUI) and Tableeghi Jamaat, set up the HJI in 1980, at the outset of the Afghan war. It was first formed to run relief camps for the Afghan mujahideen and was led by Maulana Irshad Ahmed. As the war in Afghanistan intensified, the ISI approached the HJI leadership to recruit and train the militants from Pakistan. The HJI then developed links with an Afghan resistance group, Hizb-e-Islami (Yunus Khalis faction).

A power struggle was reported within the group after Maulana Irshad Ahmed died in June 1985 during the Afghan jehad. Maulana Fazlur Rahman Khalil, the group's commander-in-chief split with the new ameer, Qari Saifullah Akhtar and decided to form Harkatul Mujahideen. Maulana Fazlur Rahman Khalil, a resident of Dera Ismail Khan became the first ameer of the HuM while Maulana Masood Alvi was appointed its central commander.

Having parted ways with the Harkat al-Jehad al-Islami, the HuM began participating in the Afghan jehad and started sending volunteers into Afghanistan on its own to assist the Afghan mujahideen The money largely came from Pakistan, Afghanistan, and Saudi Arabia, and this helped recruit and train over 6,000 volunteers from Pakistan, Algeria, Egypt, Tunisia, Jordan, Saudi Arabia, India, Bangladesh, Myanmar and the Philippines. The initial batch of HuM volunteers was trained in the use of arms, ammunition and explosives, at the training camps in Pakhtia province of Afghanistan being run by the Afghan leader, Jalaluddin Haqqani, who belonged to Hizb-e-Islami (Maulvi Yunus Khalis group) but later joined hands with the Taliban.

Soon, however, HuM set up its own training camps in Afghan territory just across Miran Shah in NWFP. Some of the best fighters of the Afghan war came from the HuM training camps. Impressed by their motivation and prowess, the CIA supplied them with Stinger missiles and trained them in their use to enable them to shoot down Soviet planes and helicopters. After the withdrawal of the Soviet troops, HuM focused on the Kashmir. The first batch of HuM volunteers entered J&K in 1991 under the leadership of Sajjad Shahid. The Harkat started its militant operations soon afterwards in Baramulla, Poonch and Anantnag areas of J&K to promote its radical pan-Islamic agenda which it has maintained since then by striking alliances with different jehadi groups.

In 1993, two leading Deobandi ulemas, Maulana Samiul Haq of the Jamiat Ulema-e-Islam and Hafiz Yusuf Ludhianvi of the Sunni Tehrik, asked leaders of the three splinter factions of the Harkat al-Jehad al-Islami to reunite. The three groups eventually merged in October 1993, to form what came to be known as Harkatul Ansar (HuA). Maulana Fazlur Rahman Khalil was appointed ameer while Maulana Shahadat Ullah became the chief commander of the new Harkat. The reunion led to an intensification of violence in J&K and the group soon carved a place for itself on the basis of some major operations in the Kashmir Valley.

While the HuA was formally launched in Pakistan, the merger of the three factions in J&K was the task of HuA general secretary Maulana Masood Azhar who had entered India on a fake Portuguese passport and reached Srinagar in February 1994. Azhar convened a meeting of twenty leaders of HJI, HuM and JuM at Matigund, Anantnag district, to discuss the merger. When returning from the meeting, Masood Azhar and Sajjad Afghani, respectively the secretary general and the military chief of the HuA, were arrested in Srinagar. With these arrests, the move to reunite the three HJI factions into HuA did not materialize.

A few months later, in April 1994, an unknown jehadi group, Al-Faran, kidnapped two British tourists from the Kashmir valley to use them as a bargaining chip for the release of Maulana Masood Azhar and Sajjad Afghani. It later transpired that Al-Faran was actually launched by two HuA commanders, Abdul Hameed Turkey and Mohammad Sikandar. The kidnappings drew so much criticism from the international community that for the first time in the US, two Kashmiri militant groups, HuA and Al-Faran, were placed on the US State Department's list of terrorist groups.

In October 1997, the then US Secretary of State Madeleine Albright notified to the American Congress, a list of thirty international terrorist organizations which the US government had decided to bring under the purview of the Anti-Terrorism and Effective Death Penalty Act. HuA was one of the organizations so notified, and the US terror tag split it into two factions.

The Harkat al-Jehad al-Islami faction blamed Maulana Fazlur Rahman Khalil of the HuM faction for masterminding the kidnapping as the two commanders who set up Al-Faran were from his group. Under intense pressure, Maulana Khalil simply disowned Al-Faran and dubbed it a creation of India's Research and Analysis Wing. Commanders Sikandar and Hameed were killed soon afterwards, making it easy for Khalil to distance himself from Al-Faran. The issue however kept hanging fire and finally led to a split in HuA, with both the groups reverting to their earlier identities. Both the groups however continued to enjoy very warm relations with the Taliban regime that allowed them to run their respective training camps in Afghanistan.

In 1995, the chief of Harkat al-Jehad al-Islami, Maulana Saifullah Akhtar, was arrested along with four officers of the Pakistan Army for planning Operation Khilafat to take over the military headquarters in Rawalpindi and establish an Islamic regime in Islamabad by overthrowing the government of Prime Minister Benazir Bhutto. The four army officers, were tried and sentenced in a court martial, but, for some unexplained reasons, Qari Saifullah Akhtar was never formally charged. He was released after the Benazir-government's dismissal in 1996 and was sent to Kabul where he once again revived Harkat al-Jehad al-Islami in support of the Taliban regime against the Northern Alliance. Saifullah's presence and activities in Kabul remained hidden from the rest of the world until his headquarter was hit in the American bombing of September 2001.

That the HuM had been associated with Osama bin Laden was proved in August 1998, when America bombed the al-Qaeda training camps near Khost and Jalalabad in eastern Afghanistan in retaliation for the bombings of their embassies in three African countries. The bombing destroyed two HuM training camps and killed twenty-one of its activists. Two days later, speaking at a news conference in Islamabad, Maulana Fazlur Rahman Khalil denied that bin Laden was indulging in terrorism and accused the US of killing fifty innocent civilians in Afghanistan. He said the camps bombed by the US in Afghan territory were actually set up by the CIA during Afghan war, and that they were now being used by HuM for imparting education to Afghan students, and denied that any of these camps were conducting training courses in terrorism.

Maulana Fazlur Rahman Khalil had then warned: 'The US has proved itself to be the world's biggest terrorist by carrying out attacks on Afghanistan and Sudan. I want to convey to the American leadership that we will take revenge for these attacks.'

Ten days later, in yet another warning to the US, Khalil said: 'The US has struck us with Tomahawk Cruise missiles at only two places, but we will hit back at them everywhere in the world, wherever we find them. We have started a holy war against the US and they will hardly find a tree to take shelter beneath.'

In September 2001, the Pakistan government announced a ban on the HuM following the Bush administration's 24 September 2001 decision to freeze all its assets. The US ban compelled the HuM leadership to rename itself Jamiatul Ansar. However, it decided to use the cover name of Harkatul Mujahideen al-Alami in order to keep functioning uninterrupted. Pakistan received the first hint of Harkatul Mujahideen al-Alami's presence and its al-Qaeda connections in 2002 when the FBI arrested an Egyptian Arab, Hisham al-Wahid from Saudi Arabia and brought him to Pakistan in July 2002. He guided the security agencies to three activists of Jaish-e-Muhammad and two of Lashkar-e-Jhangvi in Karachi. They then led the Karachi police to one Iraqi and two Yemeni Arabs.

Subsequent interrogations revealed that those arrested were connected with the al-Qaeda. The police then arrested Rafeequl Islam of Sipah-e-Sahaba who later admitted to being in charge of communications for the al-Qaeda sponsored jehadi network in Karachi.

As of today, the US intelligence agencies believe that HuM still retains links, like most of other jehadi groups, with the Taliban remnants and al-Qaeda operatives hiding on the Pak–Afghan border. They recall that Maulana Fazlur Rahman Khalil took hundreds of his men to Afghanistan after the US-led Allied Forces attacked Afghanistan in 2001. The HuM chief returned home safely in January 2002 and lived for the next six months without any constraints in an Islamabad sanctuary until August 2002 when the government placed him under house arrest. Some say he was taken into protective custody after American intelligence sleuths sought his custody for a debriefing. The Pakistani authorities, however, had refused to oblige.

The American demand for Khalil's custody came after the Afghan government captured a 17-year-old Pakistani jehadi, Mohammad Sohail, who was fighting alongside the Taliban in southern Afghanistan. The arrest was made amid allegations by the Afghan and American officials that some Pakistan-based militant groups were still training fighters and sending them into Afghanistan to wage jehad against the US-led Allied Forces and the Northern Alliance troops.

During interrogations by Afghan security officials, Sohail reportedly confessed that Pakistan was still allowing militant groups to train and organize insurgents to fight in Afghanistan. In his confessional statement, Sohail talked about his militant group and its leaders, and claimed that they had high level support from within the Pakistani establishment. Afghan intelligence officials also found on Sohail a Jamiatul Ansar membership card and a list of phone numbers of high-level group officials. In his confessional statement, Mohammad Sohail claimed he traveled with a group of fifteen jehadis from his local mosque in Karachi to a training camp near Mansehra, where they received one month of training in explosives and weapons. After the training session was over, Sohail claimed the group members went to Islamabad and met Maulana Fazlur Rehman Khalil, at his headquarters. Three months later, Maulana Khalil went to speak at their mosque and called on the group of youngsters to fight, according to Sohail said. They then went to Quetta, the capital of Balochistan, and with four other fighters, he crossed the border and drove to Kandahar.

In Kandahar, they went to a designated hotel where they were supplied a bag full of automatic weapons. The next day, they headed to a mountain base near the town of Panjwai, west of Kandahar, where they joined some fifty fighters and became involved in combat operations, before finally being arrested. Sohail was charged with taking part in a terrorist attack on the

Panjwai District centre in April 2004, in which an Afghan police officer and two aid workers were killed. He was subsequently sentenced to 20-year rigorous imprisonment by a judge in Kabul. As Kabul took up Sohail's case with Islamabad, Maulana Khalil was taken into custody by the security agencies in August 2004. Yet, the arrest seemed more a protective measure to keep him away from the FBI, which had expressed its desire to interview the jehadi leader in the light of Mohammad Sohail's confessional statement. As soon as the pressure eased off, the Musharraf administration set him free on 20 December 2004. Soon after his release, Khalil resigned in January 2005 as the Jamiatul Ansar chief, citing his poor health, and appointed his right hand man Maulana Badar Munir in his place. However, the resignation move was nothing more than an eyewash to ease off the American pressure.

Khalil's name once again popped up in the international media after the June 2005 arrests of two Pakistani-Americans in a small Californian town, Lodi, followed by a confessional statement by one of them of having been trained at a militant training camp in Rawalpindi, being run by the Jamiatul Ansar. In a 6 June 2005 FBI affidavit filed in a US court, one of the arrested, 22-year-old Hamid Hayat, was accused of getting training at an al-Qaeda camp in Pakistan to learn how to kill Americans. His father, Umer Hayat, was charged with financing of the al-Qaeda camp in Rawalpindi.

Hamid Hayat confessed to having received terrorist training for six months [in 2003 and 2004] at a Dhamial camp in Rawalpindi, which was being run by Fazlur Rehman Khalil. According to him, the Rawalpindi camp provided structured paramilitary training, including weapons training, explosives training, hand-to-hand combat and strenuous exercise. The fresh disclosures revived the interest of the American intelligence sleuths in interviewing Khalil. But the Pakistani agencies again moved swiftly and took him into their custody, only to release him in August 2005 when the dust had settled.

Since then, Khalil has restricted himself to his Islamabad headquarters, though he remains in the good books of the Pakistani agencies and still calls the shots.

While most of the jehadi kingpins who toe the establishment's line continue to enjoy freedom of movement and speech in Pakistan, there are those like the chief of the Harkat al-Jehad al-Islami (Movement of Islamic Holy War), Qari Saifullah Akhtar, who had to face the wrath of the establishment and were put behind bars, ostensibly because of their efforts to physically eliminate General Musharraf. Qari Saifullah was arrested from Dubai and extradited to Pakistan on 7 August 2004 for his involvement in the 25 December 2003 twin suicide attacks on Musharraf in Rawalpindi.

A graduate of the Banori Mosque in Karachi, Qari Saifullah was first heard of 1995 when the then chief of army staff, General Abdul Waheed Kakar, discovered a plot by a small group of Pakistan Army officers led by Major General Zaheerul Islam Abbasi to stage a coup. The plotters wanted to assassinate the then prime minister Benazir Bhutto, seize power and proclaiming formation of an Islamic Caliphate in Pakistan. Qari Saifullah was arrested for his alleged involvement in the coup plot. But strangely enough, while many army officers were court-martialled and sentenced to various terms of imprisonment, Qari was spared and turned an approver. He was released soon after dismissal of Benazir Bhutto's second government in November 1996. Major General Zaheerul Islam was set free too following Musharraf's 1999 military take over.

Qari Saifullah immediately made his way to Kabul, where he became an adviser to Mullah Mohammad Omar and was given several important assignments, such as training police and armed forces, and some administrative responsibilities. Qari's fighters were called 'Punjabi' Taliban and were given employment, something that none of the other Pakistani militant outfits could get out of Mullah Omar. When the US-led allied troops attacked Afghanistan in October 2001 after the

9/11 attacks, a large number of jehadis belonging to the Harkat al-Jehad al-Islami and the Harkatul Mujahideen lost their lives, especially in Kandahar. Qari was with the Taliban ameer Mullah Omar at the time of the attack, but he escaped from Kandahar, taking shelter in South Waziristan. He then fled to Saudi Arabia and later moved to Dubai from where he was executing terrorist operations in Pakistan with the help of his right hand man, Amjad Hussain Farooqui. Qari is behind the bars now, after the Supreme Court of Pakistan dismissed on 17 January 2005 a petition against his arrest.

9

Hizbul Mujahideen: Determined to Defy

Syed Salahuddin, the chief of the most powerful militant group fighting in Jammu & Kashmir the Hizbul Mujahideen (HM), has been under tremendous pressure from the Pakistan government to cease militant operations in the Kashmir Valley, especially after the inking of the January 2004 Islamabad agreement between India and Pakistan.

After successful talks between Gen. Pervez Musharraf and the former Indian prime minister Vajpayee in January 2004, the Pakistani government as well as the intelligence agencies had initiated back-channel diplomacy with most of the jehadi groups operating from Pakistan. The move was meant to persuade the jehadi leaders to fall in with the official line, keeping in view the rapidly changing geo-political circumstances that required a change of strategy. The authorities had reportedly asked Syed Salahuddin to direct his cadre to cease their operations against the Indian security forces in J&K. However, Salahuddin, who also heads the United Jehad Council (UJC), is reluctant to comply and bitterly criticizes Islamabad's 'U-turn' on the Kashmir issue. 'We will continue waging jehad against the Indian occupation forces in the Valley.

We can't become silent spectators of a show where the puppets are India and Pakistan, and the United States is pulling the strings,' the HM chief had stated in his reaction to the signing of the Islamabad agreement.

Leading the HM seems to be an odd thing for Salahuddin to do, given that he started off as a schoolteacher. Syed Salahuddin's strength lies in the fact that he heads a militant group that is largely indigenous and not one dominated by foreign mercenaries. As the supreme commander, Salahuddin, who ranks No. 8 on India's 'Most Wanted' list, controls a 20,000-strong jehadi cadre from Muzaffarabad.

Despite having a cadre base drawn from indigenous and foreign sources, the January 2004 assassination of the Hizb's chief operational commander made it quite difficult for its militants to continue carrying out major strikes against the 'enemy troops'. Ghulam Rasool Dar's assassination came as a major blow to the command structure of the valley's largest militant group which was already struggling to pull through the loss of a string of its top commanders over an intra-party blood-feud, sparked off by the gruesome murder of the pro-dialogue commander Abdul Majid Dar in March 2002. Ghulam Rasool Dar, alias Ghazi Naseeruddin and the HM's financial and publicity chief, Fayyaz Ahmed, were killed in January 2004 in a brief encounter with the Indian security forces at Zainakot in Srinagar valley. Calling it a major success, Indian forces claim to have almost wiped out the HM's entire top leadership. The successful military operation, carried out just ten days after the Indo-Pak accord, caused wild speculations in HM circles that the bloody shoot-out might have been the outcome of a clandestine intelligence sharing agreement between New Delhi and Islamabad.

Significantly, since the January 2004 Islamabad agreement was signed between India and Pakistan, at least a dozen front-line leaders of the several jehadi groups waging an armed struggle against the Indian security forces in J&K have lost their lives. Prominent among those killed by the Indian security forces since January 2004 was the HM 'chief commander of operations', Abdur Rasheed Pir alias Ghazi Shahabuddin, who was shot dead during an encounter with the J&K police in the in May 2004. Pir was the third successive chief commander of the HM operations killed in the last thirteen months. As the head HM's operations in J&K, Pir was responsible for many strikes against the Indian occupation forces in the Valley.

According to a J&K police press statement, as many as thirty senior commanders of the HM, LeT and Jaish-e-Mohammad have been killed by the Indian troops over the past eighteen months. Due to these killings, the pressure on the jehadi groups operating in J&K is enormous and rising. Even the Indian authorities have admitted for the first time that overt support from Pakistan, including artillery cover that was routinely provided to infiltrating groups, has diminished since the Islamabad agreement was signed. At the same time, counter-terrorist operations in J&K by the Indian security forces have also been enormously successful over the past months.

In April 2003, Indian security forces had succeeded in eliminating Ghulam Rasool Dar's predecessor: Ghulam Rasool Khan. Dar's deputy Saif-ul-Rahman Bajwa, who was a Pakistani national, was subsequently killed by the Border Security Force in November 2003. Dar's death came within fifteen hours of the killing of his deputy Mohammad Abbas Malik, who used to supervise the launching of attacks and logistics of HM.

Shortly before his death, Dar met the J&K Jamaat-e-Islami chief Syed Nazir Ahmad Kashani, to demand that the Jamaat throw its weight behind the All Parties Hurriat Conference (APHC) leader, Syed Ali Shah Geelani, who was opposed to the talks between the APHC and New Delhi. Previously, Ghulam Rasool Dar had made his way across the Line of Control back in 2000 to participate in the first and the last official contact of HM with the Indian government. He actually represented his leader, Salahuddin, who had become increasingly suspicious of

Abdul Majid Dar, the pro-negotiations HM commander who spearheaded the dialogue. Ghulam Rasool Dar's hard line stance during the talks eventually shut down the dialogue process. This created a visible divide between Jammu-based leaders seeking a dialogue with the Indian government and Pakistan-based hardliners.

Soon afterwards, as the chief operational commander of HM, Abdul Majid Dar had made a conditional ceasefire offer to the Indian government at a press conference in Srinagar in July 2000. Interestingly, the endorsement of this offer by the group's supremo Syed Salahuddin alias Pir Sahib was followed by a press conference in Islamabad. Majid Dar put forward three conditions for observance of the cease-fire: '… no use of force against mujahideen, human rights violations on the Kashmiris will end and people even with different political convictions will be allowed free expression.'

The ceasefire offer led to widespread speculations in the jehadi circles that the move might have been motivated by Jamaat chief Qazi Hussain Ahmad who had just returned from a visit to Washington. However, all the other militant groups operating in J&K unanimously rejected the ceasefire offer. An umbrella body of seventeen Pakistan-based militant groups, the Muttahida Jehad Council (United Jehad Council or UJC) rejected the ceasefire. Acting under the pressure of the United Jehad Council's other component parties, its chief, Syed Salahuddin, soon decided to disassociate himself from the ceasefire offer, and this about-turn infuriated Dar and generated a lot of tension between the two leaders.

Signs of the divisions within the HM top leadership became more evident at the 2 May 2002 meeting where the decision to remove Majid Dar was made. Immediately after Dar's expulsion, fissures showed up in the HM field commands.

The dramatic sacking of Majid Dar was quite predictable. Earlier, in October 2001, alarmed by Dar's efforts to initiate a dialogue with the Indian government bypassing Pakistan,

Salahuddin had replaced his field commanders. Matters had spiralled out of hand, and in late November 2001 the HM command council ordered Dar and his associates to return to Pakistan. Dar's subordinates however reiterated their loyalty to him and made it clear that they had no intention of leaving Kashmir until their replacements were in place.

By early 2003, Abdul Dar and many of his supporters within HM had decided to launch their own groups to take part in the upcoming J&K state assembly elections. However, as Dar was preparing to come to Pakistan to announce the formation of his political group, the Jammu and Kashmir Salvation Movement, Salahuddin's hit-squad allegedly killed him near his Sopore hometown in J&K in March 2003. Dar's assassination provoked a serious split within the HM cadre in Pakistan, though Salahuddin survived and remained firmly in control of the organization, primarily because of ISI's support.

While all the top commanders of the Majid Dar group and a majority of its mujahideen decided to join the Hizb-e-Islami, some of them, refusing to work under the new flag and leadership, returned to HM. On the other hand, Salahuddin announced that HM would not welcome back to its fold any commander from the Dar group but mujahideen seeking to rejoin were more than welcome to do so.

For their part, Majid Dar's followers had a simple response to charges, maintaining that Syed Salahuddin had betrayed the cause of jehad in J&K. They pointed to his five sons, not one of whom has had joined the ranks of the hundreds of young cadre that the HM leadership sends to their death each year.

Hizbul Mujahideen has undergone four splits since 1990, all of them aimed at removing Syed Salahuddin. However, he has survived till now and is in total control of the party. The Jamiatul Mujahideen of General Abdullah, Muslim Mujahideen of Ahsan Dar, Hizb-e-Islami of Masood and Al-Badr of Bakht Zameen, all broke away from HM. In the words of an ex-intelligence official: 'One of the oldest tricks in the book is to not allow any individual jehadi group to become too strong. This is a tried and tested mode of keeping overall control on such groups. Whenever one group is seen as getting too strong or influential, the agencies try to split it and sometimes pit one against the other. And the Hizbul Mujahideen is no exception.'

HM was designated a terrorist group by the US State Department before Deputy Secretary of State Armitage's visit to the subcontinent in May 2003. The move came after the its leadership owned up to having acquired shoulder-firing Estrela surface-to-air missiles being used against the Indian security forces in J&K. Only in January 2004, the group had claimed to killing 770 Indian soldiers and losing 232 of its fighters in 314 encounters during 2003. 'The slain Indian soldiers included one brigadier, fifteen majors, three captains, ten junior commissioned officers, one sergeant and four inspectors of the regular army and personnel of Special Operations Group and Special Task Force,' claimed HM spokesman Salim Hashmi, adding that the group's cadres would continue their attacks against the Indian security forces.

A comparatively stronger vocal statement came from Syed Salahuddin: 'Thousands of militants have sacrificed their lives pursuing their dream of liberating Kashmir. Islamabad's bowing to US pressures on Kashmir is a betrayal.' The HM chief goes on to argue: 'If the Indian government accepts the disputed status of Kashmir, stops killings and atrocities, releases all detainees and reduces the number of troops in Kashmir to the pre-1988 position, the guns will become silent automatically. The mere signing of a piece of paper by Indian and Pakistani leaders cannot convince us to lay down our weapons.'

Salahuddin's overtures apart, the fact remains that while operating from Rawalpindi, he is at the mercy of the Pakistani establishment; for there is little that he can do as long as he is on their soil. In the aftermath of the Islamabad agreement between India and Pakistan, Salahuddin has been barred from entering

Azad Kashmir, with instructions from his masters to wait and see. At the same time, there are reports that in a move that signalled its effort to address New Delhi's concern over terrorism, Islamabad had begun disarming HM cadres at militant training camps in Muzaffarabad in Azad Kashmir. As things stand, Syed Salahuddin seems to be a virtual prisoner. Though still in communication with his jehadi cadre in J&K, the HM chief seems no longer to be his own master.

HOW HIZBUL MUJAHIDEEN WAS BORN?

Launched in November 1989, the militant group called Hizbul Mujahideen has essentially three factions: The first of these was set up in Jammu & Kashmir in 1990 with the blessings of Jamaat-e-Islami and is commanded by Syed Salahuddin. The Pakistani faction of the HM was founded by Jamaat-e-Islami Pakistan and Usman Bhai was appointed its commander. Ameer, Azad Kashmir Jamaat-e-Islami Allama, Rashid Turrabi launched the third Hizb faction and Masood Sarfraz was appointed its chief commander. This faction later came to be called Pir Panjal Regiment.

A 20-member council and a 5-member Shura run the party. It has its own news agency, Kashmir Press International (KPI) and a women's wing: Banat-ul-Islam. Overseas, Ghulam Nabi Fai's Kashmir American Council and Ayub Thakur's World Kashmir Freedom Movement back it. Interestingly, besides being held responsible for the massacre of Hindus in the valley, the HM is also accused of liquidating several Muslim religious leaders in Jammu & Kashmir who were opposed to the Jamaat-e-Islami world-view.

The HM story begins in 1983 when Ameer, Jamaat-e-Islami, Jammu & Kashmir, Maulana Saad-ud-Din, returned to Pakistan from Saudi Arabia. In Pakistan, he met the then military ruler General Zia ul Haq and leaders of Jamaat-e-Islami Pakistan, including the then JI Ameer Mian Tufail Mohammad, to work out a detailed strategy for armed resistance in Jammu & Kashmir.

On the basis of this strategy, in 1984, Jamaat-e-Islami Occupied Kashmir (JIOK), as it is called, began preparing for militancy. Cadres were asked to migrate to Azad Kashmir and other areas, including Afghanistan, and to get military training. Syed Ali Gilani, the JIOK ameer, led the movement. Scores of JIOK cadres came to Azad Kashmir and went to Afghanistan to train and fight with the Afghan mujahideen. This process continued until 1987. This period also saw the rise of many organizations such as Zia Tigers, Al-Hamza and Al-Badr. The leaders of these organizations, invariably Jamaat affiliates, sought guidance from Jamaat-e-Islami Pakistan and its branches in Azad Kashmir and Occupied Kashmir.

These organizations began operating against Indian forces in Jammu & Kashmir from August 1988 onwards. However, until then, there was no concerted effort at armed resistance. This continued till mid-1989. At that point, leaders of the Jamaat in Pakistan, Azad Kashmir and Jammu & Kashmir thought it was important to set up a single organization that could coordinate the resistance effort. In a September 1989 session, the Jamaat-e-Islami leaders formally moved to set up such an organization.

This session gave birth to HM by merging two organizations, Tehrik-ul-Mujahideen and Hizb-e-Islami. The organizational structure of HM was finally put in place in October 1989. In November 1989, its formation was formally announced in the press and its constitution was promulgated in June 1990. Indian authorities, however, allege that Pakistan's ISI was actively involved in coordinating all these efforts to launch the organization.

Master Ahsan Dar, a schoolteacher in Kashmir's Pattan area, reportedly went to Pakistan in 1988 and was trained there by the ISI. He returned to the Valley in 1990 and was appointed the first HM chief. By 1991, major groups, such as Tehreek-e-Jehad-e-Islami led by Abdul Majid Dar, had merged with the new outfit. In Srinagar, another veteran, Mohammed Abdullah Bangroo, was appointed Ahsan's chief military adviser.

Within a year HM had over 10,000 armed cadres, mostly trained in Pakistan or Pakistan-occupied Kashmir. Meanwhile, the group's supreme advisory council met for two days and in November 1991 asked chief commander Master Ahsan Dar to step down. Mohammad Yusuf Shah, who goes by the name Syed Salahuddin, was named as the new patron and also the supreme commander of the group. Under Salahuddin's command, it adopted aggressive and often communal postures.

In early 1992, HM became a member of the Popular International Organization under the leadership of Sudan's Dr Hassan-al-Turabi, which made it eligible for guidance, training, funds and arms from abroad. At the same time, a mercenary Afghan organization, Harkat al-Jehad al-Islami, currently based in Pakistan, was actively collaborating with HM, providing guidance and material assistance. The Hizb sources claim that on an average it spends over Rs 5 million every month to maintain its cadres.

The HM has been under the scrutiny of the Indian authorities for a long time. The Indian government declared it an unlawful association in September 1996 and banned it in 1983. By that time, the hardliners in Jamaat-e-Islami and the HM leadership had already developed differences.

In November 1997, Salahuddin announced the disassociation of his group from Jamaat-e-Islami. 'Our outfit is not affiliated with any particular group. Ours is an armed resistance movement of all the people of Jammu and Kashmir. We have a network from Srinagar to every important capital of the world and our supporters are all Kashmiris and expatriate Kashmiris,' declared Salahuddin in 1997.

In February 1998, several press reports hinted at the possibility of Salahuddin being displaced as HM chief for dissociating his group from the Jamaat, an act that had also infuriated Pakistan's ISI. Intense rivalry subsequently surfaced between two HM groups, one loyal to Salahuddin, a Kashmiri, and the other headed by a Pakistani, Masood Sarfraz, who was deputed by the ISI to replace Salahuddin.

However, efforts to displace Salahuddin as HM chief received a serious blow in the wake of complaints against Masood Sarfaraz which ranged from arbitrary use of funds to mismanagement in the training camps to a high-handed attitude towards the party leadership. All this prompted Azad Kashmir's Jamaat-e-Islami chief, Allama Rashid Turrabi, to replace Masood Sarfraz. Sarfraz however refused to accept the orders and started confronting the Jamaat leadership by openly accusing them of harbouring sinister designs and plans to compromise the Kashmir cause under American pressure.

Following Sarfraz's refusal to step down, Turrabi himself took control of the HM headquarters in Kotli district of Azad Kashmir, thereby leading to a fierce battle between the two groups. This not only resulted in dozens of casualties within the cadres of the two factions but also claimed the lives of a few innocent citizens. The fighting also pointed towards a disturbing trend. The armed groups fighting in Kashmir were increasingly showing signs of indiscipline, a phenomenon that had already been witnessed in Afghanistan at one stage of its resistance movement against the Soviets.

When Rawalpindi-based Salahuddin announced a unilateral ceasefire against the Indian army in Jammu & Kashmir in July 2000, he was removed from the chairmanship of United Jehad Council, the collective body of leading militant groups fighting in Kashmir's. However, after India's failure to take advantage of HM's unilateral ceasefire offer, the UJC, in October 2000, restored HM membership and appointed Salahuddin as the council chairman.

With militancy going out of fashion and Pakistan apparently withdrawing its support to the Kashmiri militants, Syed Salahuddin plans to assume a new role by converting the Hizbul Mujahideen into a political party. Having already got clearance from the leadership of the Jamaat-e-Islami Pakistan, Salahuddin has started the groundwork for taking over the mantle of Syed Ali Shah Geelani, the ailing chief of Jamaat-e-Islami Jammu & Kashmir. However, his close associates say, being a hardcore Jamaat-e-Islami man, Syed Salahuddin cannot take decisions independently and that he has actually been asked by the Jamaat-e-Islami Pakistan and Jamaat-e-Islami Azad Kashmir to assume a political role in the emerging regional geo-strategic atmosphere.

The central leadership of the two Jamaat-e-Islamis believe that Syed Ali Shah Geelani, who is in his mid-70s and not in good state of health, will leave a big vacuum when he passes away. Therefore, it wants to prepare somebody who can easily take over the mantle of Ali Shah Geelani. It was against this backdrop that Salahuddin announced his support for the Srinagar-Muzaffarabad bus service, as General Musharraf started his cricket diplomacy with India in March 2005, although the United Jihad Council had opposed it in a meeting earlier that month.

10

Jamaat-e-Islami: On the FBI Watchlist

Under immense pressure from the US, a slow and gradual operation has apparently begun against Jamaat-e-Islami Pakistan which is led by Qazi Hussain Ahmed. This follows reports that the Federal Bureau of Investigation has been keeping a close eye on the activities of the Jamaat and its top leaders since the March 2003 arrest of al-Qaeda's chief operational commander, Khalid Sheikh Mohammad, from the Rawalpindi residence of a local Jamaat-e-Islami leader.

Khalid Sheikh Mohammad is a Kuwaiti national who allegedly played a crucial part in orchestrating the 9/11 attacks on the World Trade Center. Ahmed Abdul Qadoos, the owner of the house, who was sheltering Khalid Sheikh, was also arrested during the raid. Since then the American intelligence agencies have been closely monitoring the activities of the Jamaat and its top leaders, with a mandate to recommend the inclusion of the Islamic party in the US State Department's list of terrorist groups once they get substantial evidence to establish its al-Qaeda links. In January 2003, two other suspected cadres of al-Qaeda were arrested from the house of another Jamaat member in Karachi, thereby giving rise to suspicion that Jamaat office-bearers and cadres not only in the NWFP and Baluchistan, but also elsewhere in Pakistan were helping the surviving members of al-Qaeda.

Maj. Gen. Rashid Qureshi, who was then the media spokesman of General Pervez Musharraf, had claimed at an ISI-organized media briefing that the fact that some al-Qaeda members were arrested from the houses of individual JI members did not mean that the organization had links with al-Qaeda.

However, speaking in the National Assembly in August 2004, the interior minister, Faisal Saleh Hayat, asserted that 'religio-political' parties in Pakistan were supporting al-Qaeda. Faisal listed a number of instances in which members of Jamaat-e-Islami Pakistan had been tied to al-Qaeda, and called on its leadership to explain these links. Addressing a news conference at his parliament house chamber, Faisal confirmed links of JI activists with al-Qaeda members, and said that their houses were used as hideouts and shelters for terrorists. 'It is a matter of concern that Jamaat-e-Islami, which is a main faction of the Muttahida Majlis-e-Amal (MMA), has neither dissociated itself from its activists having links with al-Qaeda network nor condemned their activities,' he said.

US intelligence agents do not appear to be convinced that the al-Qaeda links were just the rogue actions of some individual members of JI. Their concerns have been heightened by the apparent links of Gulbuddin Hekmatyar's Hizb-e-Islami with al-Qaeda and Taliban in launching renewed attacks against the US-led allied troops in Afghanistan. Of all the Islamic parties in Pakistan, Jamaat-e-Islami had been the closest to Hizb-e-Islami and had maintained contacts with Hekmatyar even when he and his associates were in hiding. After 9/11, when, under pressure from the US, the Taliban expelled them, they were welcomed in Pakistani territory by the Jamaat leadership, which reportedly provided them shelter.

According to the FBI, some foreign students who attended the JI-run Maulana Maudoodi Institute in Lahore disappeared from the institute under mysterious circumstances after 9/11. FBI investigations revealed that foreign militants had used Maudoodi Institute to transfer new recruits to Pakistan and then Afghanistan. The militants applied for admission and entered Pakistan after fulfilling legal requirements, but having spent a few days at the institute, they would disappear.

Besides closely watching activities of Jamaat-e-Islami and its leadership, the American intelligence agents in Pakistan are also looking into Syed Salahuddin led HM's links with JI, Hizb-e-Islami and al-Qaeda. Expressing concern over the alleged links, the Counter-Terrorism Division of the US State Department in its report *Patterns of Global Terrorism during 2002* had placed not only HM, but also Al-Badr and Jamiatul Mujahideen, both associated with the JI and Hizb-e-Islami, in the list of 'other terrorist organizations'.

The 'other terrorist organizations' list included the names of those organizations against whom evidence regarding their likely involvement in terrorism directed against the US is not strong enough to warrant their being declared foreign terrorist organizations. The US State Department's decision to categorize HM, Al-Badr and the Jamiatul Mujahideen as terrorist organizations was taken not so much by their activities in the Jammu & Kashmir, as by their links with JI, Hizb-e-Islami and possibly al-Qaeda too.

11

Tableeghi Jamaat: Nurturing Jehadis?

Tableeghi Jamaat (TJ) or the party of preachers, a non-militant organization of practicing Muslims that claims to have never indulged in any militant or political activities as a matter of principle, has been infiltrated by jehadi elements belonging to several banned militant and sectarian groups that are using the organization as a cover to further their extremist agenda.

Tableeghi Jamaat came into existence in British India in 1940 to spread the message of the Holy Koran with two aims: to ensure that Muslims strengthen their faith and to carry out humanitarian work. The TJ headquarters for South Asia are located in India. They were originally set up for humanitarian work and have not thus far evidenced any extremist views. In sharp contrast, however, TJ's Pakistan branch has now for quite some time been found to be involved in making clandestine efforts to aid jehadi elements and to promote their agenda. Since Pakistani law treats Tableeghi Jamaat as a humanitarian groups and not as a religio-political group, there is no ban on government servants, members of the armed forces, and the scientific community concerned with nuclear and missile development, from joining the party.

According to information obtained by intelligence sources, many government servants, military officers and scientists devote at least part of their annual leave to undertake voluntary work for TJ. At least three former heads of the ISI, Lt. Gen. (retd) Hameed Gul, Lt. Gen. (retd) Javed Nasir and Lt. Gen. (retd) Naseem Rana, were and still are closely involved with TJ's preaching activities. Lt. Gen. (retd) Javed Nasir, who was appointed ISI chief during the first tenure of Prime Minister Nawaz Sharif (1990–93) had to be removed under American pressure in 1993. He subsequently got involved in preaching tours and used to lead TJ delegations from Pakistan, going to the Philippines, Indonesia, Malaysia, the Central Asian Republics, Chechnya, Dagestan and Somalia.

TJ's annual conventions at Raiwind attract the second largest religious congregation in the Islamic world after that of the Haj in Saudi Arabia. Reputed to be the richest religious organization in Pakistan, it recruits hundreds of students in other countries and brings them to Pakistan at its own expense for studies in the religious seminaries.

According to US intelligence sources, among the foreign nationals who fought in Afghanistan against the Northern Alliance troops and US-led allied forces as members of the Pakistan-based jehadi outfits were American Muslims (mostly Afro-Americans), nationals of the West European countries, Thaïs, Malaysians, Singaporeans who projected themselves as Malays from Malaysia, and Indonesians. Fact is, that HuM, LeT and Harkat al-Jehad al-Islami teams that used to visit these countries as preachers, had recruited them all. They used to bring hundreds of Muslims to Pakistan who were educated at the religious seminaries before being eventually taken to Afghanistan for jehadi indoctrination and training.

According to intelligence sources, HuM, LeT and Harkat al-Jehad al-Islami enjoy close links with TJ and recruit their cadres in Pakistan as well as abroad through TJ. Often, to avoid attracting the adverse notice of foreign intelligence agencies, recruiting teams of HuM, LeT and HJI go abroad under the guise of TJ preachers. According to American intelligence findings, reported in the international media, Osama bin Laden too had used HuM, LeT and HJI teams going abroad under the garb of TJ preachers to communicate instructions to his network of non-Arab organizations in different countries. In the 1990s, many members of the HuM travelled to the southern Philippines as preachers and trained the cadres of the Abu Sayyaf and the Moro Islamic Liberation Front, and participated in their operations against the Philippine security forces.

It has already been reported in the US media that the six persons of Yemeni origin arrested by the FBI in the US after the 9/11 terrorist attacks in its search for sleeper agents (an agent who can be used at any time but may not be tasked for upto a decade or more) were found to have links with TJ. They had all visited the TJ headquarters in Raiwind before the 9/11 attacks. John Walker Lindh, known as the American Taliban, was reportedly inspired to go to Afghanistan after travelling to Pakistan with TJ preachers. Three Australians also visited Raiwind and joined TJ before going to Afghanistan.

An investigative report carried by Pakistan's *News International* on 13 February 1995, brought to light for the first time the nexus between TJ, the HuM and their clandestine role in supporting Islamic extremist movements in different countries. The report quoted unidentified office-bearers of the HuM as saying, 'Ours is basically a Sunni organization close to the Deobandi school of thought. Our people are mostly impressed by the TJ. Most of our workers do come from the TJ. We regularly go to its annual meeting at Raiwind. Ours is a truly international network of genuine jehadi Muslims.'

The report also quoted the HuM office-bearers as claiming that among the foreign volunteers trained by them in their training camps in Pakistan and Afghanistan, were sixteen African–American Muslims from various cities of the US and that funds for their activities mostly came from Muslim businessmen of Pakistan, Saudi Arabia, Egypt and the UK.

The February 1998 issue of the Karachi-based monthly *Newsline* quoted TJ workers as saying that the organization had many offices in the US, Russia, the Central Asian Republics, South Africa, Australia and France, and that many members of the Chechen cabinet, including the deputy prime minister of Chechnya, were associated with TJ and had participated in its proselytizing activities.

TJ's activities are being closely monitored by the American intelligence community, which believes that TJ was the fount of all the Pakistan-based jehadi organizations active not only in the Central Asian Republics, Chechnya and Dagestan but also in other parts of the world. According to the US intelligence findings, amongst US-based organizations with which the TJ is closely associated, are the Islamic Society of North America (ISNA) and the Muslim Youth of North America (MYNA).

Addressing the 1995 annual convention of the ISNA, held in the US at Columbus, Ohio, Dr Israr Ahmed, the ameer of Tanzeem-e-Islami of Pakistan and a member of the TJ had said: 'The process of the revival of Islam in different parts of the world is real. A final showdown between the Muslim world and the non-Muslim world, which has been captured by the Jews, would soon take place. The Gulf war was just a rehearsal for the coming conflict.' He appealed to the Muslims of the world, including those in the US, to prepare themselves for the coming conflict.

TJ operates in the US and the Caribbean directly through its own preachers deputed from Pakistan and also recruited from the Pakistani immigrant community abroad. In its preaching to the Pakistani immigrants in the US, the TJ has been stressing the importance of cultivating the African–American Muslims in order to counter the lobbying power of the Hindus and the Jews.

12

Dawood Ibrahim: Financing Militants?

Few outside India and Pakistan have heard of Dawood Ibrahim Kaskar despite his status as a billionaire gangster, an alleged global terrorist, a nuclear black market entrepreneur, and an Islamic extremist. An impoverished street tough from Mumbai who grew up to acquire international notoriety Dawood Ibrahim formed the infamous 'D Company', one of the most feared international crime organizations in the world.

A colourful mobster with powerful friends ranging from Bollywood movie stars to members of Pakistan's intelligence establishment, his alleged crimes include murder, kidnapping, drug-smuggling and trafficking in nuclear secrets. Underworld don Dawood Ibrahim is also accused of having masterminded the 1993 Bombay serial blasts, when twelve car-bombs killed almost 300 innocent people and injured over a thousand more. Until 11 September 2001, this was the single most destructive terrorist act in modern history.

As the global consensus against terrorism grew post-9/11, in October 2003, the US State Department declared Dawood

Ibrahim a specially designated global terrorist with al-Qaeda links. The US decision created ripples in Pakistan's intelligence circles which had cared little about the security implications of harbouring a mafia don wanted by an ever-hostile neighbour. Not only did the US action change the complexion of its relationship with India, but it also brought Washington into conflict with Islamabad, its ally in the war against terror, for the latter's alleged covert support to terrorists.

Much to Islamabad's embarrassment, the US Treasury Department in its reasons for naming Dawood in the list of the world's worst terrorists, cited intelligence reports of his connection with al-Qaeda and LeT. The fact sheet on Dawood Ibrahim placed on the Treasury Department's website states: 'Dawood Ibrahim, son of a police constable, has financially supported Islamic militant groups working against India such as Lashkar-e-Toiba. Information as recent as Fall 2002 indicates that Ibrahim had been helping finance terrorist attacks in the Indian state of Gujarat by Lashkar-e-Toiba, the armed wing of Markaz Dawa Wal Irshad – an anti-US Sunni missionary organization, formed in 1989.'

According to media reports, soon after India's then deputy prime minister L.K. Advani returned from his US visit in June 2003, New Delhi received information about Dawood Ibrahim's alleged links with LeT and the Taliban, and through the latter, to al-Qaeda. On his June 2003 trip to Washington, Advani had told US leaders that India needed a visible, non-reversible action from Pakistan to demonstrate its sincerity in curbing terrorism, and what could be a more visible action than handing over Dawood Ibrahim and others from the list of twenty most wanted terrorists who according to India, are based in Pakistan. This list was handed over to Pakistan after the December 2002 attack on the Indian parliament.

Advani told US leaders, 'the name Dawood Ibrahim had the same kind of resonance in India as the name Osama bin Laden had in America.' US leaders were also told that any movement on the 'most wanted' list could completely change the dynamics in the region. In early 2002, Islamabad was repeatedly asked to hand over those named in the list, but it stonewalled, predictably rubbishing media and intelligence claims of Dawood Ibrahim residing in Pakistan. Among other things, India provided details of the 1993 Interpol red corner notice (A 135/4-1993) on Dawood and of the Pakistani passport issued to him on 12 August 1991.

Curiously, when the US Treasury Department terrorist listing was made public, it mentioned Dawood's passport number as G 869537; the number New Delhi had provided was G 866537. There was also a discrepancy in Dawood's telephone numbers: the American list said the number was 021-5892038; the numbers provided by India were 021-7278866 and 7272887. Though the US treasury did not list Dawood's address, his passport mentions his permanent residence as: 6/A Khayaban Tanzeem, Phase 5, Defence Housing Area, Karachi. It is a posh Karachi address where retired army officials live and it underscores the intimate links between Dawood and the establishment there. These discrepancies in the US Treasury Department listing, perhaps enabled Islamabad to claim that it had checked out the details but that they did not tally with their records. Indian officials, however, say the discrepancies were an error and would presumably be rectified by the US.

Obviously, it was not just Advani's proddings that pushed the US into moving against Dawood. The latter had already crossed Washington's path during the investigations into the massive bomb blasts in Riyadh on the eve of the then Secretary of State Colin Powell's visit there in May 2004. American sleuths were tracking *hawala* or money laundering operations, so it is not surprising that Dawood's name cropped up, considering the control he exercises the region.

American investigations in Riyadh, to begin with, focused the spotlight on one of Dawood's shadowy henchmen, Saud

Memon. Otherwise known as a wealthy Karachi garment exporter, it was Memon who, in January 2002, drove Daniel Pearl into a compound that he owned. It was here that Pearl was murdered. Memon subsequently disappeared from Karachi.

Meanwhile, in June 2003, when General Musharraf was in the US, the FBI nabbed eight suspected LeT operatives in the US. Charged with stockpiling weapons and waging war against India, these eight activists had apparently received arms training in Pakistan and some of them had even seen action in Kashmir. A set of official documents released by the FBI in June 2003 in Washington stated that some of those arrested had even fought against Indian troops in Kashmir and were being funded by the Dawood syndicate to conduct terrorist activity in the Indian state of Gujarat. The documents disclosed that one of the arrested men was a Pakistani citizen working as an electrical engineer in the US. FBI action subsequently led to more arrests in several other American states.

Several Pakistani and Western writers, including the slain American journalist Daniel Pearl, attempted to write about Dawood Ibrahim, but they have routinely disappeared. Author Gilbert King has attempted to reveal the secrets of Dawood's life in his book entitled *The Most Dangerous Man In The World*.[1] After his expulsion from UAE, says the book, no country other than Pakistan was willing to accord him asylum. 'But his power and capability in the underworld remain undiminished; he can still do what he wants,' the author claims.

The book also paints a disturbing picture of Pakistan's ISI and its involvement with Dawood Ibrahim. The author believes that Dawood Ibrahim is as dangerous as Osama bin Laden, though few in the West know of him. The book tries to connect the Karachi killing of US journalist Daniel Pearl to Dawood. According to King, the journalist was trying to ferret out information about Dawood and 'Mr Ibrahim was alarmed and had Mr Pearl kidnapped and killed.' However, no one had so far linked the Pearl murder to Dawood. As for the Mumbai don's future, the author says that for now he is safe in Pakistan but he could be affected on account of the close cooperation between the US and Pakistan in the war against terrorism.

According to the US Treasury Department's fact sheet: 'Ibrahim's syndicate is involved in large-scale shipment of narcotics in the United Kingdom and Western Europe. Its smuggling routes from South Asia, the Middle East and Africa are shared with Osama bin Laden and his terror network. A financial arrangement was also brokered to facilitate bin Laden's use of these routes. In the 1990s, Ibrahim travelled to Afghanistan under the protection of the Taliban.' During his much trumpeted 2001 Agra visit, Musharraf had vehemently denied that Dawood had taken refuge in Pakistan, though the Vajpayee administration believed otherwise.

The truth is that Gen. Pervez Musharraf was right in his claim because Dawood had left Pakistan in early July 2001, before Musharraf's trip to India. According to the FBI's investigations, the mafia don had left on a fake Pakistani passport for Singapore and then gone on to Hong Kong. He returned to Karachi from Dubai later in July, but only after getting clearance from Islamabad.

Taking strong exception to the US observations that Dawood, holding a Pakistani passport, was hiding in Pakistan, the foreign office spokesman in Islamabad, Masood Khan, said that the US had been asked to rectify its mistake. 'Dawood Ibrahim is not in Pakistan. I would like to point out here that we do not have any Indian suspects on our soil. Second, India has not provided any evidence or proof of their presence on Pakistani soil. I mean this story, or this controversy, was re-ignited by a determination made by the Treasury Department of the US ...'

However, the FBI agents stationed in Pakistan simply refused to buy the foreign office assertion. They view Islamabad's claim as a face-saving exercise because it is in its interest not to give the don up. Fresh inquiries by FBI operatives in Pakistan show that Dawood changed his addresses in Karachi to keep out of trouble after the US unleashed its war on terror in the aftermath of the 11 September terrorist attacks. There are reports that Dawood is now trying to dispose of his properties in Karachi and elsewhere, and has taken up residence in Islamabad, along with a couple of his close associates.

THE DON IN THE DOCK

From Mumbai to Dubai to Kuala Lumpur to Karachi, the stories associated with Dawood Ibrahim and his war with his underworld rivals can beat the best Bollywood thrillers. It is the nature of the crimes attributed to Dawood that place him at the top of India's most wanted wish list. He is the prime suspect in masterminding the Mumbai bomb blasts in 1993.

Dawood figures in a list of twenty fugitives that India wants Pakistan to hand over and is suspected to be the prime player used by Pakistani intelligence to foment cross-border terrorism in India. The Musharraf-led government seems under intense pressure and feels extremely uneasy at persistent media reports about Dawood's presence in Pakistan. In September 2000, *Newsline,* a Pakistani English monthly, ran a detailed story claiming that Dawood was, indeed in Karachi and under the protection of the ISI. The story, which detailed his lifestyle, drew an extremely harsh reaction from the Pakistani authorities. During a meeting with editors almost a year after the story was published, Musharraf himself described it as an 'indiscretion that had seriously hurt Pakistan's national interest'.

According to the CBI, Dawood was drawn into the communal infighting that swept India after Hindu zealots pulled down the Babri mosque in Ayodhya in 1992. Mumbai was badly hit by communal rioting and hundreds of Muslims were butchered in the city. It is not clear why Dawood Ibrahim chose to retaliate on behalf of the Mumbai Muslims (the

Indians allege he followed instructions from the ISI while the Pakistanis feel his motivation was primarily religious) but the CBI regards him as the mastermind behind the subsequent Mumbai bombings. Since then, India has been putting constant pressure on Pakistan for the extradition of Dawood Ibrahim who it says is wanted in India for a series of crimes including gun-running, counterfeiting currency, drugs trade, funding alleged criminals, murder and smuggling.

The story that the CBI has spun regarding Dawood's alleged connections with the Pakistani intelligence has all the elements of a thriller. The CBI claims it learnt of Dawood Ibrahim's alleged involvement in anti-India espionage while investigating the Mumbai blasts. According to the CBI, the perpetrators went to Dubai using their Indian passports where Dawood allegedly provided them with Pakistani visas on plain pieces of paper so that their passports would not carry any records of their entry into Pakistan. They landed in Karachi and were taken to a training camp in the NWFP. The CBI concludes that they were sent back to Mumbai after being trained in the use of explosives by the now defunct Harkatul Ansar.

According to the Indian government's claim, shortly after Dawood Ibrahim left Dubai for Karachi in the wake of the Mumbai bombings, he was issued a passport backdated to 12 August 1991. Soon afterwards, according to the CBI, he moved into a 6,000 square yard house in Karachi. He subsequently smuggled his family, comprising his wife, four daughters and a son, certain close associates, and their families out of Mumbai. The entire Dawood family, according to the CBI, now holds Pakistani passports.

Dawood Ibrahim further strengthened his Pakistani connection in August 2005 when he got his eldest daughter Mahrukh Ibrahim married to Junaid Miandad, the eldest son of former Pakistani cricket captain Javed Miandad. Dawood and Miandad's becoming in-laws has given credence to the Indian allegation that its most wanted fugitive hides in Pakistan despite repeated claims to the contrary by General Musharraf. The engagement ceremony in Karachi in January 2005 was a hush-hush affair as the 'globally designated terrorist' is not supposed to be residing in Pakistan.

---

1. King, Gilbert, *The Most Dangerous Man in the World*, Chamberlain Brothers, New York, 2004.

13

Sectarian Monster Haunts Pakistan

Celebrating liberal democracy during his speech to the Constituent Assembly on 11 August 1947, Pakistan's founder Mohammed Ali Jinnah famously declared, 'You may belong to any religion or caste or creed ... that has nothing to do with the business of the state. You are free, free to go to your temples, you are free to go to your mosques or to any other places of worship in this state of Pakistan.' However, fifty-seven years later, one wonders what is happening in Jinnah's Pakistan where sectarian violence has assumed menacing dimensions.

The ongoing sectarian conflict between Pakistan's Shias and Sunnis has been bloody and deadly. Available figures indicate that, between January 1989 and 31 June 2005 a total of 1,793 Pakistanis were killed, and another 4,288 injured in 1,872 incidents of sectarian violence and terror across the country. Keeping in view the current wave of sectarian violence in Pakistan, it seems that the government has simply failed to curb the activities of the banned jehadi and sectarian groups despite repeated claims by Musharraf of having adopted strict administrative measures against them. The fact remains that most of these groups continue to enjoy a free hand under the very nose of the Musharraf administration.

It would appear that the genie of sectarian violence in Pakistan refuses to be bottled and threatens the very fabric of its society. Even as Gen. Pervez Musharraf exhorts the people of Pakistan to adopt an approach of enlightened moderation, Pakistan's tentative quest for a non-discriminatory, liberal democracy continues to unravel. Indeed, the ideology of fundamentalist Islam appears to remain at the heart of the Musharraf establishment's strategy of national political mobilization and consolidation, despite the talk of enlightened moderation. Pakistan continues to be caught in the trap of extremist Islamist militancy and terror that its establishment constructed as part of its Afghan and Kashmir policies. Official support, both explicit and implicit, to Islamic terrorist groups continues, even while the state struggles to cope with the internal fallout of the burgeoning terrorist community.

Since the overall ideological direction of Pakistan's military establishment favours an Islamic state, some of the militant groups whom the regime used to support are often found involved in bloody acts of sectarian violence. The result is that the Musharraf administration's support for the jehadis fighting in J&K has indirectly promoted sectarian violence in Pakistan. The growing nexus between the Pakistan-based sectarian groups and the jehadi ones active in J&K and Afghanistan has of late resulted in a spurt of sectarian violence in the country. These militant organizations now visibly threaten the country's internal security.

While the Pakistani military establishment's support for these groups has kept the Indian army tied down in J&K, it has also created a serious principal-agent problem for Pakistan domestically. The linkages between militants active in J&K or Afghanistan and those within Pakistan are not surprising as these jehadis share the same madrassas, training camps and operatives. By facilitating the actions of irregulars in the

Kashmir valley, Pakistan actually promotes sectarian jehad and terrorism back home.

While seeking an explanation for Pakistan's sectarian menace, one is constrained to notice, that for decades, the country's Shia and Sunni sects lived side by side without any major differences. The roots of sectarian killings lie not in religious differences, but in political and social developments within Pakistan and the region. They are intimately tied up with the country's wider problem of militant extremist Islam. The origins of sectarian violence in Pakistan can be traced back to the days of Afghan jehad against the Soviet occupation troops.

Soon after the withdrawal of the Soviet troops from Afghanistan, the radical Islamists in Afghanistan formed the Taliban while their brethren in Pakistan turned their attention to J&K or to sectarian opponents within Pakistan. Each act of sectarian killing began provoking a cycle of revenge killings, with the civilian governments failing to curb the menace, either because they wanted the militants to fight Pakistan's corner in J&K or because they lacked the will and the strength to do so. That failure, in turn, allowed the religious militants to flourish and grow in strength. However, external factors besides Kashmir also promoted sectarianism. For a period, Shia and Sunni sectarian groups were sponsored by Iran and Saudi Arabia respectively.

The end result of all this was that when Musharraf seized power in October 1999, he faced a formidable foe: well-armed, well-trained and well-financed Islamist-sectarian organizations with a huge pool of recruits available in thousands of religious madrassas across the country. Dealing with such a menace was never going to be easy for an un-elected leader, but the task was made somewhat easier by the 9/11 terror attacks in New York and the worldwide backlash against extremist Islam that it unleashed. Islamabad's decision to cut support for the Kashmiri militants also boosted its drive against sectarianism. Prior to that, many sectarian groups had emerged and were being tolerated because of their links with groups fighting in J&K.

Once Islamabad decided to put the Kashmir issue on the back burner for the sake of better ties with New Delhi, it no longer had to tolerate the jehadi groups operating in J&K. The first clear sign of a shift in the Pakistan government's attitudes came in a televised speech by Musharraf to the nation on 12 January 2002. While announcing a massive campaign to eradicate the sectarian menace, the general banned three sectarian groups—Sipah-e-Sahaba Pakistan, Tehreek-e-Jafria Pakistan and Tehrik-e-Nifaz-e-Shariat Mohammadi—and put the fourth, Sunni Tehrik, on notice. Six months later, in August 2002, he banned two more sectarian groups, Sipah-e-Mohammad Pakistan (SMP) and Lashkar-e-Jhangvi, declaring them terrorist groups.

The Sunni-Shia conflict in its more modern and virulent manifestation in Pakistan can be traced to Imam Khomeini's successful revolution and the setting up of a Shia state in Iran. In response, extremist Sunni groups began to espouse the cause of transforming Pakistan into a Sunni state in which Shias would become a non-Muslim minority. A close look at the sectarian problem in Pakistan would suggest several significant trends. In the past ten years, the struggle, which essentially began between the Shia and Sunni groups due to General Zia ul Haq's Islamization drive, has become transformed from a theological to a political battle.

The military regime of General Zia fostered the growth of sectarianism in a number of ways. It created among the Shia community a perception that his government was moving rapidly towards the establishment of a Sunni Hanafi state in which the Islamization of laws was seen to reflect the Islam of the dominant community. The 1980 seige of the government secretariat in Islamabad by tens of thousands of Shias protesting against the zakat and ushr ordinance was a clear manifestation of their apprehensions about Zia's Islamization project. The selective backing of Afghan mujahideen groups resisting the Soviet occupation of Afghanistan again corresponded to a sectarian pattern of preferences that reinforced perceptions on both sides of the divide.

Under Zia, with the promulgation of the Zakat and Ushr Ordinance of 1979, the religious establishment was considerably strengthened. On joining zakat committees, maulvis became responsible for distributing money to the poor; in rural areas maulvis became ushr collectors, enhancing their status considerably as it brought them into close contact with the district administration and local government. The government's decision to provide zakat funds to madrassas resulted in their explosive growth. The induction of their graduates into government service created the prospect of upward social mobility which made madrassa education an attractive proposition.

By the end of Zia rule, the consequences of his policies were fairly obvious. There has been a major escalation in sectarian tension, the number of sectarian killings and armed sectarian groups. Among those that have gained particular prominence is the Sipah-e-Mohammad Pakistan. It is an off-shoot of Tehrik-Nifaz-e-Fiqh-e-Jafaria (TNFJ), the main politico-religious Shia party in Pakistan (later renamed Tehrik-e-Jafaria Pakistan). Then there is Anjuman Sipah-e-Sahaba, later renamed Sipah-e-Sahaba-Pakistan, an off shoot of Jamiat Ulema-e-Islam, the leading politico-religious Sunni Deobandi party. A further offshoot of the SSP, considered to be the most violent sectarian group, is the even more militant Lashkar-e-Jhangvi.

The current organized sectarian conflict can be traced to the murder of the TNFJ leader Arif Hussaini in 1988. Others date it to 1987, when Ahl-e-Hadith leaders, Allama Ehsan Elahi Zaheer and Maulana Habib ur Rehman Yazdani, were killed along with six others. Prior to this, there were serious anti-Shia riots in Lahore in 1986. In any case, the spiral of violence registered a sharp rise in February 1990 with the murder of Maulana Haq

Nawaz Jhangvi, founder of the SSP. This was followed by violent clashes resulting in dozens of casualties and numerous houses and shops in Jhang being burnt to the ground.

The pattern and scale of violence indicates some key features. The contending groups are well organized and well armed. Their ability to maintain their effectiveness and to elude the law enforcement agencies also has to do with an extensive support network that includes madrassas, political parties, bases across the border, and financial support from foreign countries if not foreign governments. It is generally believed that something of a proxy war between Iran and Saudi Arabia is going on in Pakistan, with a number of groups in Afghanistan weighing in as well.

In the process, state authority is being eroded by the sectarian groups in one way or the other. Hate literature and cassettes from the two sides, easily available across Pakistan, clearly violate the law of the land but seldom invite sanction. Offences such as murder and destruction of property do invite a state response but the administration lacks the will to take the difficult steps necessary to deal with the phenomenon. A narrow law and order approach, with a police force ill-equipped to deal with highly motivated, well trained and well organized militants, has obviously not had much of an impact, particularly when the latter have state-of-the-art weapons.

The increasing militarization and brutalization of the conflict shows that there are virtually no sanctuaries left: neither home, nor mosque nor hospital, not even jail. Being innocent is not the issue, just 'being' is enough – being Shia or Sunni, Barelvi or Deobandi. One explanation for this is that in a situation where different sectarian groups are vying to prove themselves as the standard bearers of Islam, one option is to stand out as being closer to 'true Islam' by displaying extreme hostility and intolerance to those designated as being un-Islamic by virtue of belonging to religious minorities and minority sects.

14

Sipah-e-Sahaba: The Sectarian Soldiers

Earlier known as Anjuman-e-Sipah-e-Sahaba, the Sipah-e-Sahaba Pakistan (SSP) is a Sunni sectarian group alleged to be involved in terrorist violence across Pakistan, primarily targeting the country's minority Shia community.

SSP was one of the five militant and sectarian groups to be banned by General Musharraf in January 2002 for their alleged involvement in terrorist activities. After it was banned, the party chief, Maulana Azam Tariq, renamed it Millat-e-Islamia Pakistan. He was shot dead in Islamabad in October 2003. Maulana Azam Tariq had won the October 2002 general elections from Jhang as an independent candidate and was a frequent visitor to Afghanistan during Taliban rule.

SSP was an offshoot of Jamiat Ulema-e-Islam, which has played an active role in the electoral and agitational politics of Pakistan since its inception. Maulana Haq Nawaz Jhangvi established the SSP, initially known as the Anjuman Sipah-e-Sahaba, in September 1985 in an environment of increasing sectarian hostility in Pakistani Punjab. Maulana Jhangvi, a prayer leader in a mosque in Jhang, was a product of madrassa education and was known for his anti-Shia oratory. He was groomed during the 1974 anti-Ahmedi agitation, as was the case with many other leaders of the group, and later rose to become the vice chairman of JUI, Punjab.

The origin of SSP lies in the feudal set-up of Punjab province and in the politico-religious developments of the 1970s and 1980s. The political and economic power in Punjab lay in the hands of large landowners, mostly Shias, a minority in comparison to the Sunni sect. Urban Punjab by contrast, was a non-feudalistic middle-class society which was largely Sunni.

The socio-economic rationale for SSP's origin is explained largely from the economic profile of Jhang, its home base. Located in a region that divides central from southern Punjab province of Pakistan, Jhang still has a significantly high proportion of large landholdings, leaving feudalism relatively undisturbed. Most large landlords, who are Shias, dominate both society and politics in the region. However, over the years, the area has developed as an important *mandi* (market town) gradually increasing the power of traders, shopkeepers and transport operators in the region. Seeking a political voice and role, this class, largely from the Sunni community, has been challenging the traditional feudal hold.

The most serious political challenge to the control of feudal interests has, with the formation of SSP been articulated in the form of violent sectarianism. This has meant, however, that the contest for access to resources and status, the competition for domination over the state apparatus are not framed in terms of class divisions or modernization imperatives but confrontationist sectarian identities. As in most areas affected by violence, a major contradiction has arisen. While a sizeable proportion of traders and shopkeepers continue to fund SSP in Jhang, most do not believe in the violence associated with the party. Rather, it is now a matter of buying security. Nevertheless, there has been a decline in their support for SSP in recent years as a result of the economic consequences of sectarian strife.

However, writer Hassan Abbas maintains in his book *Pakistan's Drift into Extremism* that extremists among Sunnis, especially those belonging to the Deobandi and Ahle Hadith groups, had found the Shia theological beliefs unpalatable all along, but sectarian violence was rare. 'However, the 1979 Iranian revolution changed the character and magnitude of sectarian politics in Pakistan. It emboldened Pakistani Shias who in turn became politicized and started asserting for their rights. The zealous emissaries of the Iranian revolutionary regime started financing their outfit Tehrik-e-Nifaz-e-Fiqh-e-Jafaria (TNFJ or Movement for the implementation of *jafaria* religious law) and providing scholarships for Pakistani students to study in Iranian religious seminaries.'

Abbas goes on to say:

> For Zia regime though, the problematic issue was the Shia activism leading to a strong reaction to his attempts to impose Hanafi Islam (a branch of the Sunni sect). For this he winked to the hardliners among the Sunni religious groups to establish a front to squeeze the Shias. It was in this context that Maulana Jhangvi was selected by the intelligence community to do the needful. The adherents of Deobandi school of thought were worried by the Shia activism for religious reasons anyhow. The state patronage came as an additional incentive. Consequently, in a well-designed effort, Shia assertiveness was projected as their disloyalty to Pakistan and its Islamic ideology. It was only a matter of few months that Saudi funds started pouring in, making the project feasible. For Saudi Arabia, Iranian revolution was quite scary for its ideals were conflicting with that of a Wahhabi monarchy. More so, with an approximately 10 per cent Shia population, Saudi Arabia was concerned about the expansion of Shia activism in any Muslim country. Hence, it was more than willing to curb such trends in Pakistan by making financial investment to bolster its Wahhabi agenda.

As soon as SSP was launched from Jhang, the hometown of Maulana Haq Nawaz Jhangvi, it made public its intentions to have Pakistan declared a Sunni state. SSP declared that the Shias were non-Muslims. While Shia activists followed the developing trend closely and prepared themselves to effectively counter the SSP propaganda, TNFJ chief, Allama Arif Hussain Al Hussaini was assassinated in August 1988. This dealt a severe blow to the Shias. Hussaini had lived in Iran for a while and had a close working relationship with the Iranian regime.

According to Hassan Abbas, the ISI's involvement was suspected in the murder as a serving army officer Majid Raza Gillani had taken part in this operation. Soon it was Maulana Haq Nawaz Jhangvi's turn to be assassinated on 23 February 1990. The SSP though suspected the hand of a Jhang-based Sunni political leader Shaikh Iqbal. However, Kaka Balli, kin of a former member of the National Assembly from Jhang, Amanullah Khan Sial, was convicted to lifetime imprisonment for Jhangvi's assassination. Later, Maulana Ziaur Rehman Farooqi took over the leadership of the group. He too was however killed in a bomb explosion in the Lahore Sessions Court on 19 January 1997, and was succeeded by Maulana Azam Tariq.

SSP is reported to have approximately 3,000–6,000 trained activists who indulge in various kinds of violent sectarian activities primarily directed against the Shias. The SSP extremists have so far operated in two ways: the first involves targeted killings of prominent opponent group activists. In the second, terrorists fire on worshippers in mosques operated by opposing sects. By 1992, SSP was reported to have gained access to sophisticated arms as well as the ability to use these weapons even against the law enforcement agencies. In June 1992, its activists used a rocket launcher in an attack that killed five police personnel. In Punjab, 1994 was one of the worst years in terms of sectarian violence when such incidents claimed seventy lives and over 300 people were injured. Many of these killings were the result of indiscriminate firing on people saying their prayers.

SSP joined peace efforts in 1996 which were actually initiated by the Milli Yakjeheti Council, though violence continued unabated. The second half of 1996 was notable for the fact that while the number of incidents decreased, the average casualties in these increased. News reports have indicated that SSP and other Sunni groups hold Iran as the sponsor of Shia extremist groups in Pakistan. Therefore, when any major Sunni leader is assassinated, Iranians in Pakistan are targeted for retribution. For instance, the Iranian Consul General in Lahore, Sadeq Ganji, was assasinated in December 1990 in what was reported to be a retribution for the killing of Maulana Haq Nawaz Jhangvi.

Similarly, in January 1997, the Iranian Cultural Centre in Lahore was attacked and set on fire, while in Multan seven people were killed, including the Iranian diplomat Muhammad Ali Rahimi. Earlier, in January 1997, a bomb blast at the Sessions Court in Lahore left thirty persons dead, which included the then SSP chief Ziaur Rehman Farooqi, twenty-two policemen and a journalist. According to newspaper reports the retribution continued even in September 1997 when five personnel of the Iranian armed forces who were in Pakistan for training were killed by suspected Sunni terrorists.

As with other sectarian groups, the SSP chose to lie low after the military coup of November 1999, lending credence to the hypothesis that it, like other sectarian and ethnic groups, indulges in violence only when a passive state guarantees an environment of neutrality, and even tacit support, to this violence. With a hard-line stance being taken by the military regime against internal violence within Pakistan, these groups decided to keep a low profile for the time being. In October 2001, however, a month after the 9/11 terror-attacks in the US, the SSP joined the hard line Council for Defence of Afghanistan to condemn the allied forces' bombing of the neighbouring Muslim state.

While condemning the Pakistan government's decision to extend support to the US-led air attacks, the SSP leader even warned that they would fight alongside the Taliban militia. In an interview with the BBC, Maulana Azam Tariq openly praised the Taliban and endorsed attacks on Shias in Pakistan. He was imprisoned in October 2001 as US-led forces rained bombs on Taliban-ruled Afghanistan. Pakistani authorities feared he would lead violent rallies against the attacks on the Taliban who also happen to be Sunnis. When General Musharraf held a national election twelve months later, Azam Tariq campaigned from behind the bars.

As things stand, the anti-Shia movement in Pakistan has two faces. One is Millat-e-Islamia Pakistan, the new incarnation of Sipah-e-Sahaba Pakistan, which believes in political struggle through parliament with the ultimate aim of constitutionally turning Pakistan into a Sunni state, just as Iran is constitutionally a Shia state. The other face of the anti-Shia movement is Lashkar-e-Jhangvi, which subscribes to the policy of eradication of Shias. It also grew out of SSP, formed after the killings of the SSP founder, Haq Nawaz Jhangvi, and Maulana Farooqi. To date, all of the SSP's chiefs have died in targeted killings. Although Lashkar-e-Jhangvi is a dissident group of the defunct SSP, many of its key members remained in contact with Maulana Azam Tariq as he was the only political leader whose opinions they respected.

Conversely, Azam Tariq lent LeJ a sympathetic ear. Revered by legions of Sunni Muslim followers, Azam Tariq had almost as many enemies. He led a violent militant group blamed for a spate of killings of minority Shiite Muslims and was himself charged with 103 cases of ordering the murders of rival Shiites but was never convicted. He was killed in October 2003, along with four bodyguards in a drive-by shooting in Islamabad.

Azam Tariq was elected to parliament four times from the SSP stronghold in Jhang. In the last election, he contested the election from jail and was elected.

Although Azam Tariq publicly dissociated himself from LeJ, law enforcement agencies knew the SSP and the LeJ were two faces of the same organization. Indeed, close observers say that creating the LeJ was a smart move as it allowed SSP to put a political mask on its sectarian agenda. This was proved when Azam Tariq campaigned to save the life of LeJ activist Haq Nawaz, sentenced to the gallows for killing the Iranian consul general in Lahore. Tariq even offered to pay blood money to Iran. In May 2002, after LeJ chief Riaz Basra was killed in a police encounter, his body was laid to rest wrapped in the SSP flag and his funeral was largely attended by SSP cadre.

SSP also had close links with Maulana Masood Azhar's JeM. Masood Azhar was also a close associate of Haq Nawaz Jhangvi. In fact, one of the reasons he broke away from HuM was because the party was trying to clean up its act and was moving away from the SSP-LeJ sectarian terrorists. By creating JeM, Azhar maintained his links with his sectarian brothers in arms. Because of his close connections with JeM, Maulana Azam Tariq also supported militancy in Kashmir. When Masood Azhar formed JeM to fight in Kashmir, the SSP leader pledged to send 500,000 jehadis to the disputed Valley to fight Indian soldiers.

The gruesome murder of Maulana Azam Tariq remains a mystery despite the fact that he and his group had maintained a cosy working relationship with Pakistan's powerful intelligence and security agencies for over a decade.

15

Lashkar-e-Jhangvi: The Group of Choice for Hard-core Militants

Most of the major terrorist operations carried out in Pakistan after 11 September 2001 appear to have a common link: Lashkar-e-Jhangvi (LeJ), the group of choice today for hard-core militants who are determined to pursue their jehadi agenda in Pakistan.

Launched in 1996 as a militant sectarian Sunni group, LeJ, with its own sucide-attack squad, is today, the most violent terrorist group operating within Pakistan. As with most militant groups, almost the entire LeJ leadership is made up of people who have fought in Afghanistan, and most of its cadre strength has been drawn from the numerous Sunni madrassas in Pakistan. LeJ was formed by a breakaway faction of Sunni extremists of the Sipah-e-Sahaba Pakistan, which walked out of the outfit, accusing its parent organization of deviating from the ideals of its co-founder, Maulana Haq Nawaz Jhangvi.

After Jhangvi's murder in February 1990, allegedly by Shia rivals, those who wanted to complete his mission started leaving Sipah-e-Sahaba, forming their own groups under different names.

Riaz Basra of SSP, launched LeJ in 1996 and three splinter groups decided to merge with his group. Basra, who believed in the use of force to further Jhangvi's mission, parted ways with the SSP leadership after accusing it of abandoning Jhangvi's path. However, there are those who insist that LeJ was launched with the consent of the SSP leadership. Riaz Basra was appointed the *salar-e-aala* (chief commander) of the LeJ, with twelve *salars* under his command. A network was established for an uninterrupted supply of the arms and ammunition from Afghanistan to Punjab, and from there to Karachi. Although the trained LeJ operatives never crossed the figure of 500, yet they proved themselves to be the deadliest of all.

Subsequent intelligence reports revealed that both SSP and LeJ enjoyed easy access to sophisticated arms and their cadres had the ability to use them even against the law enforcement agencies. It was during the second tenure of Prime Minister Nawaz Sharif that his younger brother Shahbaz Sharif's provincial government in Punjab moved against SSP and LeJ, and killed thirty-six of its leading militants in fake encounters within a short span of a year.

During his last days as prime minister, Nawaz Sharif, whose own life was under threat from SSP and LeJ terrorists and who had already survived an assassination attempt, went public in naming Afghanistan as the country providing shelter and training to SSP and LeJ hit men. Earlier, in January 1999, LeJ had attempted to blow up a bridge on the Lahore–Raiwind road, close to Nawaz Sharif's house, shortly before he was due to pass by. A few minutes before the prime minister's convoy was to pass, two policemen on a routine patrol, stopped their van under the bridge. Their driver pressed the button of his radio to talk. Because the van was parked only a few yards from the bridge, the rudimentary device detonated the explosives. The blast was so powerful that the two-span bridge collapsed. Prior to this incident, LeJ, in a press release, had offered a reward of Rs 135 million for killing Nawaz Sharif and his younger brother Shahbaz Sharif who was then the chief minister of Punjab.

LeJ uses terror tactics as a part of its grand strategy to force the state into accepting its narrow interpretations of Sunni sectarian doctrines as the official doctrine. Besides American interests in Pakistan, the victims of its terror tactics have been leaders and workers of rival Shia groups, bureaucrats, policemen and ordinary worshippers.

According to law enforcement officials, a typical LeJ cell is made up of two or three young men – going up to seven in exceptional cases. The cell disbands after an operation and regroups at another location. The cells are drawn from a pool of young men trained in Afghanistan who are scattered all over Pakistan. The ISI, with long-standing and murky links to jehadi groups, planted informers in the camps who reported back on consignments dispatched from Afghanistan. However, new recruits without criminal records were difficult to trace once they crossed back into Pakistan. Hits made by fresh batches left the police helpless in investigating attacks or preventing fresh ones.

After the fall of the Taliban regime in Afghanistan, LeJ militants preferred to take their chances with the Pakistani authorities – even risking liquidation – rather than fall into the hands of Northern Alliance commanders. For their part, the ISI lost what little control it had over LeJ when new internationalist militants took over. The LeJ leadership recruits hit men and operatives with care, looking for strong religious conviction and steady nerves. The trained martyrs, called the armoured corps of jehad, return to their homes and jobs to live normally until summoned. While they wait, they are under strict orders to shun beards and traditional clothes, to maintain a neat, inconspicuous appearance, to have their documents (real ones issued under fake names) in order, to carry them at all times, and to do nothing illegal or out of the ordinary.

Terrorism experts say LeJ has become media-savvy by timing

daylight attacks to catch the evening news. They believe the planners of the terror attacks watch Hollywood films for ideas. Another idea came from a local movie: LeJ organized a fake wedding procession in Multan in 1997, with a bridegroom on a white horse accompanied by musicians, singers and dancers. A cameraman recorded the event. As the noisy procession passed the heavily guarded Iranian Cultural Centre, hit men climbed over the rear wall and shot dead the centre's Shia Iranian director and six others. Fireworks set off by the wedding guests camouflaged the gunfire.

In October 2000, LeJ split into two factions with one faction headed by Riaz Basra and the other by the chief of the group's Majlis-i-Shoora (Supreme Council), Qari Abdul Hai alias Qari Asadullah, alias Talha. Qari Hai was Basra's lieutenant and ran the latter's training camp in Sarobi, Afghanistan, until the two fell out. While a majority of Hai's supporters are Karachi-based, Basra's cadres have their roots in Punjab. The issue leading to the split was reported to be serious differences between the two over the resumption of ethnic strife which had receded into a relative lull after General Musharraf's October 1999 military coup. While Basra was reported to be in favour of resuming attacks against Shia targets, Hai opposed the plan terming it suicidal for the organization, maintaining that with a military regime in power, any armed activity would invite stern action against the LeJ.

In August 2001, General Pervez Musharraf, in the face of growing public criticism of his failure to control anti-Shia violence, announced the banning of LeJ. Five months later, in January 2002, the general banned Sipah-e-Sahaba Pakistan (SSP). Soon afterwards, the government claimed to have rounded up a large number of members of the two sectarian groups. However, despite being outlawed, both the groups continue to carry out terrorist activities across Pakistan. Since 2002, LeJ has mounted a number of large-scale suicide attacks. A suicide operation in March 2002 in a church in Islamabad killed five Christians, as proxy targets for Westerners, although among them were two American nationals.

In May 2002, eleven Frenchmen, who were mistaken for Americans, were blown up in Karachi and in June 2002, twelve Pakistanis were killed in a suicide attack on US diplomats. At least five of the ten terrorists identified belonged to LeJ cadres. This was the first occasion in which the police identified LeJ as being involved in all the three incidents. One of the men, Asif Ramzi, was already wanted in the Daniel Pearl murder case and for other sectarian killings, with a three-million-rupee reward for his capture. According to investigators, the al-Qaeda network worked in close coordination with the LeJ cadres to plan both the car bomb attacks in Karachi.

In January 2003, the US State Department added LeJ to its 'List of Foreign Terrorist Organizations'. Making the announcement on Collin Powell's behalf, State Department spokesman Richard Boucher had said that the terrorist group has already claimed responsibility for the 1997 killing of four American oil workers in Karachi. 'They have ties to the al-Qaeda, ties to the Taliban, in addition to receiving sanctuary in Afghanistan for their activities in Pakistan. Moreover, the group was involved in the kidnapping and subsequent murder of American journalist Daniel Pearl,' Boucher added.

Muhammad Ajmal alias Akram Lahori is believed to be the last known *Saalar-e-Aala* (Commander-in-Chief) of LeJ. Lahori was originally with SSP Pakistan, which he had joined in 1990. He, along with Malik Ishaq and Riaz Basra, had founded LeJ. Lahori succeeded Basra, who was killed in May 2002. Lahori is himself in police custody after his arrest in Orangi Town, Karachi, in June 2004. Before he was arrested, Lahori was carrying a reward of five million rupees on his head announced by the Sindh government and another five million rupees announced by the Punjab government. It is not clear if Lahori has passed on the mantle to anyone else or continues to head the groups from his prison cell.

According to senior police officials, Lahori was involved in thirty-eight cases of sectarian killings in Sindh. Lahori reportedly confessed during interrogation that he was involved in thirty cases of sectarian killings in Punjab, including those of twenty-four persons who were attending a majlis (meeting) in Mominpura. He also revealed that his group had planned to kill Interior Minister Moinuddin Haider, but due to tight security measures, murdered his brother instead.

Lahori's predecessor, Riaz Basra, was involved in over 300 incidents of terrorism including attacks on Iranian missions, killing of the Iranian diplomat Sadiq Ganji and targeting government officials. Basra was arrested and tried by a special court for Ganji's killing, but escaped from police custody during trial in 1994 while being produced in court. Media reports said Riaz Basra, along with three of his accomplices, was killed in an encounter at Mailsi, Multan, in May 2002. Basra had allegedly been in police custody in Faisalabad since January 2002 and was being interrogated for the activities of his group.

Those involved in tracking down LeJ's terror network in Karachi, believe that the group might be working there as al-Qaeda's 'delta force'. The delta force is a special al-Qaeda unit that was trained under Khalid Sheikh Mohammad before his arrest and assigned specific high profile targets, including General Musharraf. Investigations into the attack on the Karachi corps commander on 10 June 2004 have given broad hints that it was an operation jointly planned and carried out by LeJ and their al-Qaeda associates, Dawood Badini and Mosabir Aruchi. The intelligence sources did not rule out the possibility of Badini and Aruchi's involvement in the abduction and murder of the American journalist Daniel Pearl. The FBI has already identified Khalid Sheikh as the person who killed Pearl with his own hands.

Sharing their findings with their Pakistani counterparts, American intelligence agents stationed in Pakistan are learnt to have warned that another leading al-Qaeda operative, Abu

Musab al-Zarqawi, might also be working in close coordination with the LeJ network in Pakistan to carry out some major terrorist activities. According to intelligence findings, Zarqawi shares the LeJ's anti-Shia bias and its fondness for brutal ultra-violent techniques, as exemplified by the May 2004 videotaped beheading of an American, Nicholas Berg, in Iraq.

While LeJ evidently takes some direction from al-Qaeda, the group stays focused on its home turf and its stated goal of radicalizing Pakistan. Most terrorism experts agree that LeJ operatives are the best trained and most vicious killers the world of terrorism has to offer, and the depressing truth is that they are probably right.

16

The Mullah–Military Alliance

The religious right in Pakistan, which had been a vocal supporter of the former Taliban regime, successfully moved from the periphery to the centrestage of politics in the October 2002 general elections, with Muttahida Majlis-e-Amal (MMA) – a six-party alliance of the religious parties – winning 20 per cent of the seats in the upper and the lower houses of parliament.

The religious right had been struggling to establish a foothold in mainstream politics ever since Pakistan came into being in 1947. The liberal lobby always boasted that the religious groups have never been able to muster double-digit figures, both in terms of seats or vote share, in any general election in all of Pakistan's five decade plus electoral history. However, the October 2002 elections changed all that. Even optimists in the religious alliance had not dreamt that they would actually rule the states of North West Frontier Province and Baluchistan which together account for over 60 per cent of Pakistan in terms of area. This was a first of its kind in the political history of Pakistan as six traditionally fratricidal religious parties were united on the electoral platform on the basis of a common anti-American agenda.

The MMA's surprise performance in the 2002 general

elections, in which it garnered 45 seats in the 272-member National Assembly and ruling majorities in NWFP and Baluchistan, set in motion intense analysis and speculation. According to analysts, it was principally Jamaat-e-Islami's (JeI) brain and Jamiat Ulema-e-Islam's brawn that led to the surprise victory. The alliance was able to bring together the Deobandi school of Islamic thought as represented by the JUI faction, the Barelvis grouped under the late Maulana Shah Ahmed Noorani's Jamiat Ulema-e-Pakistan, and the Shiites represented by Tehrike-Millat-e-Islami Pakistan.

The MMA was born only weeks before the 2002 elections and its principal leaders were in the forefront of the anti-US demonstrations in different parts of Pakistan post-9/11. The religious parties had come together earlier too under the banner of Milli Yakjehti Council (MYC), led by Maulana Shah Ahmed Noorani, but JeI's attempt to convert the MYC into an electoral alliance prior to the 1997 elections had not worked. The religious right had won very few seats then. But all this changed, at least on the face of it, with the launching of the US war on terror.

The MYC moulded itself into the Pak Afghan Defence Council (PADC) in the post-9/11 scenario, the latter a forerunner of the MMA. The six constituents of the MMA – JI, JUP, both factions of JUI (headed by Maulana Samiul Haq and Maulana Fazlur Rahman), Islami Tehreek Pakistan and Jamiat Ahl-e-Hadith – aspire to introduce what they call the true Islamic system in Pakistan. However, differences exist among their leaders at ideological and personal levels, including their views on the Taliban. Only two of the six entities – the JeI factions led by Maulana Samiul Haq and Fazlur Rahman – support the Taliban's world-view while JI, the largest religious party, openly denounced the Taliban version of Islam.

The rise of the religious right in Pakistan is attributable to several factors. Foremost among these surely was the manner in which the Musharraf regime had persistently and systematically de-legitimized the liberal mainstream parties. The credibility of parties such as the Pakistan Peoples Party led by Benazir Bhutto (PPPP) and the Pakistan Muslim League faction led by Nawaz Sharif (PML-N) was systematically eroded by portraying these as corrupt and incompetent to run the affairs of the country. There may have been some substance to these portrayals and an officially sponsored demonization of these formations might not in itself have been sufficient to mar their prospects in the polls as the people of Pakistan are sufficiently familiar with them.

However, the military regime's deliberate move to block the leaders of both parties from contesting the elections, through recourse to dubious legislative measures, made it clear to the people that they were not to be led by these twice-tested former prime ministers. The Pakistani voter was therefore left to pick between the second or third rung leaders of the PPPP or PML-N or the largely colourless leaders of the Pakistan Muslim League (Quaid-e-Azam) (PML-Q) for his choice of prime minister – which clearly was no choice at all. It was against this backdrop, in which none of the mainstream parties was able to galvanize the voters, that preferences were made on a constituency-wise basis. In this scenario, the MMA, which had put up a consolidated list of candidates and which seemed to promise an alternative to PML-Q – the regime's stalking horse, had a clear advantage.

Undoubtedly, anti-Americanism had played a vital role in the political ascendancy of MMA, but to ignore other pertinent factors projects a wrong picture for, despite the hype, MMA's strong showing was limited to NWFP and Baluchistan, and not spread throughout Pakistan. Of the forty-five national assembly seats it won, thirty-five were from NWFP and Baluchistan. Of the 3.19 million votes in favour of MMA, 2.8 million were from these two provinces. Though MMA won six seats in Sindh and three in Punjab, the margin was very narrow. Even in the provincial assemblies, MMA won enough seats to form the provincial government only in NWFP (52 out of 99). In Baluchistan, it won only fourteen seats out of fifty-one whereas the PML-Q in fact won fifteen.

Certainly, the electoral performance of the religious parties improved a great deal when compared to previous elections. What led to the political growth of Islamic parties in the last ten years, especially in NWFP and Baluchistan? Linking their growth to anti-Americanism alone is simplistic. If there is an anti-American feeling throughout of Pakistan, then why did MMA fail to win many seats in Punjab and Sindh? Why did MMA succeed in gaining support only in NWFP and Baluchistan?

From the time of the Afghan war against the Soviet Union, these two provinces have steadily fallen under the influence of radical Islam. The political use of religion in terms of jehad to fight the Soviets was a primary factor in militarizing the society. Jehad became a household term in these two provinces with a steady inflow and outflow of mujahideen. Some analysts believe that the failure of the federal government to adequately govern these provinces also led to the shift. Parts of the frontier area were never under the total control of the federal administration and had always been administered on the basis of local customs.

In the 1990s, the growth of Taliban culture provided less expensive, easy but swift justice rather than the expensive, bureaucratic and much delayed justice from the federal administration. Even after the military regime assumed power, welfare activities were never really organized. Therefore alienation, especially at the political and cultural levels, from the rest of Pakistan has made people in these provinces identify with the Taliban. The deciding factor in the October elections undoubtedly was the US war on terrorism and the support provided to the US for this by the Pakistani military regime. Although the other factors had existed through the 1990s, this was the element that swung the voters towards MMA.

The war affected the daily lives of people, especially the Pashtuns living along the border. First and foremost was the loss of life. Many Pashtuns from Pakistan fought alongside the Taliban against the US and were killed or injured. Most of the Pashtuns in Pakistan also have family ties across the border, and US military actions killed many innocent persons. The greater the collateral damage, the greater the animosity towards the US. The Punjabi support to the US war further alienated the Pashtuns from the rest of Pakistan. Worse, the Pakistani security forces along with the US undertook search and destroy operations in the tribal areas. All these factors played a crucial role in weaning them away from the moderate parties: Awami National Party, PML-N and PPPP. With the religious parties openly advocating resistance to US influence, it was only natural for the local people to vote for them. Factionalism within the liberal parties in Baluchistan and NWFP further divided the liberal vote bank.

The reduction of the voter age also helped MMA. With all the religious parties having their own madrassas, they were able to get the students to vote for the alliance. Also, the low turnout in these provinces had the effect of helping MMA to win a greater number seats. In NWFP, the MMA won the largest number of seats for both the provincial and national assemblies, it obtained only around 11 per cent of the total registered votes; in Baluchistan, it was around 13.5 per cent. While MMA succeeded in mobilizing its vote bank, the liberal voters simply did not vote. Thus, it is evident that the electoral success of the MMA is not conclusive proof that religious parties are increasing their influence in Pakistan as a whole.

At the same time, there are those in political circles who insist that the victory of the MMA in NWFP and Baluchistan was engineered by the military and intelligence establishments. The fact remains that the religio-political parties have always had a special relationship with the military in Pakistan. After all, it was the cadre of the religious parties that sustained the Afghan and Kashmir policies of the Pakistan Army.

Under the circumstances, many politicians still do not believe that the people really opted for the clergy. They point out that, remarkably, the MMA impact was not felt in Punjab. 'Does it mean that the people of Punjab do not love Islam or have no sympathy for their Afghan brethren or are secular?

Does it mean that the Punjab is the only secular and pro-America province while the rest of the provinces are anti-American? Isn't it true that the central offices of all the religious parties are based in the Punjab province and the Establishment that provides training, funding, hires and harbours the jehadi groups also hails from the Punjab?': thus goes their reasoning.

Whether the military regime precipitated such an outcome or not, it is undeniable that the MMA's strong presence at the centre and in the provinces has considerably enhanced Islamabad's diplomatic leeway. Pakistan's foreign and security policy establishment is now in a position to argue that it can neither proceed against offshoots of al-Qaeda nor moderate its policy on Kashmir to the degree that Washington desires as the religious formations, traditionally hard line on both counts, have shown their political relevance.

Interestingly, parliamentarians belonging to MMA played a crucial role in providing Gen. Pervez Musharraf with the constitutional legitimacy he so desperately sought in December 2003 through the 17th constitutional amendment. The amendment would not have received the requisite two-thirds majority in parliament without MMA's support, which had earlier appeared implacable in its opposition to the general. MMA also opposed several other decisions taken by Musharraf and repeatedly accused him of toeing a Western agenda, both at home and in the region. Why then did the MMA suddenly provide him with the constitutional legitimacy he so desperately sought?

Analysts point out that since the October 2002 general elections, MMA has been making efforts to keep its feet in two boats. On the one hand, the Majlis-e-Amal leadership entered into a political arrangement with the Musharraf, legitimizing the Legal Framework Order. On the other, it wants to continue as the main opposition party with a claim to the opposition leader's slot in the national assembly. MMA stayed away from the vote of confidence for Musharraf, enabling him to secure the required vote in the absence of too many negative votes.

17

Musharraf's Half-hearted Madrassa Reforms

General Pervez Musharraf's much-publicized plans to modernize the country's 10,000 religious seminaries have met with little success primarily because of his administration's failure to enforce the Madrassa Registration and Regulation Ordinance 2002, which was meant to reform *deeni madaris* (religious seminaries) by bringing them into the educational mainstream. Three years after General Musharraf promised sweeping reforms to ensure that the religious schools are not used any more to propagate extremist Islam, the country's traditional religious school system that is now rotten to the core, continues to operate as the key breeding ground for the radical Islamist ideology and as the recruitment centre for terrorist networks.

The campaign to reform the country's notorious *deeni madaris* was launched by General Musharraf in a bid to fight extremism in the aftermath of the 9/11 terror attacks on the United States. Many of the Pakistanis who fought alongside al-Qaeda and Taliban troops in Afghanistan had been educated in these religious seminaries, which are spread across the country.

The privately funded Islamic schools are commonplace throughout Pakistan and a majority of them owe their existence to General Zia's Islamization drive. The curriculum offered there is undeveloped and pertains mostly to religious instruction. Some of the books prescribed, including the one on Mathematics, date back hundreds of years. The result is that the *madaris* graduates simply cannot compete against others for employment. Absent any real understanding of society and social complexities, they seek to bring society onto their own level, and the only thing they identify with is religion.

Yet these *madaris* do provide free education along with boarding and lodging, and this attracts the poor. There are no exact figures about how many are operating in Pakistan, but rough estimates suggest that there are some one million students studying in over 10,000 *madaris*. Since the beginning of 2002, General Musharraf has campaigned to reform the religious schools. In a televised address to the nation in January 2002, the General unveiled a new strategy which would see *madaris* teach Mathematics, Science, English, Economics and even Computer Science alongside their traditional Islamic programme. 'My only aim is to help these institutions overcome their weaknesses and providing them with better facilities and more avenues to the poor children at these institutions. These schools are excellent welfare set-ups where the poor get free board and lodge. And very few *madaris* run by hardliner parties promote negative thinking and propagate hatred and violence instead of inculcating tolerance, patience and fraternity', said Musharraf in his address.

While embarking on several initiatives to combat zealotry and broaden educational offerings, the Musharraf administration announced a number of measures to make *deeni madaris* participate in the modernization programme. These reforms included a five-year Education Sector Reform Assistance (ESRA) plan with a budget of one billion dollars to ensure inclusion of secular subjects in syllabi of religious seminaries and a $100 million bilateral agreement to rehabilitate hundreds of public schools by United States Agency for International Development (USAID). The plan also aimed to increase access to quality education and enforcement of the Madrassa Registration and Regulation Ordinance 2002 which required *deeni madaris* to audit their funding and register foreign students with the government. At the same time, a Federal Madaris Education Board was established to enable the students at the religious schools to benefit from the national education system by learning Mathematics, English and vocational sciences in addition to the normal madrassa education.

However, three years down the road since Musharraf's historic January 2002 announcement, the so-called modernization campaign has largely failed, and hardly a few cosmetic changes could be introduced in the madrassa system. Most of the religious leaders and Islamist organizations rejected the government legislation requiring religious seminaries to register and broaden their curricula beyond rote Koranic learning. Under the reform programme, drafted on the advice of the Bush administration and financed by USAID, special government committees were constituted to supervise and monitor the educational and financial matters and policies of *deeni madaris*. Most of these schools are sponsored by the country's leading religious parties, be it Jamiat Ulema-e-Islam, Jamiat Ulema-Pakistan or Jamaat-e-Islami Pakistan, while many others are affiliated with jehadi groups which preach an extremist ideology of religious warfare.

The result is that the *deeni madaris* are increasingly seen as breeding grounds for the foot-soldiers of the global menace of militant Islam, who are motivated and trained to wage jehad - be it in Kashmir, Afghanistan, Bosnia, Chechnya – or other parts of the world. Thus the Bush Administration believed that there were madaris in Pakistan that, in addition to religious training, give military training to their students. Probably acting under these very apprehensions, the office of US Defence Secretary Donald Rumsfeld leaked a secret memo in October 2003, to the American media. In the memo, which was actually intended for Rumsfeld's top military and civilian subordinates, the American Defence Secretary wondered: 'Is the US capturing, killing or deterring and dissuading more terrorists every day than the madrassas and the radical Muslim clerics are recruiting, training and deploying against America?'

Three months later in January 2004, the International Crisis Group (ICG) report titled, *Unfulfilled Promises: Pakistan's Failure to Tackle Extremism* further strengthened the American fears. The report stated:

> The failure to curb rising extremism in Pakistan stems directly from the military Government's own unwillingness to act against its political allies among the religious groups. Having co-opted the religious parties to gain constitutional cover for his military rule, Musharraf is highly reliant on the religious right for his regime's survival.

The ICG report observed that Pakistan's failure to close madrassas and to crack down on jehadi networks has resulted in a resurgence of domestic extremism and sectarian violence.

> The Government inaction continues to pose a serious threat to domestic, regional and international security... If the US and others continue to restrict their pressure on Musharraf to verbal warnings, the rise of extremism in Pakistan will continue unchecked. By increasing pressure on Pakistan, a major source of jehadis will be shut off and Islamic militancy, as a whole will decrease.

Almost a year later, in December 2004, a report produced by the Congressional Research Service (CRS) presented to the American Congress pointed out:

> Although General Musharraf vowed to begin regulating Pakistan's

religious schools, and his Government launched a five-year plan to bring the teaching of formal or secular subjects to 8,000 willing madrassas, no concrete action was taken until June of that year, when 115 madrassas were denied access to Government assistance due to their alleged links to militancy... Despite Musharraf's repeated pledges to crack down on the more extremist madrassas in his country, there is little concrete evidence that he has done so. According to observers, most madrassas remain unregistered, their finances unregulated, and the Government has yet to remove the jehadist and sectarian content of their curricula. Many speculate that Musharraf's reluctance to enforce reform efforts is rooted in his desire to remain on good terms with Pakistan's Islamist political parties, which are seen to be an important part of his political base.

The Lahore-based *Daily Times* wrote in its February 25, 2005, editorial titled 'Madrassa registration has become a joke':

> The National Security Council, we are being told, is going to discuss the issue of registering the madrassas. Might we ask what has happened to the much-touted madrassa registration ordinance 2002? Apparently nothing! ... The facts are interesting. Registration forms were sent out to all the madrassas after which the Government waited for the seminaries to get themselves registered. That did not happen. The number of madrassas that did register was a bit of a joke. What did the Government do? Nothing! Why cannot the all-powerful General Musharraf follow up on an eminently sensible scheme?

However, a World Bank–sponsored working paper published in February 2005 came up with a new angle, stating that 'enrolment in the Pakistani madrassas, that critics believe are misused by militants, has been exaggerated by media and a US 9/11 report.' The study claimed that less than one per cent of the school-going children in Pakistan go to madrassas, and the proportion has remained constant in some districts since 2001. The study titled 'Religious School Enrolment in Pakistan: A Look at the Data', sought to dispel general perceptions that enrolment was on the rise saying: 'We find no evidence of a dramatic increase in madrassa enrolment in recent years.'

The World Bank study found Western media reports highly exaggerated in terms of number of student and total religious schools: 'The figures reported by international newspapers such as the *Washington Post*, saying there were 10 per cent enrolment in madrassas, and an estimate by the International Crisis Group of 33 per cent, were not correct. It is troubling that none of the reports and articles reviewed based their analysis on publicly available data or established statistical methodologies. Bold assertions have been made in policy reports and popular articles on the high and increasing enrolment in Pakistani religious schools.' The study found no evidence of a dramatic increase in madrassa enrolment in recent years, stating that the share of madrassas in total enrolment declined before 1975 and has increased slowly since then.

However, the South Asia Director of ICG, Samina Ahmed, has challenged the findings of the World Bank study, which questioned the validity of madrassa enrolment statistics provided by the ICG and other expert analysts. Ahmed was quoted in the *Dawn* newspaper on 11 March 2005, stating: 'The authors (of the World Bank report) have insisted that there are at most 475,000 children in Pakistani madrassas, yet Federal Religious Affairs Minister Ejazul Haq says the country's madrassas impart religious education to 1,000,000 children.' She asserted that the World Bank findings were directly at odds with the ministry of education's 2003 directory, which said the number of madrassas had increased from 6,996 in 2001 to 10,430. She added that the madrassa unions themselves had put the figure at 13,000 madaris with the total number of students enrolled at 1.5 to 1.7 million.

Questioning the methodology of the World Bank study, Ahmed said: 'If the findings of the World Bank study were to be taken at face value, then Pakistan and the international community had little cause to worry about an educational sector that glorified jehad and indoctrinated children in religious intolerance and extremism,' the ICG director concluded.

In short, the Musharraf regime's failure to reform the country's 10,000 religious seminaries and to crack down on jehadi networks has resulted in a resurgence of extremism and sectarian violence in the country. The Pakistani military dictator's priority has never been eradicating Islamic extremism, but rather the legitimization and consolidation of his dictatorial rule, for which he seems dependent on the clergy.

MUSHROOMING GROWTH OF MADRASSAS AND MILITANTS

After the end of British rule and the partition of India in 1947, the madrassas in India and the newly created Islamic Republic of Pakistan took different courses. The Indian seminaries stayed true to their original mission of preaching Islamic scholarship, while the Pakistani ones became progressively more intolerant and aggressive in the competition to exclusively define Pakistan's 'Islamic' character. There are currently five broad types of madrassas in Pakistan, with four of them run by the majority Sunni sect and one by the Shia minority. Among the Sunnis, the Barelvis predominate and are a moderate group seeking to be inclusive of local rituals and customs. Then there are seminaries run by Jamaat-e-Islami, which is non-sectarian but tends to be politically very active.

In the context of extremism, the remaining two types of madrassas are most important. The first of these are those which adhere to the Deobandi school of thought. The Deobandi movement which originated in the Indian town of Deoband near New Delhi has long sought to purify Islam by rejecting 'un-Islamic' accretions to the faith and returning to the models established in the Koran. Then there are madrassas which subscribe to the Ahle Hadith school which places a similar emphasis on purifying the faith as the Deobandis, but follows Salafi religious jurisprudence (*fiqh*) as opposed to the Hanafi school adhered to by the Deobandis.

General Zia ul Haq, who seized power after a military coup in 1977, was an ardent Islamist. He began with some ill-fated attempts at ushering Islamic law in Pakistan. General Zia's existing plans to turn Pakistan into an Islamic state gained urgency and acquired a fundamentalist bent after two major events: the Iranian revolution in January 1979 and the Soviet invasion of Afghanistan in December 1979.

These two events also encouraged a new movement within the Deobandi madrassas, which sought to change the way Islam was taught to students. While it is true that many madrassas dropped secular subjects like mathematics and the sciences in part or whole, what was more significant than the narrowing of the syllabus was the change in focus and interpretation in the teaching of the Koran, drawing on the incendiary combination of Muslim brotherhood and Salafi thought developed under Saudi funding.

The emphasis in madrassa curriculum was shifted almost entirely from the standard pillars of faith such as prayer, charity and pilgrimage to the obligation and rewards of jehad. The madrassas taught young students that the world was divided into believers and unbelievers. Jews, Hindus and Christians were portrayed as evil usurpers. The curriculum began emphasizing the need for Islamic warriors of jehad to liberate regions dominated by unbelievers as well as to purify Islamic nations in order to establish a single Islamic caliphate where pure Islam would be practised. The students were taught that the only means to achieve this utopian state was by waging a near-perpetual war, pursued by any and all means against unbelievers as well as impure Muslims.

Subsequently, the era of the jehadi madrassas began. The madrassas got sucked into politics under the military regime of Zia, who promoted the madrassa system as a way of garnering the support of the religious parties for his dictatorial rule and to recruit troops for the anti-Soviet war in Afghanistan. General Zia's Islamist policies opened the floodgates for funding for the madrassas. Saudi Arabia, which seeks to promote its brand of Wahhabi Islam, remains the principal source of funding for this. The Deobandis are inspired by the Wahhabi version of Islam enforced in Saudi Arabia.

It may be coincidence that the rise of JUI's militant groups, HM in Jammu & Kashmir, and the Taliban in Afghanistan happened around the same time. Most of the Pakistani madrassas where the Taliban received education are controlled and run by the JUI. Gulf petrodollars funded a sustained growth of Deobandi madrassas not only in the Pashtun areas of Pakistan near the Afghan border, but also in the port city of Karachi as well as rural Punjab. Prominent madrassas included Darul Uloom Haqqania at Akora Khattak in NWFP and Binori madrassa in Karachi. Haqqania boasts almost the entire Taliban leadership among its graduates, including Mullah Omar, the leader of the Taliban, while Binori madrassa was once considered as a possible hiding place for Osama bin Laden and is also reportedly where bin Laden met Mullah Omar to form the al-Qaeda-Taliban partnership.

After the Soviet withdrawal from Afghanistan in 1989, instead of slowing down, the rapid spread of jehadi madrassas in Pakistan continued unabated. The first and most important reason was that Saudi money continued to flow into madrassa system. The prestige and influence of the big madrassas encouraged wealthy Pakistanis to contribute more than ever before, sometimes as an expression of conviction and sometimes as a means of ingratiating themselves with what had become major power-players. The Zia regime had grown comfortable spending massive amounts of money on defence and almost nothing on education during the days of Afghan jehad when US and Saudi aid flowed freely.

In the 1990s, after the US imposed sanctions on Pakistan

because of its nuclear programme the economy almost collapsed and the education infrastructure deteriorated rapidly. For the poor, the madrassas offered a place where their children could get free boarding, food and education and it turned out to be an irresistible option in comparison to the crumbling or non-existent government-funded secular schools. The successive Pakistani governments also encouraged this to avoid spending much on education. The Pakistani army, on its part, saw the large number of madrassa-trained jehadis as an asset for its covert support of the Taliban in Afghanistan, as well as its proxy war with India in Kashmir.

While the US may feel that it has achieved a great success in convincing Musharraf to make a U-turn on the Taliban, and on stopping the inexorable tide of hate-filled messages put out by the Deobandi and Ahle Hadith seminaries, the real question is whether the Pakistani government will change its long-term policy and stop supporting jehad. The Pakistani defence for its slow progress is that madrassa reform is difficult and dangerous, so it may take a while. The problem with that argument is that the longer the madrassas operate as they do, the fewer people there will be in Pakistan who would support such a change.

18
Injecting Jehad via Textbooks

Some recent debates across three countries, the US, India and Pakistan, on the question of textbooks reveal how the ruling regimes attempt to construct nationhood amongst young minds and how textbooks are used as an instrument of ruling paradigms to develop a particular mindset. The American Council of Trustees and Alumni published a report insisting that the American universities teach courses on western and American civilization and America's continuing struggle to extend and defend the principles on which it was founded. The report was critical of several universities which were focusing on other cultures and providing critiques of US policies that did not coincide with the Bush government's interests.

In India, texts by internationally acknowledged historians were first censored and then removed by the government because they discussed issues that did not conform to the construction of a dominant Hindu nation. Instead, the Bharatiya Janata Party (BJP) government of Prime Minister Vajpayee, despite strong resistance, introduced new school textbooks that reconstructed history to suit the Hindutva ideology conforming to the ruling party's nationalistic perspective. In Pakistan, an in depth study by academics from the Sustainable Development Institute of Pakistan revealed that social studies texts for the junior grades in Pakistan's public schools instruct students in the concept of jehad and martyrdom. Thousands of the religious seminaries in Pakistan are known to have contributed large numbers of young boys to the Taliban and jehadi groups.

All these instances show how education can be used to construct a particular kind of national chauvinistic mindset and how ruling regimes intervene in education to promote certain ideologies that suit their own interests. In such circumstances, secular and multicultural history is seen as subversive, and governments try and impose a cultural uniformity through education. Textbooks are the obvious examples of how history is manipulated, especially if it is conceived by ruling regimes and written by those who want to construct a homogeneous nationality. In texts where history is simplified and distorted by glorifying conquest or constructing humiliation, there is little interest in people's history.

In March 2004, Muttahida Majlis-e-Amal (MMA), the fundamentalist alliance of religious parties in the Pakistani parliament, disrupted the national assembly proceedings and staged a walkout on the grounds that a certain reference to jehad as well as other Koranic verses had been excluded from the new edition of a state-prescribed biology textbook. MMA threatened to launch a protest movement if the Koranic verses were not reinstated. The education minister clarified that no chapter or verses relating to jehad (holy war) or *shahadat* (martyrdom) had been deleted from textbooks, adding that the particular verse referring to jehad had only been moved from the biology textbook for senior students. The education ministry in Pakistan has not found it expedient to inquire, as most people familiar with the discipline of biology would, what references to jehad were doing in the biology curriculum in the first place. This is unsurprising, as it was the ministry of education headed by a former ISI chief, Lt. Gen. Javed Ashraf Qazi, that put these references there in the first place.

The systematic slanting of the state prescribed curricula for all levels of the public education system in Pakistan was exposed in great detail by a report published by the Sustainable Development Policy Institute (SDPI), Islamabad, entitled *The Subtle Subversion: The State of Curricula and Textbooks in Pakistan*. The report shows that for over two decades the national curricula and the officially mandated school textbooks in social studies, English, Urdu, and civics have contained material that is directly contrary to the goals and values of a progressive, moderate, and democratic Pakistan, and encourages students to participate in jehad and martyrdom.

The report is abundantly clear on where the responsibility for these persistent distortions lies: 'Over the years, it became apparent that it was in the interest of both the military and the theocrat to promote militarism in the Pakistani society. This confluence of interests now gets reflected in the educational material.' The opponents of the report have taken issue with it and sought to divert attention from its findings by questioning the agenda of its authors. There is however no arguing with the facts and findings it presents in great detail, including textbook references and their page numbers. Going through the SDPI study, it becomes clear that it is not just some *deeni madrassas* that are spreading hatred, sectarianism and religious bigotry but also prescribed government textbooks.

As a matter of fact, the concepts of jehad and martyrdom were incorporated into the Pakistani curriculum after the start of the so-called Afghan jehad against the Soviet occupation troops. At that point, it suited Washington and its most allied of allies, Pakistan, to encourage and glorify the so-called mujahideen, or holy warriors, in the war against the Russians, and an American institution of higher education was asked to accordingly formulate textbooks for Pakistani schools. The University of Nebraska at Omaha, which has a centre for Afghan

Studies was subsequently tasked by the CIA in the early eighties to rewrite textbooks for Afghan refugee children.

The new textbooks included hate material even in arithmetic. For example, if a man has five bullets and two go into the heads of Russian soldiers, how many are left. Now, as the Soviets are no more, and the mujahideen have not only mutated into Taliban but have also outlived their usefulness, the same American university (University of Nebraska at Omaha) has been given an additional grant by the Bush administration to re-rewrite textbooks, excising material on subjects like jehad.

The SDPI report deals specifically with three subjects: social studies or Pakistan studies, Urdu and English, which are compulsory for all Pakistani students. The report notes that though Islamiat is not compulsory for non-Muslim students, it is taught through other subjects. Therefore, many non-Muslim students end up taking Islamiat anyway because this provides the incentive of 25 per cent extra marks. 'One may get an impression from these textbooks that Pakistan is for Muslims alone because Islamiat is taught to all students whatever their faith, including a compulsory reading of the Holy Koran,' says the SDPI report, and continues:

> The process of equating Muslim and Pakistani identities starts at early stages of school education. For example, the National Early Childhood Education (NECE) curriculum released in March 2002 stressed the need to nurture in children a sense of an Islamic identity and pride in being Pakistanis. There is no mention that this is to be done among Muslim students alone. The suggested material under this objective is Islamiat that is to be read by students of all religions. The curricula for all the compulsory subjects require every Pakistani, irrespective of his or her faith, to love, respect, be proud of and practice Islamic principles, traditions, customs and rituals.

The phenomenal growth of radical Islamic publications, especially magazines and newspapers, have introduced a new breed of jehadi journalism in Pakistan which is committed to pan-Islamic causes and advocates the waging of jehad against the infidel states: the US, Israel and India.

Twenty Pakistan-based militant organizations publish around thirty monthly, fortnightly, weekly and daily publications that are a blend of information and disinformation designed for the countless millions of young students being educated in religious seminaries, where they are taught to read, write and recite the Holy Koran by heart to the exclusion of all other disciplines. Those responsible for these publications claim they promote an alternate world-view to the mainstream press. Their critics however maintain they are doing nothing positive by radicalizing Pakistani society. Some of these periodicals have even garnered a share in the mainstream market, where their influence is growing on the back of the rising anti-US sentiment since the toppling of hardline Islamic Taliban regime in Afghanistan. The war in Iraq has added fuel to the fire.

A study conducted by Friedrich-Naumann-Stiftung a German NGO entitled, *Mediaeval Mindset, Modern Media: Kabul to Kashmir,* discussed the growing culture of hate speech and pondered how media could be instrumental in promoting the culture of religious and political tolerance and peace in Pakistan. According to the study, most of the jehadi publications have legitimate declarations issued by competent authorities, a few among them even certified by the Audit Bureau of Circulation which entitles them to official government advertisements. The study says the genre of jehadi journalism coincides with the Afghan jehad of the 1980s, when wire services like Afghan Islamic Press, Kashmir Media Service and Kashmir Press International were set up. With the Taliban seizing power in Afghanistan, these publications received a massive boost and very vocally and proactively favoured what could be described as 'Talibanization of mind and soul' in Pakistan.

The contents of these publications support the world-view of the Taliban, JeM and LeT, the German study said. Some prominent Kashmir-specific publications that make a regular appearance on the news-stands include the monthlies *Mahaz-i-Kashmir* (Jami'at-ul-Mujahideen, J&K), *Shahadat* (Urdu) and *The Message* (English), and a fortnightly *Jehad-i-Kashmir* (Jamaat-e-Islami, J&K). The monthly *Kashmir Digest* (Urdu/English) is published from Birmingham, UK, for Kashmiris. The circulation figures claimed by the publishers of these newspapers, weeklies and monthlies often rivals that of the highest selling periodicals.

19
Is al-Qaeda Becoming Stronger?

Since President Bush's declaration of war against global terrorism, the US and its allies have claimed to have killed or captured around 75 per cent of al-Qaeda's senior leaders. Yet, the frequency of terror attacks worldwide being attributed to the Osama-led terrorist network has increased, as compared to the pre-9/11 period.

Most Americans were unfamiliar with the al-Qaeda until the terror attacks of 11 September 2001. According to the CIA, using the group's trademark style of tightly coordinated and high-profile violence, al-Qaeda operatives hijacked four US airliners and successfully crashed two of them into the World Trade Center towers in New York, with a third hitting the Pentagon headquarters in Washington, and a fourth crashing in rural Pennsylvania after the passengers attempted to regain control of the plane.

Al-Qaeda, which means 'the Base' in Arabic, was founded in 1988 by Osama bin Laden who continues to be the organization's undisputed leader and driving force. Al-Qaeda goes by other names, such as Islamic Army, World Islamic Front for Jehad Against Jews and Crusaders, Islamic Army for the Liberation of the Holy Places, Osama bin Laden Network,

Osama bin Laden Organization, Islamic Salvation Foundation, and The Group for the Preservation of the Holy Sites. The aim behind al-Qaeda's establishment was to expand the resistance movement against the Soviet forces in Afghanistan into a pan-Islamic resistance movement.

The religious inspiration of al-Qaeda has its roots in the Wahhabi sect, the creed embraced by the current rulers of Saudi Arabia. The ultimate goal of al-Qaeda is to establish a Wahhabi caliphate across the entire Islamic world by working with allied Islamic extremist groups to overthrow regimes it deems non-Islamic (i.e., non-Wahhabi Islamists). It sees Western governments (particularly that of the US) as interfering in the affairs of Islamic nations in the interests of Western corporations. Having fought the US-sponsored jehad against the Soviet occupation troops in Afghanistan, bin Laden apparently developed a taste for jehad. Bin Laden left Saudi Arabia to fight against the Soviets in Afghanistan in 1979 where he sponsored and led a number of Arabs fighting in Afghanistan against the Soviet troops in the 1980s.

In the mid-1980s, bin Laden co-founded, with the Palestinian leader Abdullah Azzam, Maktab-al-Khidamat (MaK) or Services Office, to help funnel fighters and resources to the Peshawar-based Afghan resistance groups. MaK eventually established recruitment centres around the world – including the US, Egypt, Saudi Arabia and Pakistan – that enlisted, sheltered and transported thousands of individuals from over fifty countries to Afghanistan to fight the Soviets. It also organized and funded paramilitary training camps in Afghanistan and Pakistan. Osama bin Laden imported heavy equipment to cut roads and tunnels, and to build hospitals and storage depots in Afghanistan. However, bin Laden split from Abdullah Azzam in the late 1980s to extend his campaign to all corners of the world.

Bin Laden envisioned an all-Arab legion which could eventually be used to wage jehad in Saudi Arabia and Egypt, while Abdullah strongly opposed making war against fellow Muslims. That was the time bin Laden's followers started undermining Azzam's position by spreading rumours that he was an American spy. On 24 November 1989, Azzam and two of his sons were blown up by a car bomb as they were driving to a mosque in Peshawar. Although no one claimed responsibility for the killings, many were blamed, including bin Laden.

Towards the end of the Soviet occupation, many mujahideen wanted to expand their operations to include Islamist struggles in other parts of the world. A number of overlapping and interrelated organizations were formed to further those aspirations. One of these was al-Qaeda. The name 'al-Qaeda' was not self-chosen, but was rather coined by the US government, based on the name of a computer file of bin Laden's that listed the names of contacts he had made at MaK.

After the withdrawal of the Soviet troops from Afghanistan, the Osama-led al-Qaeda decided to lie low for a couple of years, quietly building a financial and operational infrastructure while bin Laden returned to his native Saudi Arabia as a war hero. He raised money for the cause from among his wealthy Saudi peers. When the Gulf War broke out in 1991, bin Laden offered to raise an army of mujahideen in defence of Saudi Arabia, but was spurned in favour of US assistance. He considered the US presence in the Persian Gulf offensive and, beginning around 1992, led the al-Qaeda into a new role with the stated purpose of driving the US forces out of the Gulf.

Al-Qaeda launched a series of terrorist attacks against US interests in the Saudi kingdom, starting with a failed attempt to target US troops in Yemen in 1992. Subsequent attacks included numerous embassy bombings, a boat attack on the *USS cole* bombings of airplanes and like actions. As Osama sought to exploit the general public sentiments against the deployment of

American troops in Saudi Arabia, he was compelled to leave the Holy Kingdom. In 1992 he moved to Sudan, whose Islamic government was fighting a civil war at that time. Money poured in from false charitable funds such as Benevolence International and several other groups that bin Laden's brother-in-law, Mohammed Jamal Khalifa, started. Bin Laden sent his men to Southeast Asia, Africa, Europe and the US. Money and arms reportedly also flowed through American cities like Chicago, Houston, Kansas City and Fort Lauderdale. In 1996, however, bin Laden was expelled from Sudan after his possible participation in the 1994 attempted assassination of Egyptian President Hosni Mubarak in Addis Ababa, Ethiopia. Laden returned to Afghanistan with some of his Sudanese operatives.

In February 1998, Osama bin Laden and his deputy, Ayman al-Zawahiri, issued a joint statement under the banner of the World Islamic Front for Jehad Against the Jews and Crusaders, saying that it was the duty of all Muslims to kill the US citizens, either civilian or military, and their allies everywhere. From 5-8 January 2000, al-Qaeda held its annual summit in a condominium in Kuala Lumpur, Malaysia. The Malaysian authorities learnt about the summit beforehand and provided videotapes to the American intelligence agencies after the summit concluded. The US agencies believe that several of the 9/11 hijackers had attended the summit. Although al-Qaeda was under watch by Western security and intelligence agencies, its members trained to fly both in the UK and in the US a year prior to the 11 September attack.

The US intelligence agencies attribute al-Qaeda's unusual capacity to withstand sustained human losses and material wastage to its unique structure and ideology. According to them, five characteristics contribute to both its survivability and force multiplication. The terror organization is neither a single group nor a coalition of, say, two-dozen large, medium and small groups. It is a conglomerate of groups spread throughout the world, operating as a network. Its affiliates include Egyptian

Islamic Jehad (EIJ), Al Jammaya-al Islamia (IJ: Islamic Group of Egypt), Armed Islamic Group of Algeria (GIA), Islamic Party of Turkestan (IPT: Islamic Movement of Uzbekistan), Jaish-e-Mohammed of Kashmir (JeM: Army of Mohammad) and the Abu Sayyaf Group of the Philippines (ASG). The constituent groups of the network have their own command, control and communication structures. However, whenever required these groups interact or merge ideologically, financially, as well as operationally.

According to an August 2002 *Jane's Intelligence Review* report, 'Peeping into al-Qaeda', al-Qaeda is a conglomerate of quasi-independent Islamic terrorist cells in countries spread across at least twenty-six countries, including Algeria, Morocco, Turkey, Egypt, Syria, Uzbekistan, Tajikistan, Burma, Lebanon, Iraq, Saudi Arabia, Kuwait, Indonesia, Kenya, Tanzania, Azerbaijan, Dagestan, Uganda, Ethiopia, Tunisia, Bahrain, Yemen, Bosnia, as well as the West Bank. 'Other countries where al-Qaeda is known to have covert operational cells, include Pakistan, the Philippines, Malaysia, the United States, Britain, France and Canada,' the *Review* reported.

Al-Qaeda reportedly provides leadership at both the international and national levels. Although Osama bin Laden has identified the US as its prime enemy, he is an internationalist. As such, he is likely to target not only Western targets, but also regimes that identify with the West: from Israel to Pakistan. However, the leaders of the other groups that work with bin Laden also have crucial domestic agendas. For instance, while deputizing for Osama, Ayman al-Zawahiri, also leads the EIJ in Egypt. The broad ideological disposition of the organization advocates pan-Islamism and not pan-Arabism. Consequently, bin Laden's ideology cuts across divisions and appeals to both West Asian and non-West Asian groups, including Asian Islamic groups.

American terrorism experts believe it is part of Osama's psyche to conduct multiple terrorist attacks. For instance, when he attacked US diplomatic targets in East Africa, both the embassies were bombed almost at the same time. Similarly, the 9/11 attacks in the US were coordinated. The three targets were to be attacked within an hour to deny his enemies both the lead time to thwart the attacks and to seek shelter. He was able to do so by meticulous planning, and through attention to detail: all qualities of a professional terrorist. Besides, he is patient, cunning and deceptive. The planning and preparations to attack the US embassies in East Africa stretched over five years.

Terrorism experts further point out that a significant characteristic of bin Laden is his ability to absorb ideas and operationalize them. According to Western media reports, the idea of airborne suicide operations actually grew from a plan conceived by the Oxford educated Ramzi Ahmed Yusuf in the Philippines and another al-Qaeda pilot to crash-dive a plane full of chemicals into the Pentagon in 1994. However, an accidental fire in Manila reportedly disrupted Ramzi's plans, which included the simultaneous bombing of eleven planes over the Pacific and the assassination of the visiting US President Bill Clinton and the Pope. After testing one of the bombs over an aircraft flying over Japan, Ramzi fled to Pakistan, from where he was arrested and extradited to the US. Although he is serving a jail term in the US for bombing the World Trade Center in 1993, Osama decided to go ahead and finally operationalized Ramzi's unique terror plan.

Soon after the 9/11 terror attacks, the operational headquarters of al-Qaeda in Afghanistan were disrupted by US air strikes. Several of the top al-Qaeda leaders have already been captured in Pakistan and several more are suspected to be hiding in the region. However, the al-Qaeda chief and his second-in-command, Ayman al-Zawahiri, a former surgeon and lifelong jehadi, are still at large. If bin Laden is the heart of the al-Qaeda, Zawahiri is considered to be its brain. He was charged with complicity in the assassination of Egyptian president Anwer Sadat, who in his opinion was acting as an American agent. Zawahiri is the second most wanted terrorist in the world according to the FBI and also carries a twenty-five million dollar reward on his head.

The invasion of Afghanistan drove most of the al-Qaeda's leadership out of the country and many of them are now thought to be in Pakistan, while Pakistan's intelligence services have been in cahoots with the terrorist network for several years. Now a US ally in the war on terrorism, Pakistan has been working closely with the CIA and the FBI to capture al-Qaeda operatives throughout the country.

The regional and international manhunts have apparently damaged al-Qaeda's ability to execute major attacks. However, substantial evidence suggests that the network still has hundreds or thousands of operatives at large across the globe, including sleeper agents and other operatives in the US. Whatever the future holds, terrorism experts believe that al-Qaeda will almost certainly continue to pose a threat to Western influence and the stability of governments across the Middle East and Southeast Asia. Since 11 September 2001, when the US vowed to eliminate bin Laden and the al-Qaeda, the terror organization has suffered numerous setbacks and has been forced to redefine its operations, tactics and targets. Bin Laden's International Islamic Front, an umbrella organization for jehadi organizations, has apparently focused its attention primarily on attacking the US and Western interests in a number of countries, which is most likely to continue.

As things stand today, it appears that al-Qaeda has been seriously damaged by a change of fortunes in Saudi Arabia and Pakistan, where it had enjoyed what amounted to be a truce with, if not active support from the powerful establishments of those countries. A number of al-Qaeda suspects are now believed to be in Saudi jails, while in Pakistan, which came under intense US pressure after 9/11, the blind eye that once gazed on al-Qaeda is now looking with 20-20 vision. As a direct result of this, al-Qaeda is expected to open some new fronts both in Saudi Arabia and Pakistan. Indeed, the ceasefire that it had adhered to in Saudi Arabia, bin Laden's country of birth, has already been broken.

Among the 14,000 male members of the Saudi royal family there is a strong but sidelined lobby of princes who support bin Laden. They do not necessarily agree with his strict Wahhabi agenda; rather, they seek to use him as a means of getting at the ruling élite. In terms of its new mission, terrorism experts believe that al-Qaeda will actively play along with this. After all, if nothing else, it still needs the funds that apparently flow from its supporters in the kingdom. In Pakistan too, the knives are literally going to be drawn.

From the early stages of the war on terror, there were media reports that al-Qaeda and the Taliban had been assured by Pakistan's military and intelligence establishment that Islamabad would wear two faces: one acceptable to the US, the other friendly to al-Qaeda and the Taliban, the latter, especially, having enjoyed long-time support from Pakistan. Consequently, General Musharraf made much of his alliance with George Bush on the international stage, while on the domestic front the crackdown on terror remained merely lip service. This did change however, and in time, Musharraf's crackdown has begun to bite.

THE AL-QAEDA NETWORK IN PAKISTAN

General Pervez Musharraf frequently harps on his intent to root out terrorism from Pakistan. And US President George Bush has been lavishing praises on Musharraf for participating in the war against terror, and putting al-Qaeda on the defensive. But the fact remains that Pakistan continues to be a site of recruitment and training for al-Qaeda.

The American intelligence sleuths stationed in Pakistan say the al-Qaeda leadership has changed its strategy; that it operates in small independent groups of five to ten members, thereby creating a chain of command that remains in operation even if there is a major bust.

The information on the current organizational structure and mode of operations of al-Qaeda was provided to the US intelligence agencies by some of the militants arrested in 2005. It shows that Pakistan continues to provide a production line of new terrorists to al-Qaeda, and the fugitives who are on the run from Afghanistan under pressure from America have been provided sanctuaries by the heavily-armed populace in the Pak-Afghan border.

Not only this, the intelligence gathered by the Americans indicates that some of the al-Qaeda training camps have already been reactivated in the tribal area of Waziristan on the Pak-Afghan border. Sources say that the overhead surveillance imagery gathered by the FBI has shown a large number of vehicles and people moving into areas known to be training sites for al-Qaeda. The US intelligence sleuths here also have in their possession a videotape showing members of al-Qaeda receiving military training at a camp there, and bearded men firing weapons and performing various physical exercises. The video has made the Americans believe that if there is one country that matters most to al-Qaeda's future, it is Pakistan.

These findings belie the Bush administration's claims that al-Qaeda has dispersed. Not only has it survived the arrest of its important leader – Khalid Sheikh Mohammed, Abu Zubaydah, Waleed bin Attash, Ahmed Khalfan Ghailani and Abu Faraj Al Libbi – it has also demonstrated its ability to thrive under immense American-Pakistani pressure and despite the arrest of nearly 500 of its activists over the last two years.

Osama bin Laden's group now utilizes its informal networks with local militant groups to obtain logistical support as well as operational collaborators. Before 11 September say sources, Osama targeted the US while his lesser-known Pakistani allies

– radical groups such as the Jaish-e-Mohammad and Harkatul Mujahideen – concentrated on waging jehad in Kashmir. These groups have now rallied behind al-Qaeda and are now trying to physically eliminate General Pervez Musharraf, provide shelter to fugitive al-Qaeda leaders and organize attacks against American targets.

Unlike the pre-9/11 al-Qaeda, say sources, the structure, central command, depth and whereabouts of the mutant cells remain largely unknown. What has been unearthed till now is that the underground al-Qaeda core in Pakistan works clandestinely and provides administrative support to its local operatives besides arranging finances to carry out operations. They reveal that the terror group has a good number of 'footsoldiers' in Pakistan who are drawn from a virtually bottomless pool of ad hoc members. These footsoldiers, usually 20-30 years old, are provided in accordance with the needs of individuals placed higher in the hierarchy. In other words, the footsoldiers never get the 'big picture' of al-Qaeda operations or its new command structure.

The nature of al-Qaeda operations is best illustrated by the example of Amjad Hussain Farooqi, who had masterminded two failed assassination attempts on General Pervez Musharraf in Rawalpindi. Killed on 26 September 2004, after a five-hour gunbattle with security forces in Nawabshah, Sindh, Amjad had been a member of the transnational terrorist organization, Harkat-ul Jehad al Islami (HUJI) and was also linked with al-Qaeda and Lashkar-e-Jhangvi. But less widely known was his role as a hijacker of the Indian Airlines flight IC-814 in December 1999.

Investigations into Amjad Farooqi's involvement in the assassination attempts revealed his ties with Khaled Sheikh Mohammad's successor as al-Qaeda's operational chief, Abu Faraj Al Libbi. This link confirmed fears of the US intelligence sleuths that many of the religious extremists in Pakistan are working in tandem with al-Qaeda operatives, making them difficult to be identified and segregated. Libbi exploited such links to orchestrate some major terrorist activities in Pakistan, including a failed suicide attack on Prime Minister Shaukat Aziz in the Fateh Jang area of Punjab in July 2004.

Pakistani police officials cite the example of the group headed by Attaur Rehman, who graduated from Karachi University, to illustrate how al-Qaeda operates through small independent groups. Attaur was associated with Islami Jamait Tuleba, student wing of the Jamaat-e-Islami. He later broke away from the Jamaat to form his own militant group, Jundullah (Army of God), which draws its cadres from the professional classes.

Although Jundullah reportedly receives orders from Osama's senior followers, it has no direct association with al-Qaeda or any other group associated with the network. That's why, police officials say, the arrest of Attaur and his accomplices could not lead them to other al-Qaeda cells. They describe Jundullah as a well entrenched al-Qaeda cell comprising a few dozen hardcore militants, most of them in their 20s and 30s. The terror group hit the headlines after a daring attack on the motorcade of Karachi corps commander Lt. Gen. Ahsan Saleem Hyat in June 2004. Now serving as vice-chief of army staff, Hyat narrowly escaped death, but eleven people, including eight soldiers, were killed on the spot.

Sources say that some twenty cells, largely splinters of banned militant outfits, are operating in Karachi, which has become the main centre of terrorist activities in the recent past. And many of those involved in the recent terrorist attacks in the city had received training in camps in Waziristan. These splinter groups are trying to cash in on the rising popular disaffection against the domestic and foreign policy decisions of the Musharraf led civilian government. And al-Qaeda is banking on them to do what they can't as a cohesive group.

THE AL-QAEDA NETWORK IN KARACHI

The port city of Karachi has become the new hub of Islamist radicalism since the 9/11 terror attacks on the US and the subsequent decision of the Bush administration to launch the war against terror. Just as Lebanon's capital Beirut was devastated by crime, terrorism, sectarian and religious fundamentalism in the 1980s, Karachi has hit the headlines for all the wrong reasons during the 1990s.

As the US concentrates its hunt for Osama bin Laden and his top al-Qaeda leaders in Afghanistan and Pakistan, many US officials say they also have to consider the possibility that bin Laden could be hiding amid the teeming millions in Pakistan's largest city, Karachi. The former capital of Pakistan is by far the nation's largest city. It is the country's financial and industrial centre, its principal port, home to the stock exchange and headquarters for 70 per cent of its industries. Taxes and revenue from Karachi make up about 65 per cent of the federal budget. Lose Karachi, the political wisdom goes, and lose Pakistan. Much has already been lost. Sixty per cent of the city consists of slums, three out of four people are unemployed, and two million illegal immigrants live here: Afghans, Bangladeshis, Arabs, Sudanese, Somalis, Egyptians, Chechens and others.

Various mafias smuggle drugs, weapons, prostitutes, indentured refugees and other contraband through the city's harbour and along its coastline. Automatic weapons, though illegal, are easily bought in Karachi markets, and the 'Kalashnikov culture' thrives. The city has endured twenty years of gruesome sectarian violence and political killings that have gone virtually unchecked. Karachi has its own style of murder: victims are killed, burned, perhaps beheaded, then stuffed into burlap grain sacks and dumped on the streets at night.

The infiltration of militants into Pakistani cities is illustrated by no less than Abu Zubaydah, the Palestinian manager of al-Qaeda's former training camp network. He and his entourage moved anonymously from one city in Pakistan to another after they slipped out of Afghanistan. Zubaydah went first to Peshawar, then to Lahore, then to Faisalabad. He was arrested in late March with the help of the FBI but, according to Pakistani intelligence reports, not before he oversaw the establishment of al-Qaeda cells in Karachi. The intelligence agencies have no doubt that al-Qaeda and Taliban fugitives are finding sanctuary among the radicals in the city's religious community.

Dozens of known foreign militants, including top al-Qaeda leaders Khalid Sheikh Mohammad and Ramzi bin al-Shibah, have in the past used Karachi as a safe haven since the 9/11 attacks. Senior security officials say many may still be here, though it is difficult to estimate their number. The al-Qaeda activity in Karachi was at its peak from 11 September 2001 until 2002. It was the kidnapping and execution of US reporter Daniel Pearl that first brought the establishment's attention to a possible al-Qaeda presence in Karachi.

On the first anniversary of the 9/11 terror attacks, Pakistani security agencies thwarted a major al-Qaeda attack in Karachi just a few hours before it was to occur. During a raid on an apartment in Karachi's Defence Society area, security agencies found themselves engaged in a gun battle with al-Qaeda operatives that lasted several hours. The encounter resulted in the deaths of two suspects while five others were captured. One of those arrested turned out to be Ramzi bin al-Shibah, who figured on the US list of terrorists wanted in connection with 9/11.

The police had raided another apartment the night before and arrested the wife of Khalid Sheikh Mohammad, the most wanted al-Qaeda operative after Osama bin Laden and Dr Ayman al-Zawahiri. Khalid Sheikh Mohammad, however, managed to escape but intelligence agencies caught up with him in March 2003 when they arrested him from a house in Rawalpindi. By this time, the al-Qaeda presence in Karachi had been firmly established and security agencies were placed on high alert.

During the year 2002-03, al-Qaeda-trained Pakistani militants attacked several targets in Karachi. The most high profile among these was the car-bomb blast targeting a navy bus which killed eleven French engineers working on the Agosta submarine project, and two Pakistanis. A few weeks later, another car bomb exploded outside the US consulate, killing twelve Pakistanis. Later, the police learnt of an al-Qaeda plot to assassinate General Pervez Musharraf, who was in Karachi as part of his referendum campaign. In May 2004, Mufti Nizamuddin Shamzai was killed in Karachi, followed by a deadly attack on the convoy of corps commander, Karachi, Lt. Gen. Ahsan Saleem Hayat in June 2004.

Militants have long favoured Karachi. Its many slum areas house thousands of madrassas, that enable militants to blend into the background. Al-Qaeda or its affiliated groups have often rented out many of the city's derelict apartments. Sometimes they even rent properties in upscale localities of the city such as Defence and Clifton.

Security agencies have arrested several Arab and Pakistani militants with links to al-Qaeda from these areas over the past two years. Last year agencies unearthed the presence of militants from a foreign-based network and arrested a student, Gun Gun Gunawan, brother of Hambali, the Indonesian militant accused of being the mastermind behind the Bali bombing. Police and intelligence agencies say they do not have the necessary resources to monitor the activities of over 3,000 madrassas in the city or its 20,000 empty apartments, which could be used by militants.

While analysing why and how Karachi became a centre of fanaticism and mayhem, journalist Wilson John writes in his book entitled *Karachi: A Terror Capital in the Making:* 'Rife with heroin, hired killers, extortionists and jehadi groups,

Karachi reflects the times and tribulations of a nation that is increasingly becoming hostage to forces of terror.'[1]

In 1986, Pan Am Flight 73 was hijacked by the Abu Nidal terrorist group and landed in Karachi. When asked why Karachi was chosen as the venue, one of the hijackers replied: 'It's so easy here.'[2]

The author goes on to say:

> With fundamentalists as perfect allies and covers and a warren of ghettos and no go areas offering anonymity, Karachi's labyrinths are terrorists' favourite hiding spots. Ramzi Yusuf, already convicted in the United States, took full advantage of Karachi's infrastructure and set up an import-export firm first. Then he started a school for terrorists in transit, boasting students such as Zacarias Moussaoui and Richard Reid. With his uncle Khalid Sheikh Mohammad's help, Ramzi planned the 1993 World Trade Center blast and flew back to Karachi with Pakistan Airlines ...[3]
>
> In December 1999, Muhammad Atta and Ziad Jarrah flew to Karachi on their way to Afghanistan for preparing the attacks that took place in the United States on 11 September 2001. Sheikh Omar Saeed, another Karachi resident, part-financed the attacks by wiring $100,000 to Atta via the ISI network. Omar Saeed and Ramzi bin al-Shib, aided by agent handler Abu Zubaydah, ran al-Qaeda's top-secret Karachi cell before and after 11 September. To camouflage the presence of the al-Qaeda and Taliban cadres in the city, the cell co-opted Harkat-ul-Ansar, JeM and LeJ activists as foot soldiers. On 1 October 2001, the cell executed a deadly attack on the Jammu and Kashmir Assembly in India. The 13 December 2001, attack on India's parliament can be traced back through telephone records to the same Karachi contacts'.[4]

Despite raids, holdups, and arrests in the port city, Wilson John concludes that the revival of the al-Qaeda cell is inevitable as its support base in Karachi is unshaken. Dawood Ibrahim and his associates remain unaffected by the war on terrorism and his syndicate has reportedly shipped Osama bin Laden's sidekick

Ayman al-Zawahiri to safety in Chittagong. Airport alertness having been beefed up, terrorists will rely more and more on the sea route, again making Karachi the epicentre of the next wave of terrorist strikes. The al-Qaeda is said to have purchased a fleet of freighters and tested them out in the October 2002 French oil tanker explosion off the coast of Yemen.

Karachi's image as a launch pad for terrorism endures. The city is a warehouse of forged travel documents and credit cards. Several fake passports were mailed from Karachi to terrorists who carried out the 1998 East African US embassy bombings. According to intelligence inputs, several hundred al-Qaeda terrorists are hiding in various quarters of Karachi such as Defence Housing Society and Korangi. They are, in the words of the US Monitoring Committee on al-Qaeda, 'poised to strike again and again, how, when and where they choose'.

IS AL-QAEDA WINNING THE WAR?

Since Musharraf joined hands with the US in its war on terror, the al-Qaeda network has suffered severe damage to its command and control structure, especially as a consequence of the arrest of its principal operatives from Pakistan. Some of the big al-Qaeda catches were Abu Zubaydah (arrested from Faisalabad in March 2002), Ramzi bin al-Shibah (captured from Karachi in September 2002), Khalid Sheikh Mohammad (arrested from Rawalpindi in March 2003), Waleed bin Attash (captured from Karachi in April 2003), Ahmed Khalfan Ghailani (detained from Gujrat in July 2004) and Abu Faraj Ali Libbi (arrested from Mardan in May 2005). Almost all those captured were handed over to the FBI for interrogation. Of these, Khalid Sheikh was suspected to have masterminded the 9/11 strikes in the US with the help of Ramzi, while Waleed was one of the suspects in the attack on the US naval ship *USS Cole* in October 2000. Zubaydah, reportedly a computer expert, was billed as the No. 3 of al-Qaeda before his arrest. Under these circumstances, the obvious al-Qaeda objectives are clearly evident – to deal with what it considers 'traitors' and the ruling agents of infidels in Saudi Arabia and Pakistan, though there are those in the Pakistani intelligence circles who refuse to believe that the Osama-led organization is as powerful and extensive as is being painted by the American intelligence agencies.

Despite the arrest of many al-Qaeda heavy-weights from various parts of the world, especially Pakistan, there is mounting concern in the West that the terror organization and its international affiliates are actually stronger now than they were prior to the 9/11 terror attacks.

A May 2004 report by the *Jane's Intelligence Digest* asked an important question that might have appeared unthinkable in the aftermath of the terror attacks in New York and Washington: Is al-Qaeda winning the war? For many people (at least in the West) the very question is provocative and even outrageous. Their argument would probably run along the lines that the US and its close allies hold both the moral high ground, and the resources and determination to defeat an international criminal network.

The invasion of Afghanistan and the ousting of the Taliban regime have denied al-Qaeda's access to training camps that operated under state protection; the pro-Western orientation of the current Pakistani leadership has limited the group's scope for geographical movement; and the capture or killing of senior al-Qaeda operatives has demoralized and undermined the movement. However, the Jane report adds that while there are elements of truth in all of the above assertions, the overall progress made by the anti-terrorist coalition led by the US is extremely limited when compared to the mounting evidence of the growing popular support for bin Laden's group and its ideology.

Yet another report published in May 2004 by the London-based International Institute for Strategic Studies (IISS) suggested that despite losing Afghanistan as a training ground for its recruits, al-Qaeda has 'fully reconstituted, set its sights firmly on the US and its closest Western allies in Europe and established a new and effective modus operandi that increasingly exploited local affiliates'. The IISS *Strategic Survey 2003/04* also warned that al-Qaeda must be expected to keep seeking to develop more effective plans for terrorist operations in the US and Europe. The authors of the IISS report suggested that there is potential for weapons of mass destruction being used by the group. None of this points to an organization in retreat or facing a crisis of morale. In fact, according to estimates quoted by the IISS, al-Qaeda is active in over sixty countries and may have as many as 18,000 potential terrorists at its disposal.

AL-QAEDA AND THE 7/7 LONDON BOMBINGS

Proving its might, al-Qaeda once again struck on 7 July 2005 in London, the heart of Europe, targeting the transport network of the British capital, killing fifty-five people and wounding over 700 others. Claiming responsibility for the bloody terror attacks carried out by four suicide bombers, an organization calling itself the Secret Organization Group of al-Qaeda said a day after the bombings that it carried out the London attacks. A 200-word statement posted by the organization on an Islamic website which previously carried statements purporting to be from al-Qaeda, threatened more attacks in Europe.

On 1 September 2005, almost seven weeks after the 7/7 bombings, Al Jazeera television aired snippets of an al-Qaeda video tape in which the network's number two, Ayman Al-Zawahiri claimed responsibility for the London bombings. Zawahiri described the rush-hour bombings on underground trains and a bus as a 'slap for the policy' of British prime minister Tony Blair and said that these operations have taken the battle to the enemy's land. The news channel, which often carries exclusive video and audiotapes attributed to al-Qaeda, showed Zawahiri with an automatic rifle next to him. The 7/7 bombings were a sharp reminder just how capable the al-Qaeda was of hitting where it hurts most.

1. John, Wilson, *Karachi: A Terror Capital in the Making,* Rupa, New Delhi, 2003.
2. Ibid.
3. Ibid.
4. Ibid.

20

Taliban: Still Alive and Robust

The Taliban and their al-Qaeda associates, backed by new volunteers from Pakistan, are reuniting and expanding their area of operations in the southern and eastern parts of Afghanistan, which were their former stronghold. Despite the fall of the Taliban regime in Afghanistan in October 2001, the US-led Allied Forces have apparently failed to uproot the Taliban and al-Qaeda fighters in Afghanistan who are gaining strength with every passing day and regrouping and reorganizing their resistance movement in the war torn country.

While the Musharraf government continues to claim having taken concrete measures to uproot the Taliban and al-Qaeda network from the troubled Waziristan region bordering Afghanistan, the Karzai government keeps questioning Islamabad's willingness to effectively eliminate the Taliban and al-Qaeda insurgents attacking the Allied Forces as well as the Northern Alliance troops from the Pakistani side of the border. President Hamid Karzai alleges that General Musharraf treats the Taliban rebels differently than he did al-Qaeda. He has repeatedly pointed out that even though Pakistan had arrested and handed over to the FBI around 500 al-Qaeda operatives, including half-a-dozen key leaders, not a single senior Taliban commander was captured from Pakistan and extradited to Afghanistan, despite repeated demands in this regard.

While attacking Afghanistan in October 2001, the Bush administrations' objective was to eliminate the Taliban militia, get hold of the Osama bin Laden-led al-Qaeda members and establish a regime in Kabul that would be protected by the Northern Alliance in particular. Yet the fact remains that the US-led Allied Forces have failed to uproot the Taliban and the al-Qaeda insurgents from Afghanistan. Before the US-led invasion of Afghanistan, Pakistan actively supported the Taliban regime in Kabul, primarily because many of its members were products of Pakistan's madrassas and had close links with the Inter Services Intelligence (ISI). Even though Musharraf formally renounced support of the Taliban when he threw in his lot with the US, action against the Taliban and their supporters has been half-hearted at best, partly because many within the Pakistan security apparatus remain close to the Taliban. Islamabad even pleads drawing moderate Taliban into the mainstream political process in Afghanistan to defuse the escalating Taliban-led unrest in the country.

The former Taliban regime of Afghanistan was actually brought to power with US's silent blessing as it dallied in an abortive new 'Great Game' in Central Asia. Keen to see Afghanistan under strong central rule to allow a US-led group to build a multi-billion-dollar oil and gas pipeline, Washington urged key allies, Pakistan and Saudi Arabia, to back the Taliban militia's bid for power in 1996.

At the beginning of the 1980s, although backed by an expeditionary force of around 117,000 Soviet troops, the Babrak Karmal regime was unable to establish authority outside Kabul. Around 85 per cent of the countryside eluded effective government control. An overwhelming majority of Afghans opposed the communist regime, either actively or passively. Afghan mujahideens made it virtually impossible for the regime to maintain a system of local government outside major urban centres. Poorly armed initially, in 1984 the mujahideen began receiving substantial assistance in the form of weapons and training from the US, Saudi Arabia, Pakistan and other outside powers.

Late in 1985, Afghan mujahideen were active in and around Kabul, launching rocket attacks and assassinating high government officials. The failure of the Soviet Union to win over a significant number of Afghan collaborators or to rebuild a viable Afghan army forced it to bear an increasing responsibility for fighting the resistance and for the civilian administration. Soviet and popular displeasure with the Karmal regime led to its demise in May 1986. Muhammad Najibullah, former chief of the Afghan secret police, replaced Karmal. As prime minister, however, Najibullah was ineffective and highly dependent on the Soviet support.

It was not until 1988 that Pakistan and Afghanistan, with the US and Russia serving as guarantors, signed an agreement settling major differences between them. The agreement, known as the Geneva accords, called for Soviet and US non-interference in the internal affairs of Pakistan and Afghanistan, the right of refugees to return to Afghanistan without fear of being harassed and, perhaps most important of all, a timetable that ensured full Soviet withdrawal from Afghanistan by 15 February 1989. About 14,500 Soviet and an estimated one million Afghan lives were lost between 1979 and the Soviet withdrawal in 1989.

Significantly, the Afghan mujahideen were neither party to the negotiations nor to the 1988 agreement, and consequently refused to accept the terms of the accords. Consequently, civil war did not end with the Soviet withdrawal in February 1989, but instead escalated. Najibullah's regime, though failing to win popular support, territory or international recognition, was able to remain in power until 1992.

The Soviet occupation force of some 115,000 troops and the Karmal government waged several campaigns to crush the uprisings with mass arrests, torture, executions of dissidents, as well as aerial bombardment and executions in the countryside. Most of the one million Afghans died during this period from aerial bombardment. These measures further expanded the resistance to the communist government in Kabul and fuelled a outflow of refugees from Afghanistan that soon reached a figure of five million out of an estimated population of about sixteen million.

That was the time when Islamic organizations became the heart of the resistance, with most of them operating from within Pakistan and Iran. Seeing the conflict as a way to extend the Cold War battleground, the US, and in particular Saudi Arabia, provided massive support for the resistance, nearly all of it funneled through Pakistan. Thousands of Muslim radicals from the Middle East, North Africa and other Muslim countries joined the resistance forces. Most fought with Pashtun factions that had the strongest support from Pakistan and Saudi Arabia, the Hizb-e-Islami of Gulbuddin Hekmatyar and Ittehad-i-Islami of Professor Abdul Rasul Sayyaf. Among them was Osama bin Laden, who reached Afghanistan in the early 1980s and built training facilities there for these foreign recruits.

In early 1992, the forces of Tajik leader Ahmed Shah Masood; General Abdul Rashid Dostum, head of a powerful Uzbek militia that had been allied with Najibullah; and the Hazara faction, Hizb-e-Wahdat, joined together in a coalition they called the Northern Alliance. In April 1992, non-Pashtun militia forces that had been allied with the government mutinied and took control of Kabul airport, preventing President Najibullah from leaving the country and pre-empting a UN peacekeeping role.

Najibullah took refuge in the UN compound in Kabul, where he remained for the next four years. On 25 April 1992, Ahmad Shah Masood entered Kabul, and the next day, the Northern Alliance factions reached an agreement on a coalition government that excluded the Hizb-e-Islami led by Gulbuddin Hekmatyar, considered to be the protégé of Pakistani establishment. Rejecting the arrangement, Hekmatyar launched massive and indiscriminate rocket attacks on Kabul that continued intermittently until he was forced out of Kabul.

In June 1992, Berhanuddin Rabbani, the Tajik leader of Jamiat-e-Islami, became president of the Islamic Emirate of Afghanistan, while Gulbuddin Hekmatyar continued to bombard Kabul with rockets. In January 1994, Hekmatyar joined forces with General Abdul Rashid Dostum to oust Rabbani and his defence minister, Ahmad Shah Masood, launching full-scale civil war in Kabul. By 1995, one-third of the city had been reduced to rubble.

That was the time a group of students from Darul Uloom Haqqania (a religious school in Akora Khattak in the Frontier Province of Pakistan) led by a one-eyed religious teacher, Mullah Mohammad Omar, made an appearance on to the Afghan war scene and successfully battled the Northern Alliance troops in various parts of Afghanistan. Most of the Taliban leaders were educated in Pakistan, in refugee camps where they had fled with millions of other Afghans after the Soviet invasion. The Jamiat Ulema-e-Islam, led by the Leader of Opposition in Pakistan's National Assembly, Maulana Fazlur Rehman, provided welfare services, education and military training for refugees in many of these camps besides establishing madrassas in the Deobandi tradition. The story goes that a group of well trained Taliban was chosen by the Inter Services Intelligence to protect a convoy trying to open a trade route from Pakistan to Central Asia. They proved an able force, fighting off rival mujahideen and warlords. The Taliban then went on to take the Afghan city of Kandahar, beginning a surprising advance that ended with their capture of Kabul in September 1996. The Taliban's popularity with the Afghan people was surprising for the country's other warring factions. Many Afghans, weary of conflict and anarchy, were relieved to see corrupt and often brutal warlords replaced by the devout Taliban, who had some success in eliminating corruption, restoring peace and allowing commerce to resume.

In areas under their control, Taliban authorities enforced their version of Islamic law, enacting policies prohibiting women from working outside the home in activities other than health care and decreeing corporal punishment for those convicted of certain crimes. The Taliban also enforced a strict dress code for women, and required men to have 'fist-length' beards and to refrain from Western haircuts or attire. Arguably, the most powerful agency within the Islamic Emirate of Afghanistan was the Ministry of Promotion of Virtue and Prevention of Vice (al-Amr bil Maruf wal Nahianal Munkir), which was responsible for the enforcement of all Taliban decrees concerning moral behaviour.

Through 2000 and 2001, fighting continued in the north-east between Masood's forces and the Taliban, with the latter taking control of Taloqan in September 2000, driving the Northern Alliance troops further east to Faizabad. On 9 September 2001, two days before the 9/11 terrorist attacks, Ahmad Shah Masood was assassinated when suicide bombers, disguised as journalists, detonated a device hidden in a video camera. Northern Alliance leaders later claimed that the Algerian assassins were linked to Osama bin Laden and the assassination was designed to deprive the Northern Alliance of its most effective leader in the aftermath of the 11 September attacks on the World Trade Center in New York and the Pentagon in Washington DC.

The US-led Operation Enduring Freedom against Afghanistan was launched on 7 October 2001 and the Northern Alliance troops entered Kabul on 13 November 2001, eventually leading to the fall of the Taliban regime. It was a twist none had expected: few had predicted a sudden Taliban collapse. In less than a week, the famed reputation of the Taliban's fighting abilities was pounded to dust under the Northern Alliance tanks. From Mazar-e-Sharif to Herat to Kabul, Taliban forces were on the run, fleeing the battlefield and leaving behind arms and ammunition. The occupation of Kabul by the Northern Alliance, with the help of US air power and the subsequent outburst of anti-Pakistan anger in Kabul and other cities of the north, led to the hasty withdrawal into Pakistan of the dregs of the Pakistani components and their Arab associates of Chechen ancestry. Similarly, the jehadis from Southeast Asia and the central Asian Republics withdrew into Pakistan in disarray.

Only the Arabs of al-Qaeda led by bin Laden stayed on in southern and eastern Afghanistan for some weeks and put up some resistance to the US. After the unsuccessful Tora Bora operation, in which the Americans managed to surround the dregs of al-Qaeda, including Laden, for some days, the latter managed to escape into the Federally Administered Tribal Areas from where they dispersed in small groups into the principal cities of Pakistan. When the US started the second phase of the operations against al-Qaeda, it sought the assistance of the Pakistan Army to seal the border with Afghanistan to prevent the dregs from escaping into Pakistan. It similarly sought the help of the Northern Alliance to prevent their escape into the central Asian states.

Since the fall of the Taliban regime in Afghanistan, the US military operations in Afghanistan have passed through three phases. In the first phase, the government set up by the Taliban regime with its administrative headquarters in Kabul and its religious headquarters in Kandahar was replaced by a provisional government headed by Hamid Karzai, an educated Pashtun enjoying confidence of the US and other Western countries. In the second phase, the training and other terrorist infrastructure of al-Qaeda and Taliban in southern and eastern Afghanistan were destroyed through aerial and ground action. In the third phase, efforts were initiated to restore law and order and governance in the rural areas liberated from the control of the jehadi forces, and to build the infrastructure of a liberal democracy in Afghanistan in the form of a constitution paving the way for free and fair elections.

However, as things stand, it appears that the Taliban movement has regrouped itself in Afghanistan, mostly along the Pak–Afghan border areas. The social, geographical and political characteristics of the whole of this tribal belt favour the Taliban fighters, and the Pakistani, US and Afghan authorities just cannot control them in the region. Earlier, between 7 October 2001 and December 2001, heavy US precision bombing had coerced the Taliban into abandoning their controlling positions and disperse to places where they could find shelter. Mullah Mohammad Omar's decision to retreat from Kabul and Kandahar forced most of his commanders to hide in the Pakistani tribal areas. Ordinary Taliban foot soldiers easily melted into the civilian Afghan population. Several disposed of their black turbans from Pakhool and joined the new Afghan administration. Many chose to return to their tribes and resume routine life as ordinary citizens.

However, since August 2003, the situation in Afghanistan has been deteriorating. Increasing numbers of better trained, better equipped and better-led Taliban cadres operating from sanctuaries in Pakistan have stepped up their hit-and-run raids into southern and eastern Afghanistan in order to demoralize the newly-raised army and police of the Hamid Karzai government in the hope of inducing large-scale desertions. Their attacks have been focused on members of the new Afghan army, police and other government departments, and foreign aid workers. They have avoided direct confrontation with US forces, lest they pursue them into Pakistani territory.

The Taliban resistance movement has apparently selected Zabul, Spin Boldak and Hilmand as areas where they need to re-establish their authority. These districts are all situated along mountainous terrain, which best serves a guerilla campaign. This terrain leads to safe routes that cut across areas demarcated by the Durand Line separating Pakistan from Afghanistan, which exists only on the map. In practical terms there is no clear demarcation of the border and there are dozens of villages located on the line, part in Afghanistan and part in Pakistan. The people on both sides of the Durand Line belong to the same tribes (the Noor Zai and the Achakzai) and have traditionally moved freely on both sides of the divide for centuries. These are the circumstances that make it possible for the Taliban to attack their targets on Afghan soil, using the mountainous terrain to strategic advantage, and then melting into the villages in the Pak-Afghan border areas. Consequently, the Pakistani tribal areas provide natural strategic depth to the Taliban fighters.

The people who live all around the Chaman area on the Pakistani side of the divide are extremely religious and numerous madrassas (numbering approximately 200) are the ideological centres of the Taliban movement. The location of these seminaries is, again, problematic as they exist along the line where a clear demarcation of Pakistani and Afghan territory is impossible. With these key factors complementing their modus operandi, the Taliban have established their writ in Zabul, Hilmand and Spin Boldak. The US forces in Afghanistan are unwilling to take casualties and consequently provide only limited aerial support to the Afghan army in their operations in the area.

On occasion, some US soldiers have been sent in to reinforce the Afghan militia's line of defence, but they rarely participate in the action and generally limit their role to guiding the operations. This has tended to demoralize the Afghan administration and forces, and they now increasingly accept the presence of the Taliban in these three districts. Although the Taliban have yet to appoint their own administration there, they have established a kind of de facto rule and a strong presence in the mountainous terrain around the area. The local administration is aware that, if they act against the will of the Taliban, the consequences will be extreme.

In Khost, Paktia, Paktika and Gazni, the Taliban seek to inflict terror on the US Forces. They do not control any significant areas in these provinces, but gather in the Northern and Southern Waziristan area of Pakistan as well as in the Kurram Agency for strikes across the border and then retreat to the relative safety of Pakistani territory. Once again, they hide in the mountains in areas where the nebulous Durand Line separates Pakistan from Afghanistan. There is a long-standing tradition within this specific area for the local Waziri tribes who live on both sides of the Pak-Afghan border to move across the divide for trade. They move as a group and always carry guns and ammunition with them. For centuries there have been no curbs on their free movement in the area, and no one has ever asked them for travel documents. The result is that neither the Afghan security guards nor the Pakistanis can distinguish between the movement of these tribal groups and that of the Taliban.

Addressing a press conference at Kabul on 7 October 2004, the then US ambassador to Kabul Zalmay Khalilzad said:

> The Taliban and al-Qaeda might be planning larger or more spectacular attacks in Afghanistan as part of a campaign against the reconstruction process. We have seen a surge in activity in recent weeks, but we also see signs that the response has been quite effective, and I think in desperation they may try, or there are indications that they may try to do something to get a lot of attention. The resurgent Taliban present a serious threat across the south and east of the country, not least on the main north–south highway between Kabul and Kandahar, a priority project supported by both President Bush and Karzai. . . . Pakistan cannot become a sanctuary for Taliban and al-Qaeda people who want to attack Afghanistan. There has to be a decrease, and at best an end, to cross-border attacks by Taliban and al-Qaeda people from Pakistan. I welcome the recent actions by the Pakistani government, but we would like to see more, in fact, a lot more.

Though the US has been saying that it is prepared for a longish stay, whatever be the cost in terms of funds and casualties to both the countries, the jehadis view this as mere bravado and have convinced themselves that the American will to fight will continue to weaken. America's continued reluctance to act against Pakistan and make it pay a prohibitive price for helping the jehadi terrorists is coming in the way of an effective counter-terrorism strategy. Encouraged by this reluctance on part of the US, the Musharraf regime continues to keep the jehadis alive and active in the hope of using them to retrieve lost Pakistani influence in Afghanistan, and to achieve its strategic objective of forcing a change in the status quo in Jammu & Kashmir.

21

Osama bin Laden: A CIA Creation

In its endeavour to assert the primacy of American national interests and strategic objectives through any means, the US has over the years, through covert CIA operations, made heroes out of surrogates, whose only qualification was that they were prepared to do its bidding. It eventually ended up with the mortification of seeing these heroes of yesterday becoming terrorists of today and endangering the very US national interests that they were initially created to protect.

This seems also to be the case with most of the Pakistani militant groups, which were once funded by the CIA, but have now turned anti-American. Saudi billionaire and the FBI's most wanted terrorist, Osama bin Laden, is a good case. Be it bin Laden or the former Taliban supreme commander Mullah Mohammad Omar, they all were originally the creation of the CIA, which was ably assisted by Pakistan's ISI.

Born in 1958, Osama bin Laden is the seventeenth of fifty-two sons of a Yemeni peasant, Mohammed bin Laden, who migrated to Saudi Arabia and became one of the richest construction magnates there. Of his total assets, reportedly worth US $ 5 billion, Osama bin Laden personally controlled assets worth US $ 300 million. His father was the favourite construction magnate of the Saudi royal family, who gave bin Laden's family huge contracts to renovate the holy cities of Mecca and Medina and build palaces for Saudi princes.

In 1980, at the age of twenty-two, barely a year after the Soviet invasion of Afghanistan in 1979, Osama, who had just graduated from the King Abdul Aziz University, left the family business and moved over to Pakistan to fight against the Soviet troops in Afghanistan with his money, and with over 6,000 Muslim volunteers recruited from Arab and other Islamic countries. The CIA and other Western intelligence agencies welcomed the assistance from bin Laden and his volunteers, and provided them with guidance, training, arms and ammunition to fight against the Soviet troops.

Osama used his money and equipment to help the Afghan rebels fight the Soviet army. Legend has it that he fought bravely against Soviet troops. However, according to former CIA officers, he was more a financier than a warrior – a philanthropist who also supported a number of health care ventures and widow-and-orphan charity organizations for Afghan refugees in Peshawar. Osama fought himself, constructed tunnels and other defensive structures along the Pak-Afghan border, and distinguished himself in the battles against Soviet troops at Jaji and Shaban. He became a legendary figure for his religiosity and courage. While recruiting volunteers for Afghanistan, he would say: 'One day of jehad in Afghanistan is equivalent to 1,000 days of namaz in a mosque'.

During his stay in Afghanistan, Osama met fellow warrior Mullah Mohammad Omar. It was bin Laden who bankrolled the Taliban's capture of Kabul under the leadership of the reclusive, one-eyed Mullah Omar and became one of his most trusted advisers. In 1996, Mullah Omar, became the ruler of three-fourths of Afghanistan. Osama in the meantime established the headquarters of al-Qaeda in Peshawar, a place where Egyptian and Saudi volunteers would rest before setting off for battle in

Afghanistan. Its name became a kind of flag uniting bin Laden's followers.

When the Soviet forces left Afghanistan in 1989, bin Laden returned home to Saudi Arabia. He soon set his sights on the last remaining superpower. He himself was extremely wary of the US. He found the new enemy in August 1990, when the US began sending troops to Saudi Arabia, to prepare for war against Iraq.

His criticism of the Saudi ruling family, and particularly of King Fahd, increased after the Gulf War of 1991. He described the king's action in allowing US and other Western troops into Saudi territory for fighting against Iraq a desecration of the holy land by armed infidels. He allegedly fell out with the officers of the CIA and demanded the withdrawal of the US troops from Saudi territory. Osama subsequently declared the Saudi ruling family 'insufficiently Islamic'. He was made to stay there till 1991 by the Saudi authorities who impounded his passport.

As a friend of bin Laden, Prince Turki, the then chief of Saudi intelligence, once again sent him to Peshawar and insisted that he remain there. One of the stories put out by bin Laden is that he went to King Fahd and promised that he would raise holy warriors who would protect Saudi Arabia. His violent opposition to the Saudi royal family began when King Fahd rejected that offer. The deployment of Americans in the land of Mecca and Medina reminded bin Laden of the medieval Crusades – the Christian religious wars against Islam. His rage transformed him into a stateless outlaw.

In November 1991, Saudi intelligence officers caught bin Laden smuggling weapons from Yemen, his father's homeland, and withdrew his passport. Bin Laden's family, concerned that his activities might jeopardize their close relations with the ruling clan, attempted to bring him back into the fold but were eventually forced to effectively disown him. The pressure mounted. In late 1996, an escape route appeared. Osama bin Laden received an offer of refuge from Hassan al-Turabi, the charismatic Islamist scholar of Sudan, which he decided to accept. In Sudan he was able to start the serious work of building al-Qaeda, a global umbrella group of Muslim extremists dedicated to overturning 'un-Islamic' governments throughout the Middle East and elsewhere in the world. Turabi believed that the total defeat of Iraq and the discrediting of 'secular' Arab regimes would lead to an opportunity to set up a 'pure' Islamic government across the Muslim world. It was a seductive message. Bin Laden fled Saudi Arabia for Khartoum, the Sudanese capital, never to return to his homeland.

Veterans of the Afghan war followed bin Laden under al-Qaeda's banner. Bin Laden set up home in a rich suburb of Khartoum with his four wives, his children and a core of close retainers. Then he flew in several hundred Arab veterans from Afghanistan to provide the basis of a broader organization. Life in Sudan was curious. There were football matches, bathing trips to the Blue Nile, long earnest college-student type arguments over whether Shia and Sunni Muslims should unite to fight the common enemy and over points of Islamic doctrine. Bin Laden even opened a personal bank account in his own name, and most of the time of 'the sheikh' was spent in making money rather than spreading global jehad.

At one point bin Laden bought a plane for $250,000 and hired a pilot, though the plane crashed soon thereafter. According to the CIA, bin Laden also set up several military training camps where hundreds of Algerians, Palestinians, Egyptians and Saudis received instructions in bomb-making and terrorist tactics. Many of them had fought in Afghanistan and now, like bin Laden, were at a loose end. There was talk of assassinating President Mubarak of Egypt, though nobody was sure how to go about it, and there was some haphazard surveillance of possible targets for a bombing in East Africa, including the US embassy in Nairobi.

In 1995, after the Saudi government revoked his citizenship, bin Laden began making scathing attacks on the royal family from Khartoum. He began engaging in limited political activity, issuing political statements and communiqués denouncing the Saudi government as corrupt and repressive. By January 1996, Khartoum was getting increasingly uneasy about its guest. Turabi contacted the Sudanese ambassador to Afghanistan, Atiya Badawi, who was based in Peshawar. Badawi, who had learnt the Pashtun language while fighting the Russians, had excellent contacts with his former comrades among the mujahideen. With Afghanistan split into hundreds of warring bandit fiefdoms, it was easy to persuade three senior commanders in the Jalalabad area that a wealthy Saudi under their protection might give them an edge over their rivals. The three men, all now dead, flew to Sudan to ask bin Laden to return to the land of jehad.

By mid-1996, Osama had returned to Afghanistan from Sudan with his wives and children. The jehad against the Russians had given bin Laden much-needed confidence, contacts throughout the Islamic world, and a taste for fame, respect and adulation. His authority and profile had been further boosted by his stance against Saudi Arabia and the consequent exile. However, in terms of military capacity and strategic thinking, bin Laden's group was still weak. In Afghanistan, he swiftly found a solution.

He had returned to a land that had known anarchy for six years. Thousands of Islamic militants were based in the old mujahideen complexes in the east of the country. Many were sponsored by the Pakistani secret services which wanted zealots to fight India in Kashmir. Others were backed by a variety of Islamic groups from all over the world. In the camps, the volunteers were trained in guerrilla warfare. Many had fought for the Taliban. Bin Laden's first problem was partially solved almost immediately. He had inherited an army.

In Afghanistan, he found himself surrounded by men who could help him, especially dozens of exiled Egyptian extremists. They included Dr Ayman al-Zawahiri, a 37-year-old surgeon and a founder of the effective and sophisticated Egyptian al-Jehad group. Another was Mohammed Atef, the group's hard and competent military commander. Al-Zawahiri taught bin Laden the political realities of global war. Atef lectured him on the military necessities. After several security scares, he moved his household to a former mujahideen base at Tora Bora, high in the mountains south of Jalalabad.

The Egyptians told him that the best form of defence was attack. After two months at Tora Bora, he wrote and circulated a twelve-page article replete with Koranic and historical references, promising violent action against the Americans unless they withdrew from Saudi Arabia. In a significant broadening of his view, indicative of the influence of the Egyptians, he also spoke for the first time of Palestine and Lebanon as well as 'the fierce Judaeo-Christian campaign against the Muslim world,' and 'the duty of all Muslims' to resist it. Bin Laden bought four Stinger missiles that had been supplied to the mujahideen by the CIA and had them smuggled to Saudi Islamic groups.

When it discovered the plot, Riyadh was incensed. The Saudi government, along with Pakistan, had supported the Taliban as a means of countering Iranian and Russian influence in Afghanistan. Now the Taliban were not only sheltering one of their most determined enemies but were also ignoring demands to hand him over. More extreme measures were needed.

In early 1997, the Taliban discovered what they said was a Saudi plot to assassinate bin Laden. The Islamic militia, who by then controlled about two-thirds of Afghanistan, invited bin Laden to move to Kandahar for his own security. To this, bin Laden agreed and moved into an old Soviet air force base close to Kandahar airport. He cemented his relationship with the Taliban's senior command by funding huge military purchases, building mosques, and buying cars for the leadership. He even helped construct a new residence for Mullah Omar and his family on the outskirts of the city and started work on a huge compound to be used for prayers at the start of Ramadan.

He also set up a system to cream off the élite from the existing training camps to al-Qaeda. The camp administrators told the volunteers that the best of them would earn an audience with 'the ameer'. When bin Laden met them, his aides would pick the most promising and send them to more specialized camps where, instead of basic infantry techniques, they had psychological and physical tests, combat trials, and finally, instructions in the acquisition of the skills necessary for the modern terrorist. Within a year, bin Laden had created the terrorist version of special forces.

Under Zawahiri's tutelage, Laden had also realized that he needed to internationalize his cause. Towards the end of 1997, he started work to unify Islamic movements under the al-Qaeda umbrella, using his money, charm and reputation to draw in leaders from around the world. He bolstered his support locally, giving money to village clerics to build mosques and, according to one Taliban source, organizing the import of 3,000 secondhand Toyota Corolla Estates from Dubai. They were given to the families of Taliban casualties to enable them to earn a living.

Finally, in February 1998, he felt strong enough to issue a fatwa in the name of the 'World Front for Jehad against Jews and Crusaders'. It was signed by bin Laden, al-Zawahiri and the heads of major Islamic movements in Pakistan and Bangladesh, and endorsed by dozens of other groups throughout the region. It was, according to one Western scholar of Islam, 'a magnificent piece of eloquent, even poetic, Arabic prose'. There was nothing poetic about its message. The fatwa stated that killing Americans and their allies, even civilians, was a Muslim duty. Shortly afterwards, bin Laden told an interviewer that there would be 'radical action' soon.

Then came the 1998 annual report of the US State Department, *Patterns of Global Terrorism*, stating that Laden had shifted from Jalalabad to the Taliban's headquarters in

Kandahar in early 1997 and that he had established a new base of operations. The report added that Muslims from around the world, including a large number of Egyptians, Algerians, Palestinians and Saudis, continued to use Afghanistan as a training ground. The Taliban, as well as many other combatants of the Afghan civil war, facilitated the training and provided indoctrination facilities for the non-Afghans in the territories they controlled. Several Afghan factions also provided logistic support, free passage and sometimes passports to the members of various terrorist organizations. These individuals, in turn, were involved in fighting in Bosnia, Chechnya, Tajikistan, Jammu & Kashmir, the Philippines and parts of the Middle East.

In the first week of August 1998, American embassies in Nairobi (Kenya) and Dar es Salaam (Tanzania) were bombed, allegedly by Osama's terrorist network, killing a total of 224, including twelve Americans, and injuring over 4,585. Thirteen days after the bombings in Africa, in retaliation against bin Laden for the bombings of the US Embassies, the US conducted Operation Infinite Reach. Seventy-five US cruise missiles slammed into six training camps in the eastern Afghan hills. Other missiles demolished a medical factory in Sudan. The Muslim world exploded in anger and outrage. Osama bin Laden was launched on to the global stage. When the US bombarded Afghanistan, two training camps being run by Harkatul Mujahideen were destroyed and twenty-one of its jehadis were killed.

After the attacks, Osama was interviewed in Afghanistan by an American TV news network. From a mountain hideout in Jalalabad, Osama threatened to kill 'terrorist Americans' and praised the 1993 bombing of the World Trade Center in New York, thereby 'implying' his complicity in the two incidents. The US took notice. There had been confusion after the World Trade Center bombing about the nature of radical Islamic threats to the US. Bin Laden was thus named in the WTC bombing for the first time. Bin Laden had further warned: 'For each of us killed or wounded in the cowardly US attack, at least 100 Americans will be killed. I may not be alive, but you will remember my words.'

By that time, Osama bin Laden's hand was already being suspected in the following acts of terrorism:

- In December 1995, the British police raided the London residence of an Algerian named Rachid Ramda and recovered communications from the Armed Islamic Group of Algeria which was involved in seven explosions in France in 1995. They also discovered records of money transfers and allegedly managed to trace them to Osama bin Laden's office in Khartoum in Sudan.
- Egyptian authorities suspected his involvement in a plot to assassinate President Hosni Mubarak in December 1995, which was foiled by the Egyptian security agencies.
- According to Egyptian security agencies, bin Laden was the major financier of a training camp at Kunar in Afghanistan, where members of two Egyptian terrorist organizations, Islamic Jehad and Islamic Group (possibly Al Jammaya-al Islamia) were being trained.
- Citing its own intelligence sources, the US State Department claimed that bin Laden helped to finance three terrorist training camps in northern Sudan, where extremists from Algeria, Tunisia and Egypt were trained.
- The State Department also suspected that bin Laden had helped finance two bombing incidents in Aden in 1992 allegedly directed against US troops transiting to Somalia. While they escaped, two Italian tourists were killed.
- The Saudi authorities suspected his involvement in the explosion in November 1995, in a centre for the Saudi National Guards at Riyadh run by US troops. They also alleged his links with an anti-monarchical organization called the Advice and Reformation Committee, which was then reportedly operating from London.

In November 1998, three months after the missile strikes, two luxury jets landed at Kandahar air base. One brought Prince Turki al Faisal, bin Laden's student friend and the head of Saudi Arabia's security services. The second was empty. It was there to take bin Laden back to Riyadh. Prince Turki, who had been crucial in getting millions of dollars of official aid for the Taliban, went straight to Mullah Omar's residence where a magnificent lunch had been laid out. The prince began to lecture the Taliban leader about his ingratitude to his former benefactors.

In the midst of his tirade, Omar reportedly took a water jug from an attendant and emptied it over his head. 'I nearly lost my temper,' he is reported to have told the astonished prince. 'Now I am calm. I will ask you a question and then you can leave. How long has the royalty of Saudi Arabia been the hired help of the Americans?' Lunch went uneaten and the second plane returned to Riyadh empty. Shortly thereafter, Osama bin Laden pledged allegiance to Mullah Omar and recognized him formally as 'ameer ul momineen' or leader of the faithful. His fate and that of the Taliban were now inextricably linked.

Osama issued a statement denying all involvement in the US embassies' attack though he said that he welcomed them. No one believed him. The Taliban then said bin Laden had 'disappeared'. No one believed them either. At the same time, the al-Qaeda infrastructure within Afghanistan continued to expand. Throughout 1999 and 2000, rattled Western intelligence services blamed bin Laden for hundreds of threats and scores of attacks all over the world. Though many were only tenuously linked to him, Osama was happy to take the credit. Clever publicity stunts helped too.

In April 2000, General Musharraf, acting on the request of the former US President Bill Clinton, met the Taliban ruler Mullah Omar to convince him that he should expel bin Laden but failed. According to an official US report, released by a commission investigating the 11 September 2001 terrorist attacks in the US: 'When Mr Clinton visited Pakistan on 25 March 2000, he raised the Osama bin Laden issue in his meeting with Musharraf. The Pakistanis asked for evidence that bin Laden had really ordered the US embassy bombings [in East Africa] a year and a half earlier. In a follow-up meeting the next day with Under Secretary of State Thomas Pickering, General Musharraf argued that Pakistan had only limited influence over the Taliban.' Despite these reservations, 'General Musharraf did meet Mullah Omar and did urge him to get rid of bin Laden,' the report said.

In early June 2000, according to the report, Pakistan's interior minister went to Kandahar with Mr Pickering and delivered a joint message to Taliban officials. 'But the Taliban seemed immune to such pleas, especially from Pakistani civilians like the Interior Minister,' the report observed. It also said that, 'Pakistan did not threaten to cut off its help to the Taliban regime.' The report also provided information about joint US-Saudi efforts to influence the Taliban regime on this issue.

No one knows where bin Laden was when the Twin Towers crumbled on 9/11, killing over five thousand people. However, soon after the attacks, President Bush signed an executive order giving the CIA mandate to capture or kill bin Laden and his associates, destroy al-Qaeda's communications, security organization and infrastructure. Interviewed in August 2001 by a London-based Arab journalist, bin Laden boasted that he and his followers were planning 'a very big one'. However, following the attacks on New York and Washington, both bin Laden himself and al-Qaeda spokesmen denied any involvement, but expressed support for and congratulated the terrorists.

Pakistani intelligence agencies wonder why the CIA did not capture Osama bin Laden despite a golden opportunity, a year before the 11 September 2001 attacks, when the ailing al-Qaeda chief had flown from Quetta and undergone a surgery at an American hospital in Dubai. Bin Laden had even met a CIA official there. Referring to a report that appeared in French daily *Le Figaro*, the Pakistani intelligence sources say that even though he was on the world's most wanted list, no attempt was made to arrest bin Laden during his two-week stay in the Dubai hospital, shedding doubt on the US resolve to track him down.[1] They maintain the US could have effected his arrest and extradition from the Dubai hospital where he was convalescing between 4 and 14 July 2000. The news report says:

> Having taken off from the Quetta airport in Pakistan, bin Laden was transferred to the hospital upon his arrival at Dubai airport. He was accompanied by his personal physician and faithful lieutenant, who could be Ayman al-Zawahiri – but on this, sources are not entirely certain— four bodyguards as well as a male Algerian nurse and was admitted to the American Hospital,
>
> While he was hospitalized, bin Laden received visits from many members of his family as well as prominent Saudis. During the hospital stay, the local CIA agent, known to many in Dubai, was seen taking the main elevator of the hospital to go to bin Laden's hospital room. A few days later, the CIA man bragged to a few friends about having visited bin Laden. Authorized sources say that on July 15th, the day after bin Laden returned to Quetta, the CIA agent was called back to headquarters.[2]

Contacts between the CIA and bin Laden began in 1979 when, as a representative of his family's business, bin Laden began recruiting volunteers for the Afghan resistance against the Red Army. FBI investigators examining the 1998 embassy bombing sites in Nairobi and Dar es Salam discovered that the evidence pointed to the use of military explosives from the US army and that these explosives had been delivered three years earlier to Afghan Arabs – the infamous international volunteer brigades involved side by side with bin Laden during the Afghan war against the Red Army. In the course of its investigations, the FBI discovered 'financing agreements' that the CIA had been developing with its 'Arab friends' for years. The Dubai meeting is then within the logic of 'a certain American policy', the news report concluded.

As far as the prospects for the arrest of Osama bin Laden are concerned, there are media reports that soon after the US-led allied forces launched attacks on Afghanistan in October 2001, he made his seven bodyguards take an oath to kill him if he was in any danger of being arrested. Otherwise, he will try to blow himself up. The real concern for the Americans must be that even if Osama is captured or killed, the movement he leads will be harder than ever to crush.

---

1. Richard, Alexandra 'La CIA aurait rencontré Bin Laden en juillet', *Le Figaro*, 31 October 2001.
2. Ibid.

22

Ayman al-Zawahiri: The Brain Behind bin Laden

An eye surgeon by profession, Dr Ayman al-Zawahiri is Osama bin Laden's right hand man and the chief ideologue of al-Qaeda. He is considered the moving spirit behind the Egyptian Islamic Jehad.

The American intelligence agencies accuse al-Zawahiri of being the operational brain behind the 9/11 terror attacks in the US. He is number two, only behind bin Laden, in the '22 Most Wanted Terrorists' list announced by the US government in 2001. Al-Zawahiri was born in 1953 to a prominent and religiously conservative family. He is remembered as a quiet and well-read student, but that may have changed in 1967 when Israel defeated the combined armies of several Arab nations. Zawahiri graduated from medical school in 1974 and then spent three years as a surgeon in the Egyptian army, posted at a base outside Cairo. This was a watershed period for many Muslims in the Middle East, and al-Zawahiri was no different.

Zawahiri joined the Muslim Brotherhood at the early age of fourteen, and in 1979 joined the even more radical Egyptian Islamic Jehad. Eventually, Zawahiri became one of the group's principal leaders who actively worked to recruit new members into its underground, anti-government operations. In April 1979, Egyptians voted to approve President Anwer Sadat's peace treaty with Israel. In response to a series of demonstrations orchestrated by Zawahiri's organization and other Islamists against President Sadat's pro-US and anti-jehad policies, the Egyptian leader banned all religious groups. Zawahiri envisioned not only the removal of the Egyptian head of state but a complete overthrow of the existing order. Stealthily, he began recruiting officers from the Egyptian military, waiting for the moment when Islamic Jehad would have accumulated enough strength in men and weapons to act.

Zawahiri's chief strategist was Aboud al-Zumar, a colonel in the intelligence branch of the Egyptian Army and a military hero of the 1973 war with Israel. Zumar's plan was to kill the most powerful leaders of the country and capture the headquarters of the army and state security organization, the telephone-exchange building, and the radio and television building. From there, news of the Islamic revolution would be broadcast, unleashing, he expected, a popular uprising against secular authority throughout the country.

On the morning of 6 October 1981, surrounded by dignitaries, including several American diplomats, President Sadat was saluting the army troops at a military parade when a military vehicle veered toward the reviewing stand. Four army men leapt out and tossed grenades into the stand besides emptying their machine gun rounds into President Sadat, killing him on the spot. After the assassination of President Sadat, the Egyptian government cracked down even harder on religious extremists. Zawahiri was arrested while trying to escape and taken into custody. At Maadi police station, the police chief reportedly slapped his face and Zawahiri slapped him back. He became known as the man who struck back.

He could not be directly linked to Anwer Sadat's assassination, though he was convicted of charges of keeping weapons and was sentenced to three years in prison. During that time he was beaten and tortured, experiences that only further radicalized him. Once released, Zawahiri decided to leave Egypt, reaching Jeddah in 1985. At thirty-four, he was a formidable figure. He had been a committed revolutionary and a member of an Islamist underground cell for more than half his life. His political skills had been honed by prison debates, and he had discovered in himself a capacity and hunger for leadership. He was pious, determined, and embittered.

Once in Saudi Arabia, Zawahiri returned to medicine and eventually reached Afghanistan, which had by that time become a rallying point for Muslim radicals from all over the world. He travelled to Peshawar along with an anesthesiologist and a plastic surgeon, and they worked for the Red Crescent Society, the Islamic arm of the Red Cross. Having spent four months in Pakistan, Zawahiri returned.

In March 1981, he returned to Peshawar for another tour of duty with the Red Crescent Society where he discovered Osama bin Laden among thousands of other radical Islamists who were drawn to Afghanistan after the Soviet invasion in 1979. For one thing, both were very modern men. Laden, who was in his early twenties, was already an international businessman; Zawahiri, six years older, was a surgeon from a notable Egyptian family. Both played an important role during the Afghan war.

After the Soviets left Afghanistan in 1989, al-Zawahiri returned to Egypt now more radical than ever and, like other Arab fighters, trained in how to use force and violence to create an Islamic state. Throughout the 1990s he was responsible for organizing and recruiting former mujahideen for the Egyptian Islamic Jehad. Because of governmental pressure he had to move to Sudan in 1992, where he joined hands with bin Laden. However, in 1996 they were both compelled to leave Sudan and return to Afghanistan. Before that, Zawahiri had already been sentenced to death in absentia by an Egyptian court in 1999 for his role in organizing a variety of deadly terrorist attacks, in particular the massacre of fifty-eight tourists in Luxor in 1997.

By the time they returned to Afghanistan, bin Laden and Zawahiri had apparently realized that each man filled a need in the other. They were both members of the educated class, intensely pious, quiet and politically stifled by the regimes in their own countries. Bin Laden, an idealist with vague political ideas sought direction, and Zawahiri, a seasoned propagandist, supplied it. The former had a substantial number of followers, but they were not organized. On the other hand, those with Zawahiri had extraordinary capabilities: doctors, engineers and soldiers. They had experience in secret work and they knew how to organize themselves and create cells.

In June 2001, two jehadi groups, the bin Laden al-Qaeda and Zawahiri Egyptian Islamic Jehad, formally merged into one and launched Qaeda al-Jehad. Although bin Laden eventually became the public face of al-Qaeda's Islamic terrorism, the fact remains that it was Zawahiri and his team members who actually provided the backbone of the larger organization's leadership. As a man of science, Zawahiri was interested in the use of biological and chemical warfare believing that the destructive power of these weapons was no less than that of nuclear weapons. According to US intelligence agencies' findings, Zawahiri pored over medical journals to research the use of chemical and biological weapons.

In the process, he met an Egyptian scientist in Afghanistan, Medhat Mursi al-Sayed, whose jehadi name was Abu Khabab. US intelligence officials believe that Khabab prepared the deadly explosives for the truck bomb that hit the Egyptian Embassy in Islamabad in August 1998. Later, during the 2001 invasion of Afghanistan, the US forces reportedly claimed to have discovered a factory under construction near Kandahar, to be used for the production of anthrax. A sample of anthrax powder was reportedly found in Zawahiri's house in Afghanistan.

On 11 September 2001, Zawahiri, bin Laden and their

followers evacuated their quarters in Kandahar and fled into the mountains, where they listened to an Arabic radio station's news flashes about the attacks on the World Trade Center and the Pentagon. According to a CIA report about the events of that morning, at 9.53 a.m., between the crash of American Airlines Flight 77 into the Pentagon and the downing of United Airlines Flight 93 in Pennsylvania, a member of al-Qaeda in Afghanistan was overheard saying that the attackers were following through on 'the doctor's programme'.

On 3 December 2001, American bombers struck a heavily fortified complex of caves near Jalalabad. When the ground troops arrived, they discovered over a hundred bodies and they were able to identify eighteen of them as top al-Qaeda lieutenants. Dr Zawahiri's wife, Azza, and their children may also have been killed but, according to the FBI, there is no evidence confirming this. After the attacks, a Northern Alliance commander announced that Zawahiri, too, had been killed in the American bombing. However, the claim was belied by the release of a videotape showing bin Laden and Zawahiri sitting on a blanket beside a mountain stream talking about 11 September.

ZAWAHIRI VS MUSHARRAF

A virulently anti-Musharraf message issued by Ayman al-Zawahiri was broadcast by the Al-Jazeera TV station of Qatar on 25 March 2004, conciding with a joint Pak-US operation to flush out the dregs of al-Qaeda allegedly hiding in the south Waziristan area of the Federally Administered Tribal Areas (FATA).

The high-profile operation, one of whose principal objectives was to capture Zawahiri, who had been projected by Pakistani army officials as hiding in that area, eventually proved to be an embarrassing fiasco for General Musharraf. The operation inflamed anti-US and anti-Musharraf anger among the tribals of the FATA, who accused Musharraf of letting himself be used by the US. The local tribals not only managed to frustrate the search by the security forces for foreigners allegedly hiding in that area, but also succeeded in inflicting heavy human casualties on them and damaging their equipment in ambushes and face to face clashes.

During the operation, which started in March 2004, at least seventy personnel of the Pakistani security forces were killed by the tribals. This includes eight who were captured in an ambush and executed at point-blank range after being held hostage for some days. They were executed after the top brass of the Pakistan Army turned down the tribals' demand for the release of the 100 tribals arrested earlier by the army. Faced with the determined resistance, the army had to halt its combing operations in the interior areas of South Waziristan.

In his message, Zawahiri called on the Pakistanis to overthrow General Musharraf. Reacting to the Zawahiri message, General Musharraf vowed that he would eliminate al-Qaeda. In an interview with ABC News, he said, 'Now as far as if he's taunting me well, I would like to say that I'm going to eliminate all of them.'

While it is not clear when Zawahiri's latest message was recorded, the virulence of its attack on Musharraf indicated that it was probably recorded after reports started appearing in the US and Pakistani media about the intensification of the hunt for bin Laden, al-Zawahiri, and their supporters by the US and Pakistani forces through coordinated but separate operations in the areas adjoining the Pak-Afghan border. The Zawahiri tirade against Musharraf was intended to exploit the anti-Musharraf anger among fundamentalists over three issues, namely, the action against Dr Abdul Qadeer Khan, the government restrictions on the jehadi groups operating in J&K, and cooperation with the US in its hunt for bin Laden and other al-Qaeda remnants in the tribal areas.

23

Mullah Mohammad Omar: One-eyed Commander

Mullah Mohammad Omar, the self-styled 'Commander of the Faithful', once headed the Taliban regime in Afghanistan, which controlled approximately 90 per cent of the country's territory. Very little is known about the personal life of the Taliban's supreme commander because he was a reclusive figure even before his militant Taliban government was overthrown by the Americans and he was forced into hiding. His refusal to surrender Osama bin Laden was the principal motivation for the US-led strike on Afghanistan in the wake of the 11 September 2001 terrorist attacks.

Born to a poor agriculturist in Mewand district of southwestern Afghanistan in 1960, little is known of Mullah Mohammad Omar until the early 1980s when he appeared as a guerrilla leader fighting against the Soviet armed forces in Afghanistan. During the fight against the Soviets, he was reportedly injured several times. The Mullah Omar and bin Laden relationship dates to their days as resistance fighters against the Soviet occupation of Afghanistan from 1979 to 1989. Bin Laden is believed to have at least partially financed the Taliban takeover of Afghanistan, from which Mullah Omar emerged as 'Commander of the Faithful', a title with great resonance in Islamic history.

Shortly before he launched the Taliban movement in the spring of 1994, Mullah Omar's assistance was sought by people of his village, Singesar, who complained that two local girls had been tied up, had their heads shaved, and were gang-raped by the mujahideen militia. Mohammad Omar gathered together thirty former guerrillas, found the girls, freed them and publicly hanged the mujahideen leaders. It was acts of savagery like this committed by the mujahideen which may have led to the austere regime of strict discipline that Mullah Omar imposed on his country. The Taliban movement was thus launched more by accident than design, to control the growing anarchy within the country after the US-backed mujahideen had ousted the communist government of Najibullah from Kabul in April 1992.

The people of Afghanistan greeted the Taliban with enthusiasm as they systematically clamped down on the mujahideen warlords and drug barons who had taken over the country. They were seen as a movement that restored a modicum of order over total chaos. A large number of the religious seminaries along the Pak-Afghan border provided a significant number of recruits to the Taliban. Mullah Omar once told the Pakistani journalist Rahimullah Yusufzai, 'We were fighting Muslims who had gone wrong. How could we remain quiet when we could see crimes being committed against women and the poor?'

In Mullah Omar's perception, the rationale of the Taliban was to overcome what he saw as Afghanistan's descent into warlordism. Mullah Omar's overriding purpose was to forge unity among the various warring factions and establish a true Islamic emirate in Afghanistan. Initially, the people of Afghanistan welcomed him as a 'harbinger of peace and stability' in the war-torn country. The Taliban, under his leadership captured Kabul in 1996 and founded the Islamic

Emirate of Afghanistan, introducing Shariah as the legal system of the country. Once approximately 90 per cent of Afghanistan was controlled by the Taliban, Mullah Omar initiated his agenda of 'transforming' Afghanistan into the 'purest Islamic state' in the world.

Some unconfirmed Western media reports indicate that Omar has close personal ties with Laden as he has married bin Laden's eldest daughter and that bin Laden has married one of Mullah Omar's daughters. Following the 11 September terrorist attacks on New York and Washington, and the US allegation that Osama bin Laden was the prime suspect in the events, Mullah Omar, while vigorously defending him, indicated that his guest (bin Laden) did not possess the wherewithal to carry out such lethal attacks.

Different media reports describe Omar as unusually tall (6 foot, 6 inches), bearded, reclusive, a lover of war stories and a speaker of Dari with an Iranian accent although he is a Pashtun from Maiwand in Kandahar. His right eye is stitched shut, the result of an encounter with Soviet soldiers when he was a mujahideen commander with the Harakat-e-Inquilab-e-Islami party. Omar's refusal to be photographed or interviewed tended to reinforce his image as a sphinx-like visitor from another plane of existence. In a bizarrely-constructed exchange with David Loyn, the BBC's South Asia Correspondent, Mohammad Omar, who was still in power at that time, explained – from behind a curtain and via a third party seated inches away – that his reluctance to hold face-to-face interviews was because he did not wish to meet anybody who was not helpful to his cause.

Mullah's Omar's first explanation of the Taliban's mission was that it had arisen to restore peace, to provide security to the wayfarer, and to protect the honour of women and the poor. Although the implication was there, no explicit mention was made of jehad and, indeed, it could not have been until the Taliban had acquired the critical mass needed to present themselves as a popular force for change. Jehad had however become rather a hackneyed concept even to Afghans after the events of 1992, when a government of bloodstained communists, which nonetheless possessed some of the legitimacy required in the traditional leadership equation, was replaced by home-grown Islamists with talents for little more than libertinism.

The culture of the military commander was a degeneration of a system that had been in place centuries earlier. However the rise of the Mullah, under the Taliban, proved to be less a return to the elusive values cherished in pre-communist times than the stupefying of a spiritual tradition that once traced its origins back to the earliest days of Islam. Determining whether the rise of the mullah was tantamount to the dumbing down of a richer spiritual and legal tradition is hampered by the opacity of the Taliban movement and the convergence of its military and religious agendas. The young Taliban who rallied to the cause, and many of the Taliban leaders, were products of the Deoband school of Sunni thought, founded 130 years earlier in Uttar Pradesh, India, which, in the absence of any domestic school of theological studies, had exerted an influence on Afghanistan's spiritual leadership equal to that of Egypt's Al-Azhar University.

The Deobandis represent an extreme attempt to regulate the personal behaviour of their pupils, having issued nearly a quarter of a million fatwa on the minutiae of everyday life since the beginning of the century. There is eyewitness testimony of children, chained to their lecterns, rocking back and forth learning the Koran by rote, written not in Pashtun, but in Arabic. Boys enter the system as wards, exchanging life in a poor family for bed, board and an austere catechism that will one day lead to life as a mullah. It is tempting to identify in this early separation from female relatives the origins of the extreme misogyny, which even more than the objective of a pure Islamic state, lent cohesion to the Taliban as they marched into, and subdued, non-Pashtun lands.

Official Taliban policy, in a very immediate sense, stigmatized females as the evil eye made omnipresent – and a cause for real fear – in the communities the rank-and-file occupied. They had to be covered, closeted and, where necessary, beaten to prevent more sin from being spewed into society. The penalty of twenty-nine lashes for women showing their faces in public was set by the Office for the Propagation of Virtue and the Prevention of Vice, the religious police established in Kabul. Part of this anxiety was sexual and could be attributed to the highly-charged rules of *pashtunwali*, by which girls embark on the perilous road to puberty at seven when they are first sequestered from boys and men. From then until marriage, youths have no licit contact with the opposite sex beyond the members of their own family.

In Kandahar, the custom of seclusion had given rise to a rich and colourful tradition of homosexual passion, celebrated in poetry, dance, and the practice of male prostitution. Heterosexual romance, by contrast, was fraught with the fear of broken honour, the threat of vendetta and, eventually, death by stoning, if discovered. In Pashtun society, man-woman love dared not speak its name; boy-courtesans conducted their affairs openly. The Taliban grew to maturity on the gruel of orthodoxy, estranged from the mitigating influence of women, family and village. This ensured that early recruits to the movement were disciplined and obedient.

According to analysts, the Taliban regime which imposed a strict and eccentric interpretation of the Holy Koran, banning all activities that distracted people from praying, may have been a reflection of the personal psyches of Mohammad Omar and bin Laden, the first, reacting against his poor origins and the second against his misspent youth, and a quest for attention. Bin Laden craved the attention of the father who had abandoned him through death when he was just ten years old. Mohammad Omar mixed traditional Pashtun lore with Islamic law in his personal fix for the ills of the country he came to dominate, more by chance than by design. The end result was a regime that imposed a prohibition of almost all earthly pleasures: lobster, television, cinema, enamel, statues, nail varnish, satellite dishes, photographs of people and animals, stuffed toys, the Internet, computer discs, non-religious music, dancing, musical instruments, cards, ties, chess, lipstick, fireworks, catalogues, poppies, human hair products, women drivers, female students, and kite flying.

Subsequently, the Taliban lost touch with their people through an excessive imposition of the shariah, which inflicted mutilations, decapitations, public stoning and torture on its people, the imposition of the burqa on women, who were denied schooling, and the prohibition forbidding male doctors from touching the bodies of women. A reclusive figure that lived in total austerity in Kandahar, the ultra-shy Mohammad Omar imposed his personal limitations on the movement he created. He was however no fool. In an interview with the Pakistani daily *Dawn*, in 1997, he declared that Afghanistan would be attacked by the US using Osama bin Laden as a pretext because the Taliban had refused to allow an American company to build a pipeline from Turkmenistan through Afghanistan and Pakistan to the Indian Ocean.

By the end of year 2000, facing drought, military problems, a lack of international recognition and sanctions, Mullah Omar became increasingly isolated and dependent on Osama bin Laden. During his last months in power, his public statements took on a pan-Islamic tone, which is more commonly encountered among militant Islamists from Egypt and Saudi Arabia. In a *Voice of America* interview on 21 September 2001, Mullah Omar said: 'God says he will never be satisfied with the infidels. In terms of worldly affairs, America is very strong. Even if it were twice as strong or twice that, it could not be strong enough to defeat us. We are confident that no one can harm us if God is with us.' The US-led military operation against Afghanistan that began on 7 October 2001, eventually led (in

November 2001) to the fall of the Taliban regime led by Mullah Mohammad Omar.

Since US-led coalition drove the Taliban and its leaders from power in Afghanistan in December 2001 for refusing to hand over Osama bin Laden, Mullah Mohammed Omar has vanished. Omar's appearance remains a mystery to many, and that presents a challenge to those on his trail.

There are persistent reports from coalition intelligence sources that he is in western Afghanistan, largely in the Kandahar region, once a stronghold of the Taliban, and nearby provinces. However, the hunt for Omar has focused recently on the areas around Uruzgan, Kandahar and Helmand. In July 2004, international media widely reported that Afghan intelligence agents had talked to Mullah Omar after commandeering a satellite phone being used by his top aide.

According to the Kandahar intelligence chief Abdullah Laghmanai, a man believed to be Mullah Omar's aide, Mullah Sakhi Dad Mujahid, was captured in the first week of July 2004 while carrying a satellite telephone containing the phone numbers of top members of the ousted government. 'We contacted Mullah Omar by Mullah Mujahid's phone,' he said, adding that at first Mullah Mujahid was forced to talk to his boss over the phone. 'But when he [Omar] realized the situation ... he cut off the phone.'

Laghmanai said subsequent efforts to contact Mullah Omar had been unsuccessful as the one-eyed Taliban boss refuses to answer phone calls 'from strange numbers'. 'Maybe Omar has found out that his friend is under our control,' he said. 'He doesn't answer his telephone.' Laghmanai alleged that intelligence reports as well as information received from Mujahid suggested that Mullah Omar was hiding in Pakistan's tribal areas near Kandahar and close to Quetta. 'The information Mujahid provided, and also our intelligence, suggests that Omar is in Pakistan's tribal areas,' he said.

24

Khalid Sheikh Mohammad: The 9/11 Mastermind

After his capture from Pakistan in March 2003, al-Qaeda's chief operational commander Khalid Sheikh Mohammad reportedly told his interrogators that planning for the 9/11 terror attacks in the US started much earlier than anyone had realized and that the attack was intended to be even more devastating.

'The original plan was for a two-pronged attack with five targets on the East Coast of America and five on the West Coast,' claimed a report in *Sunday Times* (London) on 28 March 2004. The report was based on the leaked transcripts from the interrogation of the alleged 9/11 mastermind, Khalid Sheikh Mohammad.

According to the report, 'Khalid Sheikh Mohammad has told the interrogators that he and his terrorist nephew, Ramzi Yusuf, leafed through almanacs of American skyscrapers when planning the operation. Sears Tower in Chicago and Library Tower in Los Angeles . . . were both potential targets, according to the transcripts. "We were looking for symbols of economic might," he told his captors.'

Accounts emerging since 9/11 from US intelligence officials and some non-governmental counter-terrorism experts known for their proximity to the American intelligence agencies have been projecting Khalid Sheikh Mohammad as the real action man of Osama bin Laden. In an interview to the Al-Jazeera network from their Karachi hideout in August 2002, Khalid Sheikh and Ramzi bin al-Shibah, a Yemeni member of the al-Qaeda, bragged about their role in 9/11. Khalid introduced himself as head of al-Qaeda's military committee.

The Al-Jazeera correspondent reported that he interviewed them in a hideout in Karachi. American intelligence officials then organized a massive manhunt for them in Karachi and through electronic intercepts located their hideout, which was raided by Pakistani authorities on 11 September 2002. During an exchange of fire lasting about four hours, bin al-Shibah was captured and airlifted to Diego Garcia for interrogation. According to US officials, he was to have joined the hijacking of the aircraft on 9/11, but could not do so because he could not obtain an American visa.

Almost six months later, in March 2003, a joint team of the ISI and the FBI raided a house in Rawalpindi in an area where many retired officers of the army and the ISI live, and arrested three persons, one of them a Pakistani. One of the arrested persons was identified as Khalid Sheikh Mohammad and handed over to the US intelligence officials.

According to the *Sunday Times* news report, Osama bin Laden who, like Khalid Sheikh Mohammad, had studied engineering, vetoed simultaneous coast-to-coast attacks, arguing that they would be too difficult to synchronize. Khalid Sheikh then switched to a two-wave strategy: hitting the East Coast (the eastern sea coast of the United States), first and following up with a second attack. Osama wanted the second wave to focus on the West Coast, i.e., targets along the western coast of the US. Zacarias Moussaoui, a French-Moroccan who had lived in London, was sent to Pan Am International flight school in Minnesota to train for the West Coast attack.

However, his instructor alerted the FBI after the Moroccan

showed no interest in landing planes, only in flying them. He was arrested in August 2001. Until now, it was widely believed that Moussaoui was meant to be the twentieth hijacker of the 9/11 attacks. The revelation by Khalid Sheikh Mohammad that he was part of a planned second wave is lent weight by the arrest of two other men by the FBI who were allegedly part of the West Coast conspirators. Despite the setbacks, Khalid Sheikh described the 9/11 attacks as, 'far more successful than we had ever imagined'.

The report says: 'He recounted sitting looking at the books with Ramzi Yusuf, his nephew by marriage, who was the man behind the first World Trade Center bombing in 1993. In that attack, Yusuf succeeded only in ripping a crater into the foundations with a van bomb. "We knew from that experience that explosives could be problematic," said Khalid Sheikh Mohammad, "so we started thinking about using planes."'

Despite their arrest by the FBI, a number of intriguing questions about Ramzi Yusuf and Khalid Sheikh remain unanswered. Are they related to each other as some reports claim? Are they Pakistanis (Yemeni–Baluchis) as Filipino and Western agencies seem to believe or are they Kuwaitis (this is denied by the Kuwaiti authorities) or Iraqis (in the past, the Pakistani media had been consistently referring to Ramzi Yusuf either as a person of Middle Eastern background or as an Iraqi)?

Born in Kuwait, either in 1964 or 1965, Khalid Sheikh's al-Qaeda roots run deep and wide. In 1996, he was indicted in New York for his alleged involvement in a Philippines-based plot to blow up twelve US-bound commercial airliners in forty-eight hours. The FBI believes that it was Khalid Sheikh who ordered the killing of the *Wall Street Journal* reporter Daniel Pearl. He has also been linked to the bombing of the *USS Cole* in 2000, Richard Reid's foiled 2001 attempt to blow up an airliner with a shoe bomb, the bombings at the El Ghriba synagogue in Djerba, Tunisia, and the Bali bombings in 2002. The synagogue bombings were the first al-Qaeda attacks outside Afghanistan after 11 September 2001.

Western counter-terrorism experts believe that Khalid Sheikh was the brain behind 9/11. In 1995, he and Ramzi Yusuf had together plotted from their hideouts in the Philippines a series of terrorist strikes against the US, which failed to materialize. Both fled to Pakistan after the Filipino authorities got scent of their plans. Ramzi was arrested by the Pakistani authorities in 1996 and was handed over to the FBI for trial in the 1993 New York World Trade Center explosion case. However, Khalid Sheikh managed to evade arrest and emerged as one of the principal aides of Osama bin Laden when the latter returned to Afghanistan in 1996.

Western media had quoted a senior American intelligence official saying in 2003 that if he had to decide between catching Osama bin Laden and Khalid Sheikh Mohammad, he might prefer the latter. The Western media also quoted French terrorism expert and UN Security Council consultant Roland Jacquard as saying: 'Khalid Sheikh Mohammad is probably the only man who knows all the pieces of the puzzle.' The police authorities of the Philippines had described Khalid Sheikh as a Kuwaiti-born and US-educated Pakistani.

According to the *Sunday Times* report Sheikh Ahmed Omar Saeed, already convicted in the gruesome murder of American journalist Daniel Pearl, was reported to have told the Karachi police that during a visit to Afghanistan before 9/11 he had learnt of the plans for terrorist strikes in the US and had immediately informed Lt. Gen. Ehsanul Haq, the then director general of the ISI, who was at that time corps commander, Peshawar. The reports adds that the interrogation reports make it clear that Khalid Sheikh was not only the chief planner for 11 September but it was he who introduced Osama bin Laden to Hambali, the Indonesian militant accused of the Bali bombing.

To date, Khalid Sheikh is the seniormost al-Qaeda member to have been captured. It is clear that he is talking, and that the 11 September conspiracy was much more extensive than has previously been revealed.

According to the FBI, Khalid Sheikh was born in Kuwait city, where his father was a preacher. He joined the Muslim Brotherhood as a teenager and went to the US to study engineering in North Carolina. At that time, the Afghan jehad against the Russians was in full flow. After graduating, he headed for one of bin Laden's guesthouses in the Pakistani frontier town of Peshawar. He has reportedly told interrogators that it was there that he first met Hambali. In 1992 Khalid Sheikh moved south to Karachi. Posing as a businessman importing holy water from Mecca, he acted as a fund-raiser and intermediary between young militants and wealthy sponsors in the Gulf.

His nephew Ramzi Yusuf's failed attempt to blow up the World Trade Center in 1993 inspired him to plan his own operations. The first was Operation Bojinka (Serbo-Croat for 'big bang'), a plot to blow up twelve American airliners over the Pacific. Both Yusuf and Hambali were involved. It failed after the conspirators' Manila bomb factory caught fire. The men fled to Pakistan where Ramzi Yusuf was arrested. Undeterred, Khalid Sheikh decided to start working on something 'far more spectacular' for which he 'hoped to persuade bin Laden to give him money and operatives'. He also decided to introduce Hambali to bin Laden. Riduan Isamuddin, alias Hambali headed Jemaah Islamiya (JI), which wanted to unite South-East Asia under an Islamic banner.

Hambali, who had been operating on a shoestring budget, was provided with a new car, mobile phones and computers. Osama bin Laden was apparently impressed by Khalid Sheikh's ideas and networking, and oppointed him head of al-Qaeda's military committee. From then on he was a key planner in almost every attack, including the simultaneous bombings of the American embassies in Kenya and Tanzania in 1998. Osama bin Laden dubbed him 'The Brain'. The big challenge was to attack Americans on their own soil. Initially, Khalid Sheikh proposed leasing a charter plane, filling it with explosives and crashing it into the CIA headquarters. Then the plan became more ambitious.

Osama bin Laden reportedly pointed out that on a visit to America in 1982 he had been to the Empire State building in New York and was astonished by how unprotected such key landmarks were. A committee, known as the *shura*, was formed comprising bin Laden, Khalid Sheikh and four others. It met at what was known as the war room in bin Laden's camp outside Jalalabad in Afghanistan. The plan for a two-pronged attack was formed. 'We had scores of volunteers to die for Allah but the problem was finding those familiar with the West who could blend in as well as get US visas,' revealed Khalid Sheikh, according to the *Sunday Times* article.

Two Yemenis and two Saudi pilots, Nawaf al-Hazmi and Khalid al-Midhar, were selected and given commando training in Afghanistan. 'All four operatives only knew that they had volunteered for a martyrdom operation involving planes,' said Khalid Sheikh. In 1999, the two Yemenis were refused American visas but a few months later, four jehad recruits from Hamburg arrived in Quetta, Pakistan. Led by Mohammed Atta, an Egyptian, they had originally planned to go to Chechnya to fight the Russians, but a former jehadi in Germany had given them an introduction to bin Laden.

After meeting the al-Qaeda leader in Kandahar, they took an oath of allegiance required to gain access to his inner circle and were invited to his Ramadan feast. He told them that they had been selected for a top-secret mission and promised that they would enter paradise as martyrs. They were instructed to go home and destroy their passports so that their trip to Pakistan would remain undetected. They were further instructed to shave off their beards, get new passports, and obtain pilots' licenses in the US. Khalid Sheikh reportedly told his interrogators that he had provided them with a special training manual, which included information on how to find flight schools and study timetables.

Three of the four were granted American visas. The fourth,

Ramzi bin al-Shibah, failed and returned to Afghanistan where he communicated with them through Internet chat rooms. In the spring of 2000, after a planned meeting in Kuala Lumpur, bin Laden reportedly scaled back the plan from two-prong to two-wave because they had been unable to get enough potential pilots into US. Moussaoui succeeded in entering America, but the order went out for potential recruits who were not Arab, Khalid Sheikh Mohammad told his captors. A date was set for the first wave attack codenamed 'Porsche 911', and a message went round the world for followers to return to Afghanistan by 10 September.

The messages were intercepted by several Western intelligence agencies but none apparently realized their significance. When the suicide planes struck on 11 September al-Qaeda seems to have been taken by surprise, both by the success of the attacks and by the US reaction. 'Afterwards we never got time to catch our breath, we were immediately on the run,' said Khalid Sheikh Mohammad. He said the war on terrorism and the US bombing of Afghanistan completely disrupted their communications network. Operatives could no longer use satellite phones and had to rely on couriers, although they still used Internet chat rooms.

'Before 9/11 we could dispatch operatives with the expectation of follow-up contact but after 7 October 2001 (when the bombing started) the situation changed by 180 degrees. There was no longer a war room or *shura* and operatives had more autonomy.' He told interrogators that he remained in Pakistan for ten days after 11 September and then went to Afghanistan to find bin Laden: 'I went to Jalalabad and Tora Bora, looking for him and then eventually met him in Kabul.' The al-Qaeda leader instructed him to continue operations, with Britain as the next target. 'It was at this time we discussed the Heathrow operation,' said Sheikh.

'Osama bin Laden declared [Tony] Blair our principal enemy and London a target.' He arranged for operatives to be sent from

Pakistan and Afghanistan to London, where surveillance of Heathrow airport and the surrounding areas began. However, he claimed, the operation never got beyond the planning stages. 'There was a lot of confusion,' he said. 'I would say my performance at that time was sloppy.'

One priority was to get Hambali out of Afghanistan. In November 2001, Khalid Sheikh arranged for him to go to Karachi. There he gave him $20,000 and a false Indonesian passport with which he could travel to Sri Lanka and on to Thailand from where he would help organize the Bali nightclub bombing the following year. They kept in touch through Gun Gun Rusman Gunawan, Hambali's 27-year-old younger brother who used to live in Karachi posing as an Indonesian student.

At the same time, the net was closing in around Khalid Sheikh Mohammad himself. Another *shura* member, Abu Zubaydah, had already been arrested from Faisalabad in Pakistan in March 2002. Six months later bin al-Shib was seized in the Karachi apartment that he shared with Khalid Sheikh, who managed to escape, but his flight came to an end in the early hours of 2 March 2003 in Rawalpindi. Questioned for two days by the Pakistani intelligence agencies, which say he did nothing but pray repeatedly, he was flown blindfolded to Bagram, the US base in the mountains above Kabul. It is neither clear how long he was held there nor what methods were used to get him to talk.

A few months later, the FBI also arrested Hambali in August 2003 from Thailand while his younger brother Gun Gun Rusman Gunawan was captured in September 2003 from a religious seminary in Karachi. As things stand, the investigators have been cross-checking Khalid Sheikh's confessions and revelations with those of Ramzi bin al-Shib, Abu Zubaydah, and Riduan Isamuddin Hambali. However, the most disturbing reality for the US is that despite all these arrests, al-Qaeda lives on.

25

Was the Pakistan Air Force Chief Murdered?

Abu Zubaydah, a top al-Qaeda operative captured from Rawalpindi in March 2002 and handed over to the US Federal Bureau of Investigations, claimed in subsequent interrogations that some key Saudi authorities and the late chief of Pakistan Air Force, Air Marshall Mushaf Ali Mir had prior knowledge of the 9/11 terrorist plot, writes Gerald Posner in his book *Why America Slept: The Failure to Prevent 9/11*, published in September 2003.

In the words of Posner, the Wall Street lawyer turned investigative writer, 'Abu Zubaydah was duped by the US interrogators masquerading as Saudis and using painkillers and sodium pentathol, sometimes called truth serum, to befuddle him into divulging secrets. As a result, the top al-Qaeda operative made startling revelations about secret connections linking Saudi Arabia, Pakistan and Osama bin Laden.' Details of this terrorism triangle are provided in the explosive final chapter where Posner examines who did what wrong before 11 September. Most of his book is a lean, lucid retelling of how the CIA, the FBI and the American leaders missed a decade's worth of clues and opportunities that if heeded might have forestalled the 9/11 terrorist attacks.

The book contains some very controversial material as far as Pakistan is concerned, including an account based on Abu Zubaydah's claims – as narrated to Posner by the US government sources 'in a position to know' – about what Saudi Arabia and Pakistan did, despite being allied to the US, to build up al-Qaeda and what they knew before 9/11. The tale begins on 28 March 2002, when US surveillance pinpointed Zubaydah in a two-storey safe-house in Pakistan. Commandos rousted out sixty-two suspects, one of whom was seriously wounded while trying to flee. A Pakistani intelligence officer and hastily made voice-prints soon identified the injured man as Abu Zubaydah. When questioning stalled, according to Posner, CIA men flew Abu Zubaydah to an Afghan complex fitted out as a fake Saudi jail chamber, where 'two Arab–Americans, now with Special Forces,' pretending to be Saudi inquisitors, used threats and other methods to terrify him into further confessions.

Yet when Abu Zubaydah was confronted by the false Saudis, writes Posner, 'his reaction was not fear, but utter relief. Happy to see them, he reeled off telephone numbers of a senior member of the royal family who would, said Zubaydah, 'tell you what to do'. The man at the other end would be Prince Ahmed bin Salman bin Abdul Aziz, a Westernized nephew of King Fahd and a publisher, better known as a racehorse owner. His horse *War Emblem* won the Kentucky Derby in 2002. To the amazement of the US, the numbers proved valid. When the fake inquisitors accused Abu Zubaydah of lying, he responded with a ten minute monologue on the Saudi–Pakistani–bin Laden triangle.

Abu Zubaydah, writes Posner, said the Saudi connection ran through Prince Turki al-Faisal bin Abdul Aziz, the kingdom's long time intelligence chief. He said bin Laden personally told him of a 1991 meeting in which Turki agreed to let bin Laden leave Saudi Arabia and to provide him with secret funds so long as al-Qaeda refrained from promoting jehad in the kingdom. The Pakistani contact, a high-ranking air force officer, Mushaf Ali Mir, entered the equation, Abu Zubaydah said, in a 1996 meeting in Pakistan also attended by Zubaydah himself. Osama bin Laden struck a deal with Mir, who was then in the military but tied closely to Islamists in Pakistan's ISI, to get protection, arms and supplies for al-Qaeda. Zubaydah told interrogators that bin Laden said the arrangement was 'blessed by the Saudis'.

Abu Zubaydah said he attended a third meeting in Kandahar in 1998 with Turki, senior ISI agents and Taliban officials. There, Turki promised, writes Posner, that 'more Saudi aid would flow to the Taliban, and the Saudis would never ask for Osama bin Laden's extradition so long as al-Qaeda kept its long-standing promise to direct fundamentalism away from the kingdom.' In Gerald Posner's stark judgment, the Saudis 'effectively had [bin Laden] on their payroll since the start of the decade'. Abu Zubaydah told the interrogators that the Saudis regularly sent the funds through three royal princes he named as intermediaries.

The last eight paragraphs of the book set out a startling final development. Those three Saudi princes all perished within days of one another. On 22 July 2002, Prince Ahmed was felled by a heart attack at the age of 43. A day later Prince Sultan bin Faisal bin Turki al-Saud, 41, was killed in what was termed a high-speed car accident. The last member of the trio, Prince Fahd bin Turki bin Saud al-Kabir, officially 'died of thirst' while traveling east of Riyadh a week later in the last week of July 2002. Thereafter, seven months later, Mushaf Ali Mir, by then Pakistan's Air Marshal, perished in a plane crash. The Fokker, which was used to transport VIPs, came down near the village of Taulanj, in an area of low hills about 17 miles from the town of Kohat, killing all the seventeen people aboard including Air Chief and his wife. Air Chief Marshal

Mushaf Mir was on his way to the Kohat base for a routine annual inspection.

The findings of an inquiry conducted by the PAF authorities into the Fokker crash later claimed that it was an accident that might have been caused due to an error of judgment on the pilot's part. 'The plane most likely crashed into the side of a 3,000 ft mountain covered in fog about 17 nautical miles east of Kohat, because of a human error of judgment,' said the inquiry report. However, there are much stronger arguments to suggest that the crash might have been an act of sabotage.

The arguments: The Fokker took off after getting clearance from the Visual Flight Range (VFR) and the Ground Proximity Warning System (GPWS). Before the crash, the plane neither gave any warning calls nor did its radar system show any terrain in its way. At the time of the crash, the skies were almost clear with only some clouds near the mountain peaks. Any experienced pilot would never let his plane descend to such a low level, and that too in a hilly area. There is also another route, a bit longer, which bypasses the hilly area. If the pilot was facing visibility problems due to a dense fog, he could have opted for the longer route to avoid any risk. Many villagers who were the first to reach the crash scene said that they had heard loud bangs. 'I heard a bang, followed by another big bang, and then I saw flames and smoke on the hills,' the Reuters news agency had quoted a villager as saying. The PAF authorities denied any possibility of foul play.

The plane crash investigations, however, took a new turn after the March 2003 arrests of al-Qaeda's operational chief, Khalid Sheikh Mohammad, from Rawalpindi and Maj. Adil Quddus of the Pakistan Army from Kohat. Those involved in the interrogation reportedly suspected Khalid Sheikh Mohammad's involvement in the crash. The al-Qaeda leader had moved from his Karachi hideout to Rawalpindi to facilitate an assassination attempt on Gen. Pervez Musharraf. The intelligence agents did not rule out the possibility of the PAF Fokker having been hit by Kohat-based al-Qaeda operatives under Sheikh's supervision. Having arrested Sheikh from Rawalpindi, the FBI was quick to detain from Kohat a serving major of the Pakistan Army, Adil Quddus, a relative of Ahmed Qudoos from whose residence Sheikh and another al-Qaeda suspect were captured.

While considering the possibility of al-Qaeda's involvement in the Kohat air crash, the investigators pointed out that the Kohat air base was being used by the US forces under an agreement to grant the US 'blanket overflight and landing rights and access to Pakistan's naval and air bases'. The investigators were well aware that on numerous occasions, blindfolded al-Qaeda operatives were handed over to the US commandos at Kohat airbase. Over 125 al-Qaeda suspects had been interrogated at an army base in Kohat by the FBI officials before the March 2003 plane crash.

The investigators also learnt that al-Qaeda activists often escape from tribal areas and make their way to Kohat. Keeping in view al-Qaeda activity in and around Kohat, the investigators could not rule out the possibility of sabotage in the air chief's plane crash. Another puzzling facet for investigators was the fact that the wreckage of the ill-fated aircraft was found scattered over a large area on two sides of the mountain cliff, with the tail end at one place and rest of the body at another. This raised the possibility of a mid-air blast due to a missile hit and the subsequent incapacitation of the pilot. The fact that there was no distress call from the pilot increases the possibilities of the sudden incapacitation of the crew, which is yet to be explained. Part of the debris had fallen in the tribal areas while the forward portion carrying the passengers, navigators and pilots was found near the mountains, thereby raising doubts about the plane hitting the mountain and raising the possibility that something else, perhaps a missile attack, was the cause of the tragedy.

However, there are those in the PAF who do not rule out the possibility of the plane having been shot down by US planes, that had been using the same corridor to carry out their anti-Taliban operations in Afghanistan. After all, Air Chief Marshal Mushaf Ali Mir had already been found involved in a deal with Osama bin Laden 'to get protection, arms and supplies for al-Qaeda', as claimed by Abu Zubaydah and reported by Gerald Posner in his book.

26

WTC Bombing, Ramzi Yusuf and Pakistan

The Sipah-e-Sahaba Pakistan has often been linked to Ramzi Ahmed Yusuf, the principal accused in the World Trade Center bombing in New York in February 1993. He was arrested from an Islamabad guesthouse in February 1995 and was handed over to the US.

Exploring Ramzi Yusuf's links with the sectarian group, Sipah-e-Sahaba, a report in Pakistan's English daily *News* stated: 'The Pakistani investigators are now sure of Ramzi Yusuf's ties with the Sipah-e-Sahaba, which flourished mostly in the military training camps inside Afghanistan designated for Arabs and Pakistanis. Orthodox Sunni religious schools in Pakistan serve as feeders for these military training camps.'

Though Ramzi Yusuf's nationality remains disputed, it is believed that he was a native of the Baluchistan area of Pakistan, a wild lawless border region with deep and broad ties to the former Taliban regime. Following his 1995 arrest from Pakistan, a spokesman of Pakistan's Foreign Ministry denied that Ramzi Ahmed Yusuf was a Pakistani national and asserted that his papers showed that he was an Iraqi national. This gave rise to the question: whether Ramzi and his associates might have organized the New York World Trade Center explosion in 1993 to coincide with the second anniversary of the end of the 1991 Gulf War, at the instance of the Iraqi intelligence with the assistance of some local accomplices in New York.

While the official agencies of Pakistan and the US could not collect any credible evidence to prove or disprove this suspicion, Laurie Mylorie, then of the Foreign Policy Research Institute, Philadelphia, conducted a detailed investigation into the nationality of Ramzi and published a paper based on the results of her research. According to the paper, US authorities think that Ramzi's real name was Abdul Basit, that he entered the US as Ramzi Ahmed Yusuf, an Iraqi national, and fled after the World Trade Center explosion as Abdul Basit, a Pakistani national. For reasons that remain unclear, they chose to prosecute him as Ramzi Yusuf and not as Abdul Basit.

According to the FBI investigations, Ramzi Yusuf was out of the US before the smoke had cleared from the World Trade Center's halls. He escaped to Pakistan just hours after the bombing, where he first visited his family and then decided to stay at an Islamabad guesthouse. Ramzi then reacquainted himself with his uncle, Khalid Sheikh Mohammad, and organized several terrorist acts, some of which succeeded. In a meeting with Khalid Sheikh and Abdul Hakim Murad, an old friend of Yusuf's, the three discussed airplanes and pilot training. After a few months, say the FBI findings, all three were dispatched to Manila under the orders of Osama bin Laden to begin plotting direct strikes on the US.

As with many elements of Yusuf's life, it remains a mystery exactly when he first joined forces with al-Qaeda. There is some evidence that the first WTC bombing might have been assisted or facilitated by bin Laden, but there is a great deal of evidence that Yusuf's Manila cell was an al-Qaeda shop financed by bin Laden's brother-in-law, Mohammed Jamal Khalifa. There is a school of thought in the American intelligence community that Yusuf might have been working for Iraq rather than al-Qaeda, particularly as the first WTC bombing took place on the anniversary of the liberation of Kuwait by allied forces in the first Gulf War. However, most theories closely tying Ramzi Yusuf to the government of Iraq tend to have many loose ends and the connection has thus never been proven.

According to US intelligence reports, with funds flowing from al-Qaeda, Ramzi Yusuf sat down with Khalid Sheikh and together they devised what would have been the biggest and most devastating terrorist act in history, and they came within two weeks of pulling it off. Project Bojinka was the devious brainchild of these sessions. The plan was ruthless. In 'Phase One' of Bojinka, a minimum of five al-Qaeda operatives would work in concert to destroy twelve US-bound airliners over the Pacific almost simultaneously on 21 January 1995. The terrorists would board planes bound for the US with stopovers all across Asia. They would plant bombs timed to explode on the second leg of the flight, then get off during the layover, and repeat the process for another plane.

The FBI findings say the plan was elegant and carefully coordinated, as all the five operatives would have escaped to Pakistan unharmed. If the plan had succeeded, it would have killed an estimated 4,000 people and completely shut down all air travel around the world for days or even weeks. The bombs were ingenious constructions, using Casio digital watches as timers and virtually undetectable liquid nitroglycerin as the explosive. Ramzi Yusuf tested the device on a flight from Manila to Tokyo on 11 December 1994. He built his bomb in the lavatory and left it under his seat when he disembarked in Philippines. It exploded on the way to Japan, killing the businessman unfortunate enough to have taken over Yusuf's seat. The plane managed to land successfully thanks to a heroic effort by the pilots. Yusuf resolved to increase the potency of the explosive.

On 5 January 1995, one of Yusuf's compatriots accidentally ignited a small chemical fire in the apartment where the bomb supplies were being mixed. The conspirators fled, leaving documents and a laptop computer behind. Watching smoke pour out the apartment window, Ramzi Yusuf calmly sent Abdul

Murad back to retrieve the computer after the fire department left, but the police were already on their way and Murad was arrested. Yusuf left the country a day or two later and Khalid Sheikh Mohammad was not far behind. Murad, left to the ministrations of the Philippines police, began a lengthy confession under torture. During the course of his confession, he revealed 'Phase Two' of Bojinka. Murad reportedly told his interrogators that he had been selected for the great honour of martyrdom. Murad, who was trained as a pilot in the US, had been instructed to hijack a commercial airliner and crash it into a US landmark. Possible targets included the World Trade Center, the Pentagon and the CIA headquarters.

Ramzi Yusuf and Khalid Sheikh subsequently fled to Pakistan. A month later, FBI agents tracked down Ramzi and arrested him. The joint team of FBI agents and Pakistani intelligence officials, which arrested Ramzi from Islamabad was so busy patting themselves on the back that they completely ignored Khalid Sheikh, who was sleeping in the room next door. Yusuf was flown back to the US and into New York, where an outstanding indictment for the WTC 1993 bombing awaited him. As the story goes, as soon as Ramzi's plane landed, an FBI agent pointed out the World Trade Center towers to the terrorist, and commented, 'They're still standing.' Ramzi Yusuf reportedly responded, 'They wouldn't be if I had enough money and explosives.'

Ramzi Ahmed Yusuf was convicted in a New York courtroom for both the WTC bombing and the Bojinka plot, and sentenced to life in prison without parole. Judged a high escape risk, he was sent to serve his sentence at the Supermax prison in Colorado. Ramzi might have been locked away but on 11 September 2001, he still managed to take one last shot at his favourite target, and this time he succeeded. An al-Qaeda operation led by Ramzi's uncle Khalid Sheikh finally made the Bojinka plan a reality, hijacking four jets and crashing three of them into their targets: the World Trade Center towers and the Pentagon. With a body count of around 3,000, it was only a little less mayhem than would have been caused had Yusuf's first draft of the plan succeeded.

27

Lt. Gen. Mahmood Ahmad and the 9/11 Attacks

Well-known journalist and analyst Pepe Escobar writes in one of his investigative pieces. 'If the 9-11 Commission is really looking for a smoking gun, it should look no further than at Lieutenant-General Mahmood Ahmad, the director of the Pakistani Inter Services Intelligence (ISI) at the time.'[1]

The 9/11 Commission was created by congressional legislation in late 2002 to prepare a full and complete account of the circumstances surrounding the 9/11 terrorist attacks. It is important to remember that on 13 September 2001 Islamabad airport was shut down, allegedly because of threats against Pakistan's strategic assets.

According to Pepe Escobar:

> On 14 September Islamabad declared total support for the US: the airport was immediately reopened. Mahmood Ahmad remained in Washington until 16 September – when the war on Afghanistan was more than programmed, and Pakistan was firmly in the 'with us' and not the 'against us' column. Million-dollar questions remain. Did Mahmood know when and how the attacks of 11 September would happen? Did Musharraf know? Could the Bush administration have prevented 11 September? It

seems hard to believe high echelons of the CIA and FBI were not aware of the direct link between the ISI and alleged chief hijacker Mohammed Atta. On 7 October Mahmood was demoted from the ISI. By that time, Washington obviously knew of the connection between Mahmood, Sheikh Ahmed, Omar Saeed and Mohammed Atta: the FBI knew it. The official version is that Mahmood was sacrificed because he was too close to the Taliban – which, it is never enough to remind, are a cherished creature of the ISI.

Pakistan's spy chief Lt. Gen. Mahmood Ahmad was in Washington when the 9/11 attacks occurred. He arrived in the US on 4 September 2001, an entire week before the attacks. He had meetings at the State Department after the 9/11 attacks, but he also had regular meetings and consultations with his US counterparts at the CIA and the Pentagon during the week prior to 11 September.

What was the nature of these routine pre-11 September consultations? Were they in any way related to the subsequent post-11 September consultations relating to Pakistan's decision to cooperate with Washington? Was the planning of war being discussed between Pakistani and US officials? On 9 September 2001, while Mahmood Ahmad was in the US, the leader of the Northern Alliance, Commander Ahmad Shah Masood was assassinated. The Northern Alliance had informed the Bush Administration that the ISI was allegedly implicated in the assassination. The Bush Administration consciously took the decision in the post 11 September consultations with Lt. Gen. Mahmood Ahmad to directly cooperate with Pakistan's military intelligence (ISI) despite its links to Osama bin Laden and the Taliban, and its alleged role in the assassination of Commander Masood, which coincidentally occurred two days prior to the terrorist attacks.

Meanwhile, senior Pentagon and State Department officials had been rushed to Islamabad to put the finishing touches on America's war plans. On the Sunday prior to the onslaught of the bombing of major cities in Afghanistan (7 October 2001), Lt. Gen. Mahmood Ahmad was sacked from his position as head of the ISI in what was described as a routine reshuffle. In the days following Mahmood's dismissal, some American media reports, quoting US intelligence sources 'revealed' the links between Mahmood Ahmad and the presumed ringleader of the WTC attacks, Mohammed Atta. These reports alleged that it was Lt. Gen. Mahmood Ahmad who ordered the UK-born Omar Sheikh to send US$ 100,000 to Mohammad Atta. Omar Sheikh has already been convicted in the murder of *Wall Street Journal* reporter Daniel Pearl.

In his bestseller *Qui a tué Daniel Pearl?* (Who killed Daniel Pearl?), Bernard-Henri Lévy suspects collusion between al-Qaeda and ISI to destroy the Twin Towers in the US. He writes: 'The possible Pakistani responsibility in the 11 September attack remains the great unsaid in George Bush and Donald Rumsfeld's America ... to admit that [Sheikh] Ahmad Omar [Saeed] wired the money ... wouldn't it be to question the whole foreign policy which, already at the time, made Iraq as the enemy and Pakistan as an ally?'[2]

In April 2003, an in-depth investigative report in *The Sunday Times* had further explored links between the ISI and Omar Sheikh. The report said the Britain-born Sheikh knew too much about this connection to ever be allowed to leave Pakistan alive. The report said that General Musharraf is reported to have told the then US Ambassador to Pakistan, Wendy Chamberlain, 'I would rather hang Sheikh myself than have him extradited.'

One 'bizarre clue' the report mentioned was the demand by Pearl's kidnappers to honour an agreement to sell F-16 fighter aircraft to Pakistan. 'This hardly squared with the outlook of a militant Muslim organization fighting a jehad in Afghanistan and Kashmir,' the report said. The next clue came with the revelation that Omar Sheikh was in custody. On a visit to the US, Musharraf announced on 12 February 2002 that Omar Sheikh had been captured by police in Lahore. However, Sheikh shouted out in court that he had turned himself over to the Home Secretary Punjab Brig. (retd) Ejaz Shah, on 7 February, i.e. a week earlier. Omar had surrendered to Ejaz Shah, a former chief of the ISI, Punjab, presently working as director general of the Intelligence Bureau (IB), as he was afraid that the police might torture him once he was arrested.

'It would appear that the ISI had its own reasons for holding Sheikh for a week before announcing to the world that he was in custody,' *The Sunday Times* report said. 'One thing it would have wanted to do was to make sure its protégé did not give away more than absolutely necessary about his relationship with Pakistan's intelligence services.' This 'missing week' shed new light on media reports in October 2001 that the ISI chief, Lt. Gen. Mahmood Ahmad, had been forced into retirement after the FBI agents uncovered credible links between him and Omar Sheikh in the wake of the 11 September 2001 attacks.

The Sunday Times report further stated: 'There is a further angle that implicates the ISI...' It had strong reasons for tailing Pearl: he was normally based in India, which to the ISI was prima facie evidence that he was reporting back to Indian intelligence.' When the ISI discovered that Pearl was trying to find out who was financing terror groups, it was the final straw, the report said.

It was 10 a.m. on 12 September 2001, a day after the devastating terrorist attacks on New York's World Trade Center and the Pentagon headquarters in Washington, when Lt. Gen. Mahmood Ahmad, the then ISI chief, arrived at the State Department for an emergency meeting with the US Deputy Secretary of State, Richard Armitage. The general, who was on an official visit to Washington, was to leave for home but was left stranded as all airports had been closed. Journalist Zahid Hussain writes in a 2002 issue of the monthly *Newsline* that Richard Armitage told General Mahmood that the US required Pakistan's full support and cooperation. 'We want to know whether you are with us or not, in our fight against terror,' Armitage is reported to have added.

The meeting was adjourned for the next day after Gen. Mahmood Ahmad had assured Armitage of Pakistan's full support. 'We will tell you tomorrow what you are required to do,' Armitage reportedly said as they left the room. Meanwhile, at 1.30 p.m., Collin Powell spoke to General Musharraf on the phone. 'The American people would not understand if Pakistan did not cooperate in this fight with the United States,' Powell said candidly, as one general to another. Gen. Musharraf promised to cooperate fully with the US. It was 12 p.m. on 13 September, when General Mahmood returned to the State Department for the second meeting.

'This is not negotiable,' said Armitage, as he handed over a single sheet of paper with seven demands which the Bush administration wanted him to accept. The general, who was known for his hard-line pro-Taliban position, glanced through the paper for a few seconds and replied: 'They are all acceptable to us.' The swift response took Armitage by surprise. 'These are very powerful words, General. Do you not want to discuss with your President?' he asked. 'I know the President's mind,' replied General Ahmad. A visibly elated Armitage asked the general to meet George Tenet, the CIA chief at his headquarters at Langley. 'He is waiting for you,' said Armitage.

The list of demands included:

1) Stop Al-Qaeda operations on the Pakistani border, intercept arms shipments through Pakistan, and all logistical support for bin Laden
2) Blanket over-flights and landing rights for US planes.
3) Access to Pakistan's naval bases, airbases, and borders.
4) Immediate intelligence and immigration information.
5) Curb all domestic expression of support for terrorism against the US, its friends, and allies.
6) Cut off fuel supply to the Taliban and stop Pakistani volunteers going to Afghanistan to join the Taliban.

7) Pakistan should break diplomatic relations with the Taliban and assist the US in destroying bin Laden and his al-Qaeda network.

Islamabad's support was important for the US. Its geographical proximity and its vast intelligence information on Afghanistan were seen as crucial for any military action against the Taliban and al-Qaeda. Pakistan was one of the two countries – the other was Saudi Arabia – which had formally recognized the conservative Afghan Islamic government. The American demands, which General Ahmad had acceded to so promptly, required Pakistan to abandon its support for the Taliban regime and provide logistical support to the American forces.

Interestingly, a few days earlier, General Ahmad in his talks with the CIA chief in Washington, had defended Mullah Omar, describing him as a pious humanitarian not a man of violence. Pakistan's patronage of the conservative Taliban regime, which had provided a base for Osama and thousands of other militants from different nationalities, had strained Pakistan's relations, not only with the US, but also with neighbouring countries. It is clearly apparent that the post-September turnaround was forced on the military regime and not the result of a considered policy review.

Astonishingly, within the course of a week, the military government took an about turn to become a lynchpin in the US-led military operation in Afghanistan that ousted the Taliban regime. Pakistan was back as the US's strategic partner in the region and was now involved in a new war against terrorism. The military government did not have any option other than an unconditional and rapid about turn which surprised even the American authorities.

Just a few months before surrendering to America's arm-twisting, the powerful military authorities in Pakistan were vehemently defending their support for the Taliban regime, which, according to them, provided Pakistan 'strategic depth'. It was the same General Ahmad who sought to convince the

American administration positively about the Taliban when Thomas Pickering, deputy secretary of state in the Clinton administration, warned Pakistan against the consequences of being 'in bed with the Taliban'.

Events following within a week of 9/11 in Washington and Islamabad provide an interesting insight into the ad hoc and arbitrary decision-making process in Pakistan on crucial national security and foreign policy issues. Like the policy to support the Taliban regime, the decision to surrender the country's sovereignty was also taken by just a few generals. There were no consultations at any level when General Musharraf abandoned support for the oppressive and reactionary regime in Afghanistan and gave the American forces complete access to Pakistani territory. It was all done in the best national interest, he later declared. However, the military leader had offered the same argument when they got Pakistan into a messy situation by supporting the Taliban. The pro-Taliban policy had not only isolated Pakistan, but had also encouraged Islamic extremism within the country, creating an enormous domestic problem.

Musharraf was addressing a meeting of local *nazims* on the evening of 11 September 2001, when he was interrupted by an urgent call from Maj. Gen Rashid Qureshi, who informed him about the terrorist attack on America. 'I realized the gravity of the whole issue of this terrorist attack,' Musharraf said. The next day he flew to Islamabad where he went into consultations with his military commanders and members of the National Security Council. On 12 September in the evening he received a phone call from General Ahmad in Washington briefing him about his meeting with Armitage. 'He did tell me the gravity of the situation, and the shock and anger that is being expressed in all the US government and also the shock of the nation,' said Musharraf. Later, US Ambassador Wendy Chamberlain met with him and conveyed a formal message from the American leader seeking cooperation. The general assured her of Pakistan's full support.

There was no consultation with political leaders on the paradigm shift in the strategic course of the nation. Musharraf took his handpicked cabinet into confidence almost three days after his ISI chief had already consented to the US demands. His line was that Pakistan was itself a victim of terrorism and the Taliban government was providing refuge to the religious extremists involved in sectarian killings in Pakistan. 'We had given a long list of the terrorists who we wanted to be handed over to us. At least they should have turned over the terrorists to us.' He told the ministers that the decision to cooperate with the US was necessary to safeguard Pakistan's nuclear assets and its Kashmir policy.

General Musharraf was concerned about the possible reaction from right wing Islamic groups and the domestic fallout of his policy shift. He expressed his concern to the American Ambassador during his long meeting with her on 15 September. With Lt. Gen. Ahmad in charge of the powerful ISI, it was not easy to effectively implement the new policy on Afghanistan. In a last bid to prevent a US attack on Afghanistan, Musharraf, in the third week of September, dispatched the ISI chief to Kandahar to persuade Mullah Omar to hand over bin Laden to the US.

The general met the Taliban leader without any aide for several hours and later informed Musharraf that he was hopeful that Mullah Omar would cooperate. In September, Musharraf sent three missions to Mullah Omar, two of them led by General Ahmad, and also sent a delegation of religious scholars to persuade the Taliban leader. The central point he conveyed was his surrender of Osama bin Laden for the sake of peace in Afghanistan. 'I was constantly conveying a message that they must understand realities and prevent the suffering of the people of Afghanistan by surrendering Osama bin Laden. And I was also trying to drill home to him that he should not make people of Afghanistan suffer for a person who's not even an Afghan, but someone who has come from outside.'

In an interview, Musharraf said: 'Mahmood, on one occasion, did manage a breakthrough. He said, "We sat separately, without the interference of anybody, and Mullah Omar seemed to show a little bit of flexibility. Unfortunately, however, he did not agree on the issue of surrendering Osama bin Laden. The maximum that he agreed to was to form a court, an Islamic religious scholar's court, to try him. He would not agree to more than that."' Some highly-placed sources believe that Mahmood may have been playing a double game. Musharraf was also not very happy with Mahmood's arrogant style and for not consulting him before agreeing to Armitage's seven-point demand. 'Though Musharraf would have given his consent, he did not like being bypassed,' a senior official said.

General Musharraf acted swiftly and replaced the hard-line Ahmad with Lt. Gen. Ehsanul Haq a former Military Intelligence chief (MI) and corps commander, Peshawar, who was known for his anti-Taliban views, as the new ISI chief. Through a series of purges at the top level, Musharraf consolidated his position, with the new commanders backing him fully on the new policy on Afghanistan. Interestingly, General Musharraf informed the US ambassador about Mahmood's retirement on 6 October a day before the decision was made public. 'Yes, I did tell her, I did surprise her,' he said in an interview. Shortly thereafter, the agency that had been deeply involved with the Taliban since its inception was guiding the US-led Allied forces into Afghanistan.

---

1. Escobar, Pepe, '9-11 and the smoking Gun', *Asia Times Online*, 8 April 2004.
2. Lévy, Bernard-Henri, *Qui a tué Daniel Pearl?* 2003 Melville House Publishing, Hoboken.

28

The 9/11 Commission and Pakistan

Prior to 11 September 2001, although US intelligence agencies had wind of several possible al-Qaeda schemes involving an attack on the World Trade Center and the hijacking or destruction of airplanes, the precise plans for that fateful day were so closely guarded that even Osama bin Laden did not know the details until 1 September.

This emerged from investigations carried out by Pakistani agencies that worked in tandem with FBI agents who interrogated at least three senior al-Qaeda members after their arrest from the port city of Karachi.

Following the 1993 attack on the World Trade Center in New York which killed six people and injured over a thousand, al-Qaeda members concluded that given the architecture of the twin towers, they could not be destroyed from their base. This led to the extraordinary plan to fly airplanes into the buildings. In August 1998, the Clinton administration fired cruise missiles through Pakistani airspace into Afghanistan in an abortive strike intended to kill Osama bin Laden in retaliation for suspected al-Qaeda attacks on three US embassies in Africa. Earlier that year, bin Laden, after forming the Coalition against

Crusaders, Christians and Jews, also known as the International Islamic Front, issued a fatwa declaring that it was the 'duty of Muslims everywhere to kill Americans, including civilians'.

According to an April 2004 news feature by the web newspaper *Asia Times Online*, the American attack on Afghanistan acted as a catalyst for several al-Qaeda cells to seriously begin planning a major attack on US soil. Details of this reportedly emerged from intelligence sources familiar with the case of al-Qaeda operative Ramzi bin al-Shibah, who was arrested after a shootout with Pakistani security forces in Karachi on 11 September 2002, the first anniversary of the 9/11 attacks. The ISI and the FBI interrogated him jointly and separately. After these sessions, he was finally handed over to the US authorities. According to the *Asia Times Online* report, Ramzi's account of events disclosed several new aspects which clearly show why the US intelligence failed to detect the 11 September plot. Ramzi was supposed to be the 20th hijacker on 9/11 but failed to obtain a US visa.

According to Ramzi the final execution of the attacks was plotted in Hamburg, Germany, where an important al-Qaeda cell was based. Its members had never carried out any missions against US interests, and they were highly motivated and extremely secretive. Ramzi bin al-Shibah reportedly informed his interrogators that he was assigned to tell bin Laden about the plan. He travelled from Germany via Bangkok to Afghanistan, where he met bin Laden. From Afghanistan he returned to Germany, where he learnt that his application for a US visa had been refused. He rushed to Spain to submit a fresh application, but was again unsuccessful. He therefore returned to Afghanistan, leaving only when Kabul fell in late 2001. He ended up in Karachi where he was arrested on 11 September 2002.

According to the information extracted by the interrogators from Ramzi bin al-Shibah, the nature of the Hamburg cell was typical of the manner in which al-Qaeda operates. Once members of a particular cell are assigned a specific task, the details of its planning and execution remain with them alone and they do not know what other cells are doing. Take the case of Khalid Bin al-Attash. He was arrested on in April 2003 in Karachi, and as a hard core al-Qaeda member and a close associate of bin Laden was regarded as the biggest-ever catch in the 'war on terror'. The one-legged operative was a suspect in the attack on the warship *USS Cole* at Aden, Yemen, in October 2000. He was later passed on to the ISI and then the FBI but after exhaustive questioning, it became obvious that he did not have a clue about the planning for 9/11.

Similarly, Ramzi bin al-Shibah was part of the 11 September team, but interrogators soon realized that he was unaware of any other al-Qaeda activities. The same was true of Abu Zubaydah, arrested in 2002 from Faisalabad. Zubaydah is known to be a part of Laden's inner circle but he was unable to supply any information on 11 September, or on al Qaeda's future plans, except for some general information. Against this backdrop, it was not surprising that the 9/11 plan went undetected. According to *Asia Times Online*, a CIA memo dated 6 August 2001 indicating that the al-Qaeda planned to attack the US was no more than a piece of intelligence analysis, primarily extracted from al-Qaeda's track record and bin Laden's call for an attack on the US. Beyond that, no specifics were available. This raises the strong possibility that, just as in Hamburg earlier, a highly secretive al-Qaeda cell might at this very moment be planning another major attack.

THE ROOTS OF 9/11

As the 9/11 Commission begun its proceedings in April 2004 to prepare a full and complete account of the circumstances surrounding the 11 September 2001 terrorist attacks, the Bush administration started feeling the heat for perceived failures to respond to the terrorist threat to the US.

However, as *Washington Post* editor Steve Coll has made clear in his book, *Ghost Wars: The Secret History of the CIA, Afghanistan, and bin Laden* there can be far more serious finger-pointing at previous US administrations, led by President Clinton. 'Their mistakes, naiveté and wrongdoing over Afghan policy not only indirectly led to thousands of Afghan deaths and the rise of the ultra-conservative Taliban, but also gave succour to the anti-American Osama bin Laden, helping to lay the groundwork for the terrorism exploding around the world today,' says the writer.[1]

According to Coll, 'it all began back in the 1980s with the United States government's misplaced multi-million dollar anti-Soviet policy in Afghanistan. During that time, an Afghan royalist mujahideen commander offered this warning to the US: "For God's sake, you are financing your own assassins." With his warning, the commander and supporter of long-exiled Afghan king, Zahir Shah, was not saying do not fund the Afghan freedom fighters or those battling the Russian communist forces who had invaded Afghanistan in 1979 (many saw the mujahideen as a just cause), his gripe was that when it came to the choice of who in the mujahideen to back, Washington was funding the wrong guys.'[2]

Steve Coll, who was *Washington Post's* South Asia Bureau Chief from 1989 to 1992, states in his book that it is easy to talk with hindsight, but even back in the mid-1980s, in the midst of the Cold War, warnings were given to Washington on the dangers of backing hard-line Islamic fundamentalists who increasingly spat venom at the US. That warning, by a moderate commander, was prophetic. Few however in the CIA and in the halls of power in Washington were willing to listen. Instead, a policy was followed that not only backed the wrong mujahideen in Afghanistan, but also helped provide Osama bin Laden with a crucible for developing terror.

As one American policy-maker put it back in the 1980s, militant Islam and militant Christianity should cooperate in the common cause of defeating communism. Such a statement sounds ludicrous today. The irony is that Washington was setting itself up for the very thing the CIA claimed it was founded for: to ensure there will never be another Pearl Harbour. American policy, however, allowed bin Laden in the 1980s to set up training camps for Arab militants and Muslims of other nationalities. Mesmerized by the glint of oil from Central Asia in the 1990s, Washington further backed Taliban leader Mullah Mohammad Omar, in his 'cleansing of Afghanistan'. The US hoped to profit from an oil pipeline through Afghanistan but instead saw a pulverized Third World country thrown back to the Dark Ages.

Suspecting that the 9/11 terrorist attacks on US targets were the work of Afghanistan-based bin Laden, Washington failed to capture or kill him, despite cruise missile strikes on one of his bases. Today, Osama bin Laden may be a tired and harried man as he tries to avoid the 'hammer on the anvil' posed by US Special Forces on the Pak-Afghan border, yet, he must be delighted at the way the US has indirectly helped him stir up so much sympathy and brought so many angry recruits to his cause.

PAKISTAN WAS A PATRON OF TERRORISM

'Pakistan, not Iraq, was a patron of terrorism and had closer ties with Osama bin Laden and al-Qaeda leading up to the September 11 attacks. The Taliban's ability to provide al-Qaeda chief Osama bin Laden a haven in the face of international pressure and UN sanctions was significantly facilitated by Pakistani support. Pakistan broke with the Taliban only after September 11, even though it knew the Afghan militia was hiding al-Qaeda chief Osama bin Laden,' said the June 2004 interim report of the National Commission on Terrorist Attacks upon the United States, also known as the 9/11 Commission.

The report said Pakistan benefited from the Taliban-al-Qaeda relationship, as Osama bin Laden's camps trained and equipped fighters for Pakistan's ongoing struggle in Kashmir. The Taliban faction that seized Kabul was itself supported by Pakistan, said the twelve-page report, and added that even when it had its headquarters in Sudan, al-Qaeda had used Pakistan and Afghanistan as regional bases and training centres, supporting Islamic insurgencies in Tajikistan, Kashmir and Chechnya. The training at al-Qaeda and associated camps was multi-faceted in nature, it said:

> A worldwide jehad needed terrorists who could bomb embassies or hijack airliners, but it also needed foot soldiers for the Taliban in its war against the Northern Alliance, and guerrillas who could shoot down Russian helicopters in Chechnya or ambush Indian units in Kashmir. Thus, most recruits received training that was primarily geared towards conventional warfare. Terrorist training was provided mostly to the best and most ardent recruits. The quality of the training provided at al-Qaeda and other jehadist camps was apparently quite good. There was coordination with regard to curriculum and great emphasis on ideological and religious indoctrination. Instruction underscored that the US and Israel were evil, and that the rulers of Arab countries were illegitimate.

According to the report, Osama bin Laden used his personal wealth and connections with rich Arab contributors to facilitate the flow of fighters into Afghanistan. He provided extensive financing for an entity called Maktab al Khidmat or the 'Bureau of Services'. The bureau apparently operated a recruiting network in Muslim communities throughout the Middle East, Southeast Asia, Western Europe and the US. 'It provided travel funds and guesthouses in Pakistan for recruits and volunteers on the road to the Afghan battlefield. Osama bin Laden also used his financial network to set up training camps and procure weapons and supplies for Arab fighters. Major Afghan warlords who led forces in the battle against the Soviets also benefited from the use of these camps,' the report said, continuing:

Following the defeat of the Soviets in the late 1980s, bin Laden formed an organization called 'The Foundation' or al-Qaeda which was intended to serve as a foundation upon which to build a global Islamic army. By 1992, bin Laden was focused on attacking the United States. The camps created a climate in which trainees and other personnel were free to think creatively about ways to commit mass murder. According to a senior al-Qaeda associate, various ideas were floated by mujahideen in Afghanistan: taking over a launcher and forcing Russian scientists to fire a nuclear missile at the United States; mounting mustard gas or cyanide attacks against Jewish areas in Iran; dispensing poison gas into the air-conditioning system of a targeted building; and, last but not least, hijacking an aircraft and crashing it into an airport terminal or nearby city.

As time passed and al-Qaeda repeatedly and successfully hit US targets, said the report, Osama bin Laden became a legendary figure among militants both inside and outside Afghanistan. 'He lectured at the camps. His perceived stature and charisma reinforced the zeal of the trainees. Bin Laden also personally evaluated trainees' suitability for terrorist operations. The camps were able to operate only because of the worldwide network of recruiters, travel facilitators, and document forgers who vetted would-be trainees and helped them get in and out of Pakistan.'

The 9/11 Commission report urged the US government to make a long-term commitment to the future of Pakistan so long as its leadership remains willing to stay the course in the fight against terrorism. The Commission, which released its 575-page report on 22 July 2004, recommended that US should make the difficult long-term commitment to the future of Pakistan so long as Pakistani leaders remain willing to make difficult choices of their own. The recommendation on Pakistan notes that, '... if General Musharraf stands for enlightened moderation in a fight for his life and for the life of his country, the United States should be willing to make hard choices too, and make the difficult long-term commitment to the future of Pakistan.

'Sustaining the current scale of aid to Pakistan, the United States should support Pakistan's government in its struggle against extremists with a comprehensive effort that extends from military aid to support for better education, so long as Pakistan's leaders remain willing to make difficult choices of their own.'

---

1. Coll, Steve, *Ghost Wars: The Secret History of the CIA, Afghanistan, and bin Laden, from the Soviet Invasion to September 10, 2001,* Penguin Press, New York, 2004.
2. Ibid.

29

Fugitives vs the Federal Bureau of Investigation

Having set up a high-tech espionage network in the four provincial capitals and the tribal areas of Pakistan to accelerate the ongoing hunt for the remaining al-Qaeda and Taliban fugitives, the FBI is slowly but surely prying open Pakistan's sensitive national security system.

The American investigation agency had to set up its own espionage network in Pakistan due to lack of cooperation from the ISI in locating the remenants of al-Qaeda and Taliban. As the ISI has had deep and long-standing ties with the Taliban and is largely believed to be beyond government control, the FBI also decided to form its own ad hoc group of locals called the Spider Group, which is a band of former army and intelligence officers, some of whom had reached the ranks of brigadier and colonel. Spider Group members include hundreds of experts in the fields of intelligence, interrogation, linguistics, cyber crime, communications and forensic investigations.

Many of those in the US-organized espionage service in Pakistan have had long experience in dealing with Afghanistan, which can be traced back to the American-sponsored war against the Soviet troops in the 1980s and as recently as the Taliban rule from the mid-1990s till 2001. The members of the Spider Group are entrusted with the task of tracking the activities of the fugitive al-Qaeda and Taliban operatives in the border areas as well as in the larger cities of Pakistan. The Spider Group has been formed to ensure that the FBI agents who had previously worked with the ISI under restrictions could have access to a free flow of information that would help them locate al-Qaeda and Taliban fugitives allegedly hiding in Pakistan.

In 2003, two years after Pakistan opted to become a frontline state in the US-led war on terror, some high profile arrests of several leading al-Qaeda fugitives by the FBI from the Pakistani soil exacerbated the public perception that the country is swarming with FBI agents. The work of the US intelligence agents in Pakistan has led to some of the greatest successes so far in the hunt for the most wanted FBI fugitives, especially the March 2002 arrest of al-Qaeda's third most important operative, Abu Zubaydah, from Faisalabad. Another FBI operation led to the September 2002 arrest of Ramzi bin al-Shibah from Karachi, who allegedly planned the September 2001 suicide hijackings in the US. Similarly, al-Qaeda's operational chief, Khalid Sheikh Mohammad was arrested from Rawalpindi in March 2003, followed by the capture of Waleed bin Attash from Karachi in April 2003, that of Ahmed Khalfan Ghailani in July 2004 from Gujrat and Abu Faraj Al Libbi in May 2005 from Mardan.

Despite these high-profile arrests, the FBI still appears to have a lengthy anti-terrorism agenda for Pakistan. According to the US intelligence findings, the terrorism infrastructure in Pakistan and Afghanistan still consists of strong remanents of the al Qaeda, the Taliban, and the International Islamic Front with its five components: Lashkar-e-Toiba, Jaish-e-Mohammad, Harkatul Mujahideen, Harkat al-Jehad al-Islami and Lashkar-e-Jhangvi.

While aiming at these targets in Pakistan, the FBI initially kept a low profile and confined itself to assisting the ISI operatives in tracking down the most wanted fugitives. However, as things stand today, the FBI works autonomously and has even established its own organizational set-up here in

Pakistan, which includes communications to track mobile and land telephone calls as well as sophisticated bugging devices. The FBI field offices have literally established direct control over the Pakistani law enforcment agencies, such as the police, who take orders from the bureau agents.

Not all are happy with this state of affairs. The FBI was involved in some operations that touched a nerve with hardliners. Musharraf's support for the US war on terror has already become a rallying cry for resurgent Islamic hardline groups in Pakistan, which rode a strong anti-American platform to unprecedented success in the 2002 polls. Time and again, Muttahida Majlis-e-Amal (MMA) has expressed its concern over the presence of a large number of FBI agents in Pakistan, and urged the government to expel them. However, the director general of the Interior Ministry's National Crisis Management Cell, Brig. Javed Iqbal Cheema, refuted the MMA claim that the FBI rules the roost in Pakistan. According to the brigadier, 'Every white person in Pakistan is mistaken as an FBI agent. Though it is just a misperception, there are vested interests here that want to catch on to the public sentiment to give a false impression.'

According to US embassy sources in Islamabad, the number of FBI agents in Pakistan has fluctuated between two to twelve since the 11 September 2001 attacks. General Musharraf made almost a similar claim in a television interview in 2003, saying, 'Hardly a dozen FBI agents are present on the Pakistani soil.' Whatever the actual number might be, the officials of the Pakistani intelligence and law enforcement agencies believe that the FBI agents had been involved in almost every important anti-terror operation in Pakistan since the war on terrorism began.

Contrary to Musharraf's own claim, an FBI official, speaking in Washington in November 2003, had informed the American media that 'between several dozen and a hundred' FBI agents remain in Pakistan at any one time, working closely with local and federal police and intelligence officials. According to well-informed interior ministry insiders, around 200-250 FBI agents are currently working alongside their Pakistani counterparts in the border areas and the large cities including Peshawar, Rawalpindi, Lahore, Quetta, Karachi and Faisalabad. They added that the FBI varies its presence in the country according to the requirements of its hunt for al-Qaeda suspects.

A senior official of the ministry of interior said requesting anonymity: 'Around 200 more support-people generally known as permanent legal attaches or legats (mostly belonging to the Spider Group) are assisting the FBI agents. These agents are often directly involved with interrogation of terrorist suspects or criminals and sometimes submit questions to those conducting the interviews, including the American Central Investigation Agency officers. The legats feed information gleaned from the interviews back to the US for further investigation, sometimes resulting in more suspects being put under surveillance or homes being searched.'

The interior ministry official also said that the FBI had so far set up twenty-eight field offices inside Pakistan, including the border areas and the cities, to track down al-Qaeda and Taliban fugitives. 'Around a dozen such offices were established in the border areas of Pakistan while sixteen others continue working in the cities. Working under tight security being provided by the Pakistani agencies, the FBI offices are equipped with high-tech surveillance equipment.' After the 11 September attacks, the official said, the Bush administration had approached General Musharraf to set up at least 100 such offices, carrying signboards and security. 'However, permission was granted for only two dozen offices, after Pakistan signed a mutual bilateral pact with the US to fight out terrorists under a joint working-group programme.' Under the programme, the FBI could establish field offices in Pakistan and take assistance from its intelligence agencies.

A massive army operation was launched in South and North Waziristan agencies in March 2004 in the wake of repeated assertions by the American intelligence agencies that the remnants of al-Qaeda and Taliban, and their local aides were regrouping in the border areas of Pakistan and were launching raids against US-led coalition troops in Afghanistan. The tribal operations were followed by reports in the American media that the US military was planning an offensive that would reach inside Pakistan to destroy the al-Qaeda network. A few weeks before the Waziristan operation was launched, the *Chicago Tribune*, in a report from Washington, said citing military sources that the plan involved thousands of US troops, some of them already in neighbouring Afghanistan. The Pakistani government issued the usual denial that it would allow such an operation, and the Pentagon declined to confirm that such a plan was being worked on. Director-General, Inter-Services Public Relations, Major General Shaukat Sultan contradicted the news report, saying that no foreign forces would be allowed to use Pakistani soil. 'Only Pakistani forces will carry out operations from its sources,' he said. The US media however kept reporting that the plans were advanced and their execution would depend on events on the ground.

The Pakistani government circles believe that such an intervention by some of the 11,000 US troops in Afghanistan would be political suicide for Musharraf, but the fact remains that the FBI Director Robert Muller has had some lengthy discussions with the former during which plans to capture bin Laden and other al-Qaeda leaders were discussed. The official circles say Musharraf had bowed to Muller's demand for setting up a permanent intelligence system in the tribal areas, allowing the FBI to monitor the Pak-Afghan border. The monitoring is being carried out with the help of sophisticated electronic surveillance equipment, all-terrain vehicles and helicopters. An American communication and intelligence centre has been set up in the tribal area on the Pakistani side to help coordinate the hunt for al-Qaeda fugitives by providing spy satellites, electronic-eavesdropping planes and special ground sensors.

According to media reports, about 100 army and intelligence officers were sent to the US in mid-2003 for various short courses. They became part of a Special Investigation Group (SIG) to track down members of the al-Qaeda network in Pakistan.

While the government of Pakistan maintains that the officers were sent to the US for training after it had realized that Pakistan's investigative machinery was simply incapable of delivering in the highly sensitive law-enforcement operations; there are also those in the country's intelligence circles who maintain that having army and intelligence officers trained by a foreign intelligence apparatus was like handing over the keys of the country to another nation as it allowed them undue influence in the armed forces. However, hardly concerned with any such apprehensions, the Musharraf administration continues to bow to the ever-increasing FBI demands. The authorities have allowed the FBI to freely use Echelon software to run its communication monitoring operation, though in collaboration with the ISI. Echelon, developed by the US National Security Agency, is a secret network that is designed to detect and capture 'information packets' couriered through Internet, telephone or fax.

The intelligence sources further added that the FBI has, in addition, installed a hi-tech Transaction Tracking Server (TTS) at Quaid-e-Azam International Airport, Karachi, and the Allama Iqbal International Airport, Lahore, which poses a serious threat to Pakistan's sensitive security operations and covert movements. The TTS was installed by the FBI to monitor the arrival and departure of the passengers.

The entire apparatus is located in the Intelligence Bureau (IB) headquarters in Islamabad and its Karachi offices where the US experts along with the IB officers control its operations. The system was basically installed to check the large number of fleeing Afghans and Arab volunteers who participated in the war against the US alongside the Taliban. According to a retired intelligence official, acting under the increasing American pressure, the Musharraf regime has also allowed the FBI access to the Pakistani communication network. The permission was granted despite a serious question being raised within the security agencies: whether the bugging of telecommunication network would remain confined only to the tracking down of the al-Qaeda operatives and their jehadi aides in Pakistan?

30

The 7/7 London Attacks, Suicide Bombers, and the Pakistani Connection

On 7 July 2005, London's transport network was attacked by four suicide bombers, killing 55 people and wounding over 700 others. The British intelligence agencies later discovered that three of the four suicide bombers were British-born youth of the Pakistani origin, who had traveled to Pakistan in November 2004. The 7/7 attacks brought to the world's attention the growing threat posed by 'human bombs' from Pakistan who, in one way or another, are found involved in the tragic stories of death and destruction. Despite repeated claims of clamping down on the terror network, the Musharraf regime clearly seems guilty of exporting terror to different parts of the globe.

For Pakistan, 7/7 is another 9/11 as the country is once again standing at the crossroads between the military and the mosque. After leaving its footprints in the United States, Afghanistan and India, the Pakistani terror trail just moved to the United Kingdom in July 2005.

Following the 7 July 2005 bombings, the situation has reached a point where most Pakistanis rush to their television sets in nervous anticipation whenever a devastating terrorist attack occurs anywhere in the world. In their hearts is the question: does the latest dastardly militant attack have the imprint of a Pakistani?

The British intelligence agencies had already concluded that the three British-born Pakistani bombers went to madrassas (religious schools) in Pakistan in December 2004.

While no religious seminary in Pakistan is ready to admit that the three London suicide bombers ever visited them, the Pakistan government itself declared that the three came to Pakistan between November 2004 and February 2005. Muhammad Siddique Khan and Shehzad Tanweer stayed in Lahore and Faisalabad, while Hasib Hussain chose Karachi. Their bloody acts of terror six months after their return from Pakistan could change Europe much more than the 9/11 tragedy changed America.

During their stay at the Pakistani religious seminaries, the bombers reportedly learnt to make explosives from recovered al-Qaeda manuals. The information provided to Islamabad by the UK authorities shows that Khan and Tanweer came to Pakistan in November 2004. After landing in Karachi, the two militants traveled to Lahore from where they proceeded to Faisalabad. In between, they were at the Jamia Manzurul Islamia, an extremist Sunni madrassa situated in Lahore Cantonment, run by Pir Saifullah Khalid. In Faisalabad, they used to visit the Jamia Fathul Raheem, another extremist Sunni madrassa which is run by Qari Ahlullah Raheemi.

British intelligence agencies are collaborating with their Pakistani counterparts to ascertain whether the three bombers were in touch with the al Qaeda or other Islamic groups in Pakistan, or if there was a Pakistan-based mastermind behind the London attacks. What the British authorities have asked the ISI to find out is how many more Muslim volunteers of Pakistani origin present in the UK are ready to carry out suicide bombings for their cause. The MI5 (the British intelligence agency) investigators have already concluded that the

September 1, 2005 video message of Mohammad Siddique Khan, one of the British suicide bombers, was recorded in Pakistan during his 2004 visit to Pakistan. The British intelligence agencies believe Khan, the eldest of the four London bombers, was the likely leader of the attacks.

The Siddique Khan video was broadcast by al-Jazeera television, through which al-Qaeda claimed responsibility for the July 7 attacks and threatened more attacks in Europe. It was the first explicit claim of responsibility for the blasts by al Qaeda. The broadcast also showed pictures of Ayman al-Zawahiri and Siddique Khan. A portion of the tape showed a young bearded man, identified as Khan, speaking in English and saying that he would take part in the attacks. In what appeared to be a defence of attacks on civilians, he warned westerners that they would not be safe if they elected governments that commit crimes against humanity.

In the tape, Khan was shown wearing a red-white checked turban and a dark jacket. He had a trimmed beard and appeared to be sitting against a wall lined with an ornate carpet. In the video, his image resembled photos of him published after the deadly 7/7 attacks. Zawahri appeared in black turban and white robes with an automatic weapon leaning against the wall beside him. "Until we feel secure, you will be our targets and until you stop the bombing, gassing, imprisonment and torture of my people we will not stop this fight," said Siddique Khan in the tape.

"I'm going to keep this short and to the point because it's all been said before by far more eloquent people than me. And our words have no impact upon you; therefore I'm going to talk to you in a language that you understand. Our words are dead until we give them life with our blood," Khan said.

He further said: "I and thousands like me are forsaking everything for what we believe. Our driving motivation doesn't come from tangible commodities that this world has to offer. Our religion is Islam - obedience to the one true God, Allah, and following the footsteps of the final prophet and messenger Muhammad . . . This is how our ethical stances are dictated. Your democratically elected governments continuously perpetuate atrocities against my people all over the world. And your support of them makes you directly responsible.'

Interestingly, the British intelligence agencies want their Pakistani counterparts to interrogate Sheikh Ahmed Omar Saeed, the killer of American journalist Daniel Pearl, in connection with the London bombings, because of his British background and his Jaish-e-Mohammad connection. The British agencies believe that since his arrest, Omar has somehow remained in touch with his friends and followers across Pakistan and Britain, and that he used to advise them on the future course of action.

The 7/7 attacks and the involvement of the British nationals of Pakistani origin shows that just as the West has failed in winning its war against terrorism, Musharraf is unsuccessful in winning his war against extremists because of lack of political will. Although Musharraf insists publicly he is determined to end all forms of terrorism, there is hardly any evidence that his government has tried to dismantle the jehadi network on Pakistani soil. For long, Pakistan has been the nerve-centre of the jehadi mafia, providing safe haven to the ideologues of terror, masterminds of spectacular and horrifying attacks, and innumerable, hapless foot soldiers — the cannon fodder of jehad.

As the international pressure increased on Musharraf to take practical measures to uproot the jehadi mafia and dismantle its infrastructure from the Pakistani soil, the general appeared on the state-run Pakistan television and addressed the nation on 21 July 2005. As usual, he ordered a countrywide crackdown against extremist jehadi and sectarian elements, prompting the security agencies to pick scores of them from religious schools across Pakistan. But analysts described Musharraf's address to the nation as an updated version of his

January 2002 televised speech, since the administrative measures he announced for combating terrorism were similar to those announced in the past.

General Musharraf's July 21, 2005 speech also raised two pertinent questions. What happened to the first campaign against terror which he had launched in January 2002? If these measures did not produce desired results in the past, how will they do a better job this time? Analysts say given the military background of General Musharraf, his government's counter-terrorism policy was confined to administrative measures pursued through the civil administration, police and intelligence agencies. The narrow strategy comprised police raids on seminaries and arrests of some activists of militant outfits. However, this policy didn't offer a sustainable solution because the government's priorities shifted and the arrested jehadis were released later.

Another problem that adversely affected the 2002 campaign against terrorism was the divided official opinion about the role of militant groups in the insurgency in Jammu & Kashmir. This is why for a long time after September 2001, Pakistan's officials insisted on distinguishing between terrorism and wars of liberation. Some groups involved in Jammu & Kashmir were advised by Pakistani intelligence agencies to keep a low profile. The underlying assumption was that if needed, these groups could be reactivated to pursue the official agenda in Kashmir.

Analysts have varying explanations about why the Musharraf administration hasn't yet destroyed the militant groups and their training infrastructure. Yet, the real problem seems to be that there is sympathy for Islamic extremists in Pakistan's military and intelligence establishments. At the same time, there is a widespread feeling that Pakistan is actually fighting the war for the West. Therefore, analysts believe that unless Pakistan makes the war on terror its own war, it cannot win it.

HUMAN BOMBS: MADE IN PAKISTAN

The deadly phenomenon of suicide bombings hit Pakistan in the backdrop of the 9/11 terror attacks. As many as twenty human bombs have blown themselves up across Pakistan since March 2002, killing over 200 people and wounding as many as 500 others. With the avowed aim of purging the land of the pure of the forces of infidel, the new breed of lethal bombers seeks to strike not only the western interests, but also the Shia minority in Pakistan.

The alleged American atrocities against Muslims in Afghanistan and Iraq are supposed to be the main motivation for most of the bombers to explode themselves for what they consider to be a noble cause. None of the suicide bombers belonged to the country's elite classes: thirteen of them belonged to the lower middle class, while the remaining seven came from middle class families. Apart from their jehadi mindset, their anti-American sentiments and their poor family background, another thing they had in common was illiteracy. Most of the human bombs belonged to the splinter groups of several leading jehadi and sectarian outfits that were launched as a reaction to the post-9/11 crackdown against militants in Pakistan.

Smaller and more isolated than their parent organizations, these splinter groups of the jehadi and sectarian outfits reportedly receive financial backing from al-Qaeda and its affiliated groups, and draw their recruits from the ranks of the poor and enraged. They are recruited for different purposes, with agendas ranging from killing Shia 'kafirs' (infidels) to liberating Muslims from the clutches of the 'infidels'. Interestingly, most of the suicide bombers in Pakistan so far were veterans of the 'holy wars' fought in Afghanistan and Jammu & Kashmir, and they were desperate to win a one-way ticket to heaven.

After the 11 September attacks, Pakistan became a key player in the US-led alliance and reversed the previous decade's policy of trying to influence Afghan politics through the Taliban. The policy reversal immediately brought the state into conflict with the jehadi groups active in Afghanistan and Jammu & Kashmir. These groups have for years been mobilized, ideologically motivated and trained in Pakistan for export in the neighbourhood - particularly to Jammu & Kashmir and to Afghanistan. Therefore, the emerging phenomenon of suicide bombings in Pakistan needs to be viewed within the context of Islamabad's alliance with the US and al-Qaeda's reach within Pakistan.

A scrutiny of the pattern of the suicide attacks in Pakistan would indicate several al-Qaeda traits, such as the targeting of Western civilians, absence of immediate claims of responsibility and the quantity of highly explosive material being used. The targets were varied: foreigners, Christians, Shias and the Muslim leaders who are considered pro-America. The data compiled by Pakistani agencies shows that the new breed of the suicide bombers, which generally is made up of the unemployed and illiterate coming from the poorer strata of the society, perceives the US as an aggressor, be it in Iraq or Afghanistan. And somehow, they have been led to believe that a suicide attack in the service of Islam against the infidels would gain them victory here and in the hereafter.

Even otherwise, it is open knowledge that for years, the Pakistani intelligence agencies have indoctrinated, motivated and trained the jehadi cadres for export in the neighbourhood - to Jammu & Kashmir and Afghanistan. The J&K had witnessed the first suicide attacks in 1999, and since then, there has been a steady stream of deadly suicide operations. These human bombs had, however, till recently excluded their home ground in Pakistan from the scope of their holy war. But, even as suicide attacks decline sharply in the Kashmir valley, Pakistan appears to be emerging as a favoured target.

It was the Jaish-e-Mohammed that introduced suicide missions to Pakistani cadres. The Jaish endorses suicidal bombing in jehad and its expertise in this field has spread to other terrorist groups active in Pakistan. Set up to target the Indian forces in J&K, the Jaish is among the best-funded terrorist groups active in the Valley today. Its first successful suicide operation was carried out on 25 December 2000, when 24-year-old Bilal, a Muslim from Birmingham, rammed his explosives-laden car into the Indian army's headquarters in Srinagar, killing nine people.

While suicide bombings were introduced by the Jaish, the fidayeen missions were introduced by the Lashkar-e-Toiba, which views suicide bombing as un-Islamic. The distinction between the fidayeen and the suicide bomber is extremely fine. The fidayeen do not believe in exploding themselves to instantaneous death. Their philosophy, though, condones death by martyrdom: they fight till the end, often launching attacks in situations where death is inevitable.

The decision to become fidayeen is usually voluntary. There is no monetary benefit, only the promise of a better hereafter involving, among other things, the promise of joys only seventy-two heavenly virgins can provide in paradise. In the bargain, they believe they leave behind, through their sacrifice, a slightly better world for their brethren.

The data compiled by the Pakistani intelligence agencies indicates that a suicide bomber is often a brainwashed religious-minded militant who is spotted by a jehadi leader, who looks out for potential suicide bombers and usually finds the unemployed and uneducated youth with the help of a cleric at a mosque or madrassa. The potential bomber is then scrutinized for his motives. The scrutiny is meant to clarify for the boy himself his real reasons for volunteering and the strength of his commitment.

During the preparation for the mission, he is told that this is a temporary life, one that ends with *shahadat* (martyrdom) they are to achieve by reducing the number of *kafirs* (infidels). The potential suicide bomber needs to be very clear that there is no drawing back in such an operation. Subsequent preparation bolsters his conviction and helps remove fear. The preparation follows a therapy, in which the boy goes through some spiritual exercises, including the recitation of the Holy Koran, particularly those chapters which dwell upon jehad.

The intelligence sources say that the suicide-bomber cells mostly operate in small groups of five to seven people, never staying at one place for more than two nights. Moving in small cells has become a necessity for members of the larger splinter groups, which have been thrown into disarray by a government crackdown after President Musharraf and Premier Shaukat Aziz became targets of their abortive assassination attempts. The sources claimed that most of the human bombs are on the run, and short of resources, yet they conceded that they remain a big threat.

The growing incidents of suicide bombings in Pakistan have already begun to worry the Musharraf-led civilian government. A careful study (carried out by the Inter Services Intelligence) of the life history of suicide bombers points out that of the twenty attackers, twelve were aged between 15-25 years, five fell in the age group of 25-30, while the remaining three bombers were above 30. Most of these human bombers were affiliated with sectarian and militant organizations like Lashkar-e-Janghvi (LeJ), Jaish-e-Mohammad (JeM), Harkatul Mujahideen Al-Alami and Harkat al-Jehad al-Islami. And none of them was even a matriculate (high school graduate).

Though suicide is forbidden in Islam, Islamic extremists have gotten around this problem by describing suicide attacks as acts of martyrdom. The suicide killings have been justified as attacks on infidels and therefore a part of the holy war or jehad. Therefore, a suicide mission in which, the bomber is able to take the lives of Westerners and Hindus is not un-Islamic because both are non-believers. The members of a rival sect, too, are regarded as infidels and therefore their killing through a suicide attack is not un-Islamic. What is particularly worrying about the recent spate of suicide attacks in Pakistan is that both Shias and Sunnis, who used guns and bombs against their rivals in the past, are now deploying suicide bombers to settle scores.

Therefore, mosques, processions and rallies have become vulnerable targets of suicide attacks by rival sectarian outfits which are out to kill each other. Since the aim is to create terror and cause maximum damage to the rival sectarian group, suicide bombers target mosques on Fridays, when thousands of worshippers attend prayers. Unlike suicide bombers elsewhere who simply detonate their explosive-strapped bodies, Pakistan's sectarian suicide bombers first hurl grenades and shoot into the crowd to inflict maximum damage, and then top off their operation by detonating themselves. They are also known to position themselves near pillars so that the explosion can bring down the roof causing more casualties.

There is no single reason for the rise in militancy and in the number of suicide bombers in Pakistan. Poverty, unemployment, lack of education, social rejection, an unhappy family environment, a romanticized notion of jehad and a growing influence of the religious seminaries have all played a role in the indoctrination of culturally dispossessed Pakistani youth. Most young men who have joined the violent world of militancy find themselves working round the clock without any significant financial gains. However, belonging to a militant organization gives these otherwise powerless men a strong sense of identity in an increasingly fragmented social structure.

Perhaps the transcripts of the statements made by some of the arrested militants would help understand the mind of a jehadi. Take Saifur Rehman Saifi, a top Jaish-e-Mohammed activist allegedly involved in a number of terrorist acts in Pakistan. He never learnt the Koran in its entirety and was unable to find a decent job after completing his C. Com certification. After working at some book stores, Saifi realized that a salary of Rs 2,000 was just not what he had in mind. All that changed when he became a militant: money started flowing in and both family and friends started respecting him now that he had become a 'man of God'.

The case of Mohammed Ayaz alias Waqar Ahmed, another suicide bomber affiliated with the Jaish-e-Mohammed is strikingly similar. Again, his failed attempts at education and employment led him straight to the welcoming doors of the nearest Jaish-e-Mohammed office. Mohammed Izhar, on the other hand was introduced to the life of militancy by his local prayer leader, Maulvi Ghulam Allah. Again the lack of decent income steered Izhar into militant circles. However, not all militants are driven into the cause by poverty.

Mohammed Ataullah's inspiration came from within his own family. The son of a prayer leader, Ataullah was raised in an environment conducive to religious militancy and other extremist thoughts. When attempts to earn an honest living proved fruitless, Ataullah was quickly snapped up by a local unit of Jaish-e-Mohammad. Since one of his brothers was already in a similar line of work, Ataullah was easily swayed. The icing on the cake was a salary of Rs 5,000 a month, which was far more than what the mainstream job market could offer a man of his credentials.

FATWA AGAINST SUICIDE BOMBING

A group of fifty-eight religious scholars from Pakistan representing all major schools of Islamic thought issued a fatwa (semi-mandatory religious edict) on 19 May 2005 saying that Islam strictly forbids suicide attacks against Muslims and that those committing such bloody acts at places of worship and public congregations cease to be Muslims.

Interestingly, however, the decree issued by the Pakistani religious scholars does not apply to bombings in either Jammu & Kashmir or Palestine. Suicide attacks are used by Pakistani militant groups like Lashkar-e-Toiba and Jaish-e-Mohammad in the Indian-administered Jammu & Kashmir. The religious scholars led by Mufti Munibur Rehman, clarified at a press conference a day after the issuance of the *fatwa* in Lahore that the line of demarcation between terrorist activity and a freedom struggle has to be clearly defined. They said the *fatwa* applies only to conditions in Pakistan and those waging jehad and running freedom movements against foreign occupants in places like Palestine, Iraq, Jammu & Kashmir and Afghanistan are beyond its scope.

The *fatwa* declares that the murder of Pakistani citizens, including non-Muslims, is a great sin. It also forbids the killing of any non-Muslim who is under the protection of the state of Pakistan or who is living in Pakistan on valid visa. It clearly states that it applies only in Pakistan where both the rulers and the majority of the people are Muslims and the state is officially an Islamic republic. The *fatwa* holds that killing of innocent human beings is forbidden in Islam and carries death penalty. Killing a fellow Muslim without Islamic and legal reasons is an even bigger crime, it said.

What the Pakistani media did not report was the fact that some leading religious scholars of the country, despite agreeing to the contents and spirit of the *fatwa*, refused to support it, maintaining that the government-sponsored move could be used by the United States to justify its propaganda against suicide attacks. Dr Sarfraz Naeemi, the country's top most religious scholar, said he backs the *fatwa* but the timing and manner in which the fatwa was hurriedly announced reflected government pressure. 'There is a need to issue a decree against Americans as well who have been slaughtering Muslims in Iraq and Afghanistan,' said Dr Naeemi in an interview with the BBC soon after the fatwa was issued.

While on the face of it, the move was seen as an attempt to discourage suicide bombings being carried out on places of worship in Pakistan, many believed the decree was part of the official campaign to sell a soft image of the country to the West. However, the outcome of the fatwa came exactly a week later, on

27 May 2005, when the Shia shrine, the Hazrat Bari Imam, in the vicinity of the heavily guarded Diplomatic Enclave in Islamabad, witnessed a powerful suicide explosion that killed twenty-five people and injured more than a 100. The message to the Musharraf regime was loud and clear: the fatwa meant nothing and the suicide bombers would continue to sacrifice their lives for the sake of God Almighty.

31

The Terror Charities

Despite being declared as terrorist support organizations by the United States and having their bank accounts frozen by Pakistan for their alleged al-Qaeda links, three banned Islamic charities — Al-Rashid Trust, Al-Akhtar Trust and Ummah Tameer-e-Nau – took full advantage of the 8 October 2005 earthquake in the Pakistan-administered Azad Kashmir, using it as an opportunity to come out in the open, revive themselves and resume their so-called social welfare activities.

The banned Islamic charities actively participated in the relief operations in the quake-hit areas as a result of the Pakistani government's failure to get aid to the most remote areas. Islamic charities in Pakistan collect billions of dollars every year, much of which, they say, is used for the benevolent causes these charities openly support. But as a matter of fact, large sums are overtly and covertly channeled to many of the leading militant groups still operating in Pakistan, despite being banned by the government.

Over the years, most of the Pakistan-based jehadi groups established an efficient network to generate as well as transfer funds from one place to another. The most common sources of their funding include donations from well-off businessmen committed to the cause of Islam, donations collected through *zakat* (the compulsory 2.5 per cent of their annual savings that every Muslim has to donate as charity every year) and collection from places of worship. But lately, Muslim charity organizations have become a major source of financing for militant groups in many countries, especially Pakistan.

These charities were proving to be problematic for the US law enforcement agencies because of the difficulty in determining whether the money collected for a particular cause was actually being used for the originally specified purpose. However, after the American intelligence agencies came to know that the World Trade Center bombing was financed through money coming from a Muslim charity organization called the Alkifah Refugee Centre in Brooklyn, New York, they immediately turned their scrutiny to Muslim charities, resulting in the eventual closure of several operating from Pakistan, including Ummah Tameer-e-Nau, Al-Rashid Trust and Al-Akhtar Trust.

Al-Rashid Trust, a Karachi-based charity, now active in Azad Kashmir, was the first one to be outlawed by the US Treasury Department after it found a clear link between the trust and al-Qaeda. According to the US intelligence findings, the trust was directly linked to the 23 January 2002 abduction and subsequent murder of the *Wall Street Journal* reporter Daniel Pearl. The abductors, linked to a mixed crew of Pakistani Islamic militant groups, including Maulana Masood Azhar's Jaish-e-Mohammad, held Pearl in a two-room hut in the compound of a commercial nursery in Karachi owned by Al-Rashid Trust, where he was finally murdered.

Founded by Mufti Rashid Ahmed in 1996 in Karachi, Al Rashid Trust was one of the twenty-seven groups and organizations which were black-listed by the US on 22 September 2001, for their involvement in financing and supporting a network of international Islamist terrorist groups. A day after the US announcement of the ban on the outfit, the

State Bank of Pakistan issued a circular, asking banks to freeze the accounts of Al-Rashid Trust. The trust documents indicate that it secures most of its finances from *zakat* and overseas donations.

According to US intelligence findings on the basis of which Al Rashid Trust was banned, it is one of Osama's many sources of income and is closely linked with the Taliban and Jaish-e-Mohammad. The trust and Jaish still share office spaces across Pakistan with even certain overlapping of their cadres. The American findings show that the trust is in charge of the Jaish's foreign funds as well. The biggest source of funds for the trust is the Middle East, South Africa and Pakistan.

With charity and relief work as its professed goals, the trust management denies having links with al-Qaeda or any other terrorist organization. The trust in-charge in Islamabad, Mohammad Arshad, says its activities include providing financial and legal support to jailed Muslim militants around the world, and that all of its actions are purely humanitarian. One of its original charters was to carry out welfare projects within Pakistan. Over time, it expanded its mandate to carry out relief activities for Muslims in Chechnya, Kosovo and Afghanistan.

Interestingly, it perceives the various NGOs currently working in Afghanistan as 'enemies of the Muslims' and, according to media reports, one of its objectives is to push Western NGOs out of Afghanistan. Like the Taliban, the trust subscribes to the Deobandi school of thought. The trust also promotes the concept of jehad among Muslims, especially in places where it sees Muslims as being 'oppressed'.

One of the numerous booklets of the Al Rashid Trust, written by Mufti Rashid Ahmed, states: 'The holy war is an essential element of Islam. Any Moslem must carry the weapons, even with the mosque, if the need would be felt to make fire on a not-Moslem.' (*sic*) The trust literature also denounces the United States for its policies toward Israel, Iraq and Saudi Arabia, and praises Islamist terrorists. Among the trust's objectives is providing assistance to illegally jailed Muslim prisoners. Its founder, Mufti Rashid Ahmed, once considered close to Osama bin Laden, also runs a madrassa in Karachi – Darul Ifta-e-Wal Irshad.

Before the US-led Allied Forces attacked Afghanistan in October 2001, the Al-Rashid Trust operations in Afghanistan were located at Kabul, Jalalabad, Kandahar and Mazar-e-Sharif. Besides running a private radio station, which propagates jehad, Al Rashid Trust also publishes an Urdu newspaper *Zarb-e-Momin* as well as English paper, *Dharb-e-Momin*, which contain anti-American and anti-Western propaganda. They carry reports on the jehadi activities of the Taliban and Jaish-e-Mohammed (JeM).

During his detention in Jammu & Kashmir, JeM chief Maulana Masood Azhar used to send articles clandestinely to the Rashid Trust, which were published by *Dharb-e-Momin*. The trust in-charge in Islamabad, Mohammad Arshad, says that they have asked the Pakistan government to de-freeze its accounts so that it could resume its welfare activities. Yet, the fact remains that despite being banned, Al Rashid Trust continues to freely operate in Pakistan.

The Karachi-based Al Akhtar Trust is the second charity active in Azad Kashmir despite being designated by the US Treasury Department as a terrorist support organization in October 2003. Earlier, US Treasury Department's secretary John Snow had stated: 'Today's designation strikes at the lifeblood of terrorists - the money that funds them. Shutting down the Trust will cripple yet another source of support for terrorists and possibly help undermine the financial backing of terrorists staging attacks against American troops and Iraqi civilians in Iraq. The activities of the Trust demonstrate the dangerous alliance between corrupted charities and terrorists.'

Nevertheless, despite being tagged as a terrorist support organization, the trust management seems unmoved and sounds confident about its future. 'All the trust operations are being carried out according to normal routine and from the same platform – Al Akhtar Trust. We are not afraid of anyone, except for God and we are not going to change the name of the trust. Despite the US action, the Pakistan government has not imposed any restriction on our working. May Allah show right path to those who are accusing us of backing terrorists,' says Zahid Ahmed Khan, a director there.

The US Treasury Department's Executive Order banning the charity stated: 'Al Akhtar Trust is a Pakistan based charity known to have provided support to al-Qaeda fighters in Afghanistan. Al Akhtar is actually carrying on the activities of the previously designated Al Rashid Trust. The organization is also suspected of raising money for jehad in Iraq and is connected to an individual (Saud Memon) with ties to the kidnapping and murder of the *Wall Street Journal* reporter Daniel Pearl.'

The Al Akhtar Trust management claims that it was running through donations contributed by generous Muslims around the world. Besides managing Al-Akhtar Medical Centre in Karachi, the trust had established Akhtarabad Medical Camp at Spin Boldak in Afghanistan, soon after the Allied Forces attacked Afghanistan. Asked about the ongoing operations in Afghanistan, Maulana Mohammad Ibrahim, the vice president of the trust, said it was carrying out humanitarian relief work especially in such areas where the poor Afghanis are in dire need of basic necessities of life such as potable water, clothes, food and shelter.

On the other hand, the US charge sheet said the trust had been financing the Taliban fighters in Afghanistan. "As the US launched Operation Enduring Freedom on 7 October 2001, reports started pouring in about Al Akhtar Trust secretly treating wounded al-Qaeda fighters at its medical centres in Afghanistan and Pakistan. During a custodial interview in early 2003, a senior al-Qaeda detainee informed that Al Akhtar and

Al-Rashid Trusts were the primary relief agencies used by al-Qaeda to move its supplies into Kandahar."

The charge states: 'Al Akhtar Trust was providing a wide range of support to the al-Qaeda and many of the Pakistani-based jehadi groups, specifically Lashkar-e-Taiba, Lashkar-e-Jhangvi and Jaish-e-Mohammed. All the three groups have already been branded as terrorist outfits by the US. This support included providing financial and logistical assistance and arranging travel for Islamic extremists. Moreover, there are credible reports that an associate of the trust was attempting to raise funds to finance 'obligatory jehad' against the US troops in Iraq.'

However, Maulana Mohammad Mazhar, the president of Al Akhtar Trust insists that the trust is purely a welfare and charity organization and the US sanctions are based on misinformation. However, he said, 'Al Akhtar Trust does not discriminate when it comes to serving humanity. While treating injured people, we are least bothered to see to which organization or faith the patients belong to.'

The third al-Qaeda-linked banned charity active in Azad Kashmir and running its relief camps is Ummah Tameer-e-Nau (UTN) - (Reconstruction of the Muslim *Ummah*), led by the Pakistani nuclear scientist, Sultan Bashiruddin Mahmood. The purported aim of the organization, launched in 2000, was to conduct relief and development work in Afghanistan. The charity was founded by Mahmood after he left the Pakistani Atomic Energy Commission, in protest against the government's intention to sign the Comprehensive Test Ban Treaty (CTBT).

Shortly after the US Allied Forces attacked Afghanistan, the Pakistani authorities detained Mahmood and other UTN board members amid charges that their activities in Afghanistan had involved helping the al-Qaeda in its quest to acquire nuclear and biological weapons as well. On 20 December 2001, the US government, which pressed for their arrest, placed them and their organization on its list of individuals and organizations supporting terrorism. President Bush ordered the organization's assets to be frozen and also froze the assets of three key UTN directors – Sultan Bashiruddin Mahmood, Chaudhary Abdul Majeed and Sheikh Mohammed Tufail.

A fact sheet distributed by the White House at the time of the announcement alleged that the nuclear scientists had close ties to bin Laden and the Taliban. During their repeated visits to Afghanistan, they met with bin Laden, al-Qaeda leaders and Mullah Mohammad Omar to discuss the development of chemical, biological and nuclear weapons. In one meeting, a bin Laden associate indicated he had nuclear material and wanted to know how to use it to make a weapon. According to the fact sheet Sultan Bashiruddin had also provided al-Qaeda information on the infrastructure needed for a nuclear weapons programme. After the fall of the Taliban regime, it said, searches of the UTN locations in Kabul yielded documents outlining basic physics related to nuclear weapons. The UTN also had links with the Al Rashid Trust and WAFA Humanitarian Organization – an NGO with ties to al-Qaeda, which has also been designated as supporter of terrorism.

32

Waziristan Operation: Osama Still at Large

The American intelligence agencies are sure of one thing: Osama is not dead. He is hiding somewhere on the Pak-Afghan border.

The hunt for Osama bin Laden has proved a major embarrassment for the Bush administration to date. The American record on the attack on Tora Bora, Operation Anaconda and Operation Snipe is dismal. Laden himself, the al-Qaeda leadership and thousands of Arab fighters managed to escape from Tora Bora despite Allied Forces' efforts to track them down. Anaconda, employing 2,000 GIs, 2,000 Afghans, B-52s and Apache helicopters, supposedly cleared out the Chah-e-Kot valley in the Paktia province. However, most Arabs and Taliban eventually managed to escape to the east. Snipe, employing 1,000 Royal Marines, intervened in Khost and just managed to push the al-Qaeda fighters further inside the Federally Administered Tribal Areas (FATA) of Pakistan. There they blended in everywhere: in Miran Shah, South Waziristan Agency and deep in the tribal areas.

The operation to find Osama has proceeded in fits and starts since October 2003, with frequent changes of code names for the hunt. However, more hype than concrete result has been the outcome so far. Initially, the Musharraf regime deployed mainly paramilitary forces, but more and more regular troops joined later. This was partly under US pressure and partly on their own volition after the two al-Qaeda-sponsored attempts to assassinate General Musharraf in Rawalpindi in December 2003.

The tribal zone of Pakistan, which borders Afghanistan, had played an important role in turning ordinary residents of the area into hardline mujahideen when the Reagan administration in the United States hired General Zia ul Haq to fight the Soviet troops in Afghanistan in the 1980s. That was the time when the mujahideen established their headquarters and military training camps in the tribal areas which had advantages over other areas. Firstly, the tribal areas were mostly inaccessible to ordinary people and could serve as secret hideouts. Secondly, there was no easy land route available to these areas even from Afghanistan. And last but not the least, there were places in these mountainous areas where the mujahideen could remain entrenched for months and years without coming into harm's way.

The Afghan fighter groups used to bring young Afghans to be trained in these camps, only to be sent back to Afghanistan to fight a guerrilla war. The tribal zone proved an ideal place to launch the US-sponsored war on its superpower rival in Afghanistan. Defence experts believe that without this belt, it would have been a lot more difficult to carry on that war. The same camps also trained Pakistanis and Muslims from all over the world to take part in the so-called Afghan jehad. Both the North Waziristan and the South Waziristan agencies in Pakistan were preferred places of the mujahideen groups because of their dense forests. They set up their camps in the inaccessible jungles of these agencies. They also built their madrassas across the agencies. In the process, Wana and Mirali became their headquarters. With the advent of the Taliban, the mujahideen further strengthened their infrastructure in the two Waziristan agencies. Subsequently, the mujahideen of the past and the terrorists of today have developed deep roots and following among the local populations of the tribal areas. And it would take many years to undo what the once US-backed militants have done in the last quarter century.

On 15 March 2004, a few hours before a major operation was launched in the Wana area of the tribal belt against those sheltering al-Qaeda fugitives, General Pervez Musharraf addressed representatives of the tribal jirga at the Governor's House in Peshawar and claimed that the investigations into the twin suicide attempts on his life in December 2003 have turned the needle of suspicion on an absconding Libyan member of the al-Qaeda. However, he said, it was yet to be probed who ordered the Libyan activist of the al-Qaeda to carry out such an attack. 'Such elements also hired services of a Pakistani in return for Rs 1.5 million to Rs 2 million. And the master source of the network is here,' he said without directly referring to the tribal belt. The general added that 500 to 600 foreign elements were still hiding in the tribal areas, thus posing a serious threat to the future of the country.

Then, waving a copy of *Time* magazine in his hand, General Musharraf said the world was expecting practical steps from Pakistan. Elaborating, he said, the magazine contains something different, wherein harsh words are used against Pakistan. He said actions speak louder than words and emphasized that some practical steps are needed which is impossible without the support of tribal elders. 'In the wake of certain allegations against Pakistan, we need to eradicate the trend of extremism and terrorism. The allegations are: terrorism is penetrating from tribal regions of Pakistan into Afghanistan; Pakistan is also encouraging extremism and terrorism in Indian Occupied Kashmir; misuse of nuclear capabilities; and encouraging trend of militancy.'

The general then informed the tribal elders that his government was left with no other option but to take practical steps to nip the evil of terrorism in the bud. 'Otherwise Pakistan's very own survival could be endangered.' The Wana operation was subsequently launched a few hours later to smoke out the dregs of the al-Qaeda terrorists. Intelligence sources say that two closely coordinated operations were launched – one on the Afghan side by a large number of US troops aided by a small number of British and Afghan troops. The other operation began on the Pakistani side of the border with a total of 7,000-plus army troops and para-military forces.

In the first week of March 2004, without a blip in many a strategic radar screen, Commando 121, that had captured Iraqi President Saddam Hussain from Tikrit, was transferred from Iraq to the Pak-Afghan tribal belt. While there was no common military command and control system, there was definitely a common intelligence command and control. The National Security Agency (NSA), the Technical Intelligence Agency (TECHINT) of the United States, the Central Intelligence Agency (CIA) and the US Defence Intelligence Agency (DIA) led the intelligence component of the hunt.

However, the operation proved futile as none of the 'high-value targets' – either Osama or his number two, Ayman al-Zawahiri, could be captured. But it was not less than a coincidence then, that a tape-recorded message by Zawahiri surfaced on the Al-Jazeera TV station of Qatar on 25 March 2004, only a day after the Pentagon leaks claimed that they had al-Qaeda surrounded, with the Americans just waiting for some authorization to capture them. The Zawahiri tape came as a clear hint that most of the al-Qaeda leaders hiding in the tribal area had already managed to slip out of the cordon that the troops had laid in a 50 sq. km area in Azam Warsak and its surrounding villages.

The failed operation was a replay of the Tora Bora in December 2001, when US-led forces were convinced of having trapped Osama in the mountainous range of Afghanistan, only to learn that he had actually moved on long before the worst of the massive American assault on the area. The failure came despite the fact that the plan to smoke out the al-Qaeda fugitives was well thought out and straightforward: the US-led coalition forces would drive from inside Afghanistan into the last real sanctuary of the insurgents, and meet the Pakistani military driving from the opposite direction. There would then be no safe place left to hide for the Taliban and al-Qaeda remnants or presumably, for Osama and Zawahiri themselves.

The implementation of the plan had begun with the start of the operation 'Mountain Storm' around 15 March 2004. But the insurgents had a plan of their own. International media reports said that, conceived by foreign resistance fighters of Pakistani and Arab origins, it was a classic guerrilla stratagem that involved enmeshing United States' military forces and its allies in numerous local conflicts, diverting them from their real goal and dissipating their strength. As the insurgents' plan was put into effect, fierce fighting broke out in the tribal agency of the South Waziristan. The resistance fighters and their tribal sympathizers took on the Pakistani military and para-military troops in a big way and literally routed them.

No doubt, it was an anti-climax. Instead of launching its next round of military operation against Islamic militants in the South Waziristan tribal region, the Pakistan Army was compelled to change its strategy and instead make peace with tribesmen placed on top of the 'most wanted' list. On 24 April 2004, Corps Commander Peshawar Lt. Gen. Safdar Hussain traveled to Wana and decorated former Taliban commander, Nek Mohammad, while striking a peace deal with him. Interestingly, a day before the deal was struck, Director General, Inter Services Public Relations, Major General Shaukat Sultan had described Commander Nek and his companions as terrorists.

As if by magic, sworn enemies became brothers and pledged to remain friends in future. The setting for this grand reconciliation between the law enforcers and the 'terrorists' said it all. The Corps Commander and other civil and military officers publicly embraced the militants to ink the deal. The militants gave the Peshawar Corps Commander so many gifts, including Kalashinkov rifles, Waziristani daggers, prayer-mats and copies of the Holy Koran, that his bodyguards needed help to carry the load to his waiting helicopter. The atmosphere was so friendly that one could never imagine that the two sides were daggers drawn only a week ago.

The venue was a *deeni* madrassa, not very different from the hundreds of seminaries that had produced thousands of Taliban. The place was Shakai, a remote village in the mountains that had served as a hideout for the wanted tribesmen led by their 27-year-old commander Nek Mohammad. Armed fighters loyal to him ringed the place and some of the 'most wanted' men secretly carried pistols on their persons. Shakai had been the militants' choice of venue for the reconciliation agreement that was mediated by two Muttahida Majlis-e-Amal parliamentarians from the South Waziristan Agency.

While the Shakai reconciliation was widely welcomed in Pakistan, shrill voices started coming from Washington, expressing displeasure over the deal. The top commander of US forces in Afghanistan, Lt. Gen. David Barno, declared that foreign fighters in Pakistan had to be 'killed or captured' instead of being given amnesty by Islamabad. The US forces in Afghanistan crossed the border and conducted search operations in border villages. This was followed by violation of Pakistani air space. These intrusions were in fact a clear message that if Islamabad did not take action in accordance with General Barno's warning, the US was prepared to take unilateral action.

On the other hand, differences had already developed between the government and the militants over interpretation of the terms of the Shakai agreement. Subsequently, on 10 June 2004, the government ordered its security forces operating in South Waziristan to 'capture or kill' five tribal militants who had earlier been granted amnesty. A government spokesman said the amnesty has been revoked after the five militants had reneged on their word to get foreign militants under their protection registered with the authorities.

Corps Commander Peshawar Lt. Gen. Safdar Hussain had granted amnesty to Nek Mohammad, Haji Sharif, Noor Islam, Maulvi Abbas and Maulvi Abdul Aziz on 24 April 2004 in return for their pledge to remain peaceful and not to use the Pakistani soil for activities against any other country. The government claimed that it was further agreed that the foreigners harboured by the militants must be registered in order to avail themselves of the amnesty under Shakai deal. But Nek Mohammad claimed the registration of foreign militants was not part of the agreement.

At a subsequent meeting held in Islamabad and presided over by General Pervez Musharraf, he was informed that with the help of sympathetic Pashtun tribesmen in the tribal area, the fugitives have established themselves in a belt stretching from North Waziristan to South Waziristan and into Afghanistan's remote area of Shawal, a veritable no-man's land now serving as the base for Afghan resistance movement. Subsequently, besides issuing 'capture or kill' orders against Nek Mohammad and his companions, Musharraf decided to withdraw the amnesty granted to the militants.

Though Nek Mohammad was a great fighter, he was not bigger than his 'intelligence creators'. On 18 June 2004, the former Taliban commander, who was fond of talking, was giving an interview to the BBC radio on his satellite telephone when his hideout near Wana in South Waziristan was pinpointed. A precision-guided missile subsequently hit the home of Sher Zaman Ashrafkhel around 9.45 p.m. in Dhok village, four kilometres north of Wana. Nek who received serious injuries in his head, arm and leg was rushed to a hospital in Wana where he expired at 2.30 a.m.

While an Inter Services Public Relations Spokesman claimed it was a hundred percent Pakistani operation with no US involvement, eye-witnesses were quoted by national newspapers as saying that the missile which killed Nek was actually fired from a plane which flew into the Wana area from Afghanistan and went back to Afghanistan after firing the missile. Well-informed sources in the para-military forces deployed in the area say that Nek was actually killed by a missile fired from a CIA Predator plane.

For the Musharraf administration, the killing of Nek Mohammad drew the curtain. But as things stand, it appears that Nek's death has given birth to a wider insurgency in the South Waziristan Agency.

ABDULLAH MAHSUD, THE NEW HERO OF THE TRIBAL EXTREMISTS

Abdullah Mahsud, the one-legged ex-Guantanamo Bay prisoner and the 'Most Wanted' commander of the Islamic militants fighting the Pakistan Army in the country's South Waziristan region, has gradually filled the shoes of Commander Nek Mohammad to become the new hero of the tribal extremists who view with contempt the United States' occupation of Afghanistan and Iraq.

The name of the 29-year-old Abdullah Mahsud hit the headlines in the international media for having directed the October 2004 kidnapping of two Chinese engineers belonging to the Sino Hydro Company who were on their way to work at the construction site of the Gomal Zam dam. The hostage-crisis ended in bloodshed with the killing of one of the Chinese engineers in a rescue operation mounted by the US-trained Special Services Group (SSG) of the Pakistan Army. Mahsud is considered to be a battle-hardened Taliban fighter who took up arms against the Pakistan Army ever since his March 2004 return from the US-run Camp X-ray in Cuba to the South Waziristan Agency in the Federally Administered Tribal Areas of Pakistan.

Within a week of his unexplained release from the Guantanamo Bay and his arrival in Kabul along with other twenty-two Taliban militants, the black-bearded jehadi who wears prosthesis on the lower part of his left leg, made his way to his tribal homeland in South Waziristan, only to confront the Pakistani forces hunting al-Qaeda fighters out there. Mahsud, whose real name is Noor Alam, is a Pashtun by caste, the same ethnic group as the Taliban and belongs to the Mahsud tribe, which inhabits South Waziristan on the border of Afghanistan.

A band of well-trained, well-equipped and religiously motivated guards protect him round-the-clock. He has been constantly on the move since his comrade Nek Mohammad's death, calling for jehad against 'foreign invaders' in Afghanistan and against the army troops in the tribal areas.

A brother of Mahsud's is a serving Major in the Pakistan Army and four of his first cousins had retired as Army officers. As the Chinese hostage crisis deepened in October, the government sent these relatives of his in one last attempt to make him change his mind and agree to the release of the Chinese hostages. But Mahsud simply refused to entertain requests from his four close relatives and told them point-blank that he was answerable to his fighters and nobody else.

In a telephone interview with the BBC, Abdullah Mahsud said he led his fighters by example, taking risks and surviving in tough conditions. Criticizing the American policies toward the Muslims, he said the US occupation of Iraq and Afghanistan was a provocation for the followers of Islam and must be avenged. He said he never wanted to take up arms against the Pakistan Army but had to wage jehad against the government of General Musharraf, who he accused of siding with infidels by carrying out US policies in the region to protect its vested interests. 'There is no going back for me and my colleagues. We would fight America and its allies, including the Musharraf government, until the very end. When the Chinese are kidnapped they are worried, but not when their own people were being killed in South Waziristan.'

ABU FARAJ AL-LIBBI – THE BIG CATCH

The May 2005 high-profile arrest of Abu Faraj Al-Libbi, the chief operational commander of al-Qaeda, from Pakistan's Frontier province, came as a significant blow to the terror network as the captured leader is considered one of those few who could possibly know the general whereabouts of Osama bin Laden and his deputy Ayman Zawahiri. The capture has already triggered speculations that Libbi can provide crucial leads and put life back into the stalled American efforts to hunt down the fugitive al-Qaeda leader.

Abu Faraj Al-Libbi was captured from the Mardan city of the country's North Western Frontier Province (NWFP), adjacent to the mountainous Waziristan region on the Pak-Afghan border. Well-placed diplomatic sources in Islamabad say the intelligence sleuths who captured Libbi were acting on a tip from none other than the head of US Central Command, General John Abizaid. According to diplomatic sources, the American General provided some specific intelligence information to Musharraf that finally led to the capture of Abu Faraj Al-Libbi the same day.

Before that, the sources say, the Federal Bureau of Investigations (FBI) had spotted Libbi in Mardan city. Washington and Islamabad had announced rewards of five million dollars and twenty million rupees respectively as head money for information leading up to Libbi's arrest. Pakistani intelligence agencies finally captured Libbi and handed him over to the US.

While his Pakistani interrogators were most interested in acquiring details about two assassination attempts against General Pervez Musharraf in December 2003 in Rawalpindi, the US counterterrorism officials are more anxious about Libbi's possible role in a wide variety of terrorist operations in Pakistan, Afghanistan, Europe and beyond, where he had been coordinating the movement of fighters, and other logistical and planning activities.

Highly-placed Pakistani intelligence sources say it is not yet clear whether or not Libbi knows Osama's possible whereabouts or those of Zawahiri. But they do expect to glean important clues about al-Qaeda's future operations in the region.

But as things stand, there are reports that despite tough interrogation, including torture and drugs, Libbi has so far refused to divulge any vital information he is expected to have about al-Qaeda's network and plans. Such plans could include another attempt on Musharraf or a major terrorist attack in United States.

PAK-US TIFF OVER THE WAZIRISTAN OPERATION

The war on terror being waged in the tribal areas on Pakistan's north-western borders has not been without its share of controversies, charges and counter-charges. This is inevitable given the difficult nature of the military operation, the enigmatic relationship of the partners involved in fighting terror and the paradoxical stands taken by the political parties in Pakistan.

The American commander of the US-led coalition forces in Afghanistan, Lt. Gen. David Barno stated on 18 April 2005 that terrorists were infiltrating into Afghanistan from Pakistan, and Islamabad has been asked to begin a fresh operation against remnants of Taliban and al-Qaeda presently hiding in the Waziristan region of Pakistan. However, two days later, Peshawar Corps Commander Lt. Gen. Safdar Hussain was quick to dismiss Barno's claim, describing it as a highly irresponsible remark. 'Lt. Gen. David Barno should not have made that statement. It was a figment of his imagination. There is no bloody operation going on until we have the right intelligence,' Safdar added while ruling out joint military operations with the US-led coalition forces, saying, 'My strategy is to achieve the end goal without firing a shot.'

The Peshawar Corps Commander's statement was followed by Director General Inter Services Public Relations (ISPR) Maj. Gen. Shaukat Sultan's rejoinder, saying 'no such military operation is being launched, and we decide for ourselves what needs to be done and when and where.' Barno made his statement during a meeting of Tripartite Commission of the United States, Afghanistan and Pakistan that was held in Islamabad. According to Pakistani media reports, the US General said during the meeting that the remnants of Taliban and al-Qaeda are planning to stage some high visibility attack over next six to nine months that would get them back on the scoreboard after suffering major strategic defeats. 'The coming spring would therefore see a fresh operation in North Waziristan to nip their planned offensive in the bud,' Lt. Gen. Barno was quoted as saying.

Ten days later, on 28 April Lt. Gen. David Barno made yet another statement to the *New York Times* in an interview in Kabul, saying 'The Americans have been training Pakistanis in night flying and airborne assault tactics to combat foreign and local fighters in the tribal areas of Pakistan near the Afghan border.' Significantly, it was the first time the American military acknowledged the training. Barno further admitted that the presence of the American troops in Pakistan is regarded as extremely delicate, adding that he had visited the Special Services Group headquarters of the Pakistan Army at Cherat, near Peshawar, recently where he watched a display by the units trained by the Americans in their new Bell 4 helicopters.

However, the *New York Times* report quoted ISPR Director General Maj. Gen. Shaukat Sultan as saying that there were no American military trainers at Cherat and that Barno had probably been referring to joint military exercises between the two countries. He told the newspaper in a phone interview, 'The Pakistan Army has been training with many countries of the world. We have also been conducting joint military training with the US army many a time earlier. They benefit from each other's experience. They learn from each other. That's what has been happening, and nothing else.' Yet, contrary to the claims of the Pakistani Generals, the *Times* report stated that the Pakistan Army was gearing up to go into the last hideouts of al-Qaeda and foreign fighters – the tribal area of North Waziristan near the border with Afghanistan.

In all likelihood, Lt. Gen. David Barno did not shoot his mouth off. He just made public something General Safdar and his superiors did not want the Pakistani people to know. There have been many instances when the Pakistani military has kept its cooperation with the US hidden from the nation. The Pakistan Army has been fighting the invisible enemies in Waziristan without much success. Often, it gives an impression that it has failed. But whatever the truth may be the statements and counter statements by the American and the Pakistan generals clearly indicate that the trouble in the Waziristan region is far from over. Nobody knows what is actually going on in Waziristan as the military authorities have banned the entry of newsmen into the region. The only available source of information is the ISPR spokesman, whose claims are always contested by the opposition and the media in public.

As a matter of fact, Corps Commander Peshawar declared in January 2005 that the back of the terrorists had been broken and that only a few of them were now alive 'roaming around in small batches.' The Corps Commander's statement came two years after the Pakistan Army started operations in South Waziristan in January 2003. The army had to launch the operation after being alerted by the Americans to the presence of the Taliban and al-Qaeda elements in Waziristan region. The Corps Commander had further announced in January 2005 that out of the 6,000 foreign terrorists, 600 have already been captured and another 150 killed. He also admitted that during the operations, 200 Pakistan Army personnel were also killed at the hands of the terrorists. But the remnants of the militants were successful in making their way into North Waziristan.

As things stand, it appears that the operation launched in South Waziristan has, by and large, failed to achieve the two targets set by its planners: nabbing the most wanted tribesmen accused of harbouring foreign militants and eliminating, arresting or at least getting registered whatever foreign militants were in the area. Given the fact that Pakistan continues to serve as a recruitment and training ground for South Asia and beyond, concerns about Islamabad's role in the war on terrorism merits further monitoring. Even in the absence of dedicated al-Qaeda recruitment infrastructure in Pakistan, there are many reasons to remain watchful of developments within Pakistan in the war on terrorism.

33

Is General Musharraf a Liberal or a Jehadi?

General Pervez Musharraf claims to have a liberal world-view and presents himself as a vocal proponent of enlightened moderation. However, a scrutiny of the international media reports on his pre-coup military career and his post-coup internal and external policies presents an extremely conflicting and contradictory picture of Pakistan's first commando president.

In the aftermath of the 9/11 terror attacks in the US, General Musharraf effected a complete turnaround in Pakistan's Afghan policy that had actually been devised by the powerful military establishment. Musharraf publicly ditched the Taliban and instantly became a 'trusted ally' of the US in its global war against the bin Laden led al-Qaeda terrorists. However, the Western media's response to the general's U-turn on its Taliban policy was clouded with suspicion.

Pakistan's relationship with radical Islamic terrorism remains dangerously ambiguous. Historically, military leaders, including General Musharraf, openly used the Taliban and terrorist groups in Kashmir to advance Pakistan's strategic objectives. That is now supposed to have stopped. After the 9/11 terrorist attacks in the United States, Musharraf broke ties with the Taliban government and let Washington use bases on Pakistani soil to support the invasion of Afghanistan. He sent Pakistan's army into the tribal territories bordering Afghanistan, in a not tremendously successful effort to hunt down Taliban and al-Qaeda fighters. But the General still lets Taliban leaders operate and recruit elsewhere on that border.

According to those close to Musharraf, he is always conscious about projecting himself as being very liberal and modern. His critics say he is a conservative in his approach and liberal only in his attitude. His personal life to some extent bears this out. Unlike orthodox Muslims who consider dogs to be 'unclean', and therefore do not keep them as pets, Musharraf has several of them. He is quoted to have said in an interview, 'My dogs love me. And I love my dogs.' In an article in the *Washington Post*, Pamela Constable wrote:

> Musharraf's personal life is distinctive in a number of ways. He is a mohajir, one whose family migrated from India in the 1940s, in an army dominated by clannish natives of what is now Pakistan. He enjoys Western music and occasionally drinks alcohol, even in his Islamic country. He speaks precise English, his son and brother live in the US and both his parents are naturalized US citizens—all of which augurs well for his stated desire to develop friendly relations with the United States.

Many Western experts shared such a benign view during the Kargil conflict with India in 1999, and in the aftermath of Musharraf's coup that toppled the elected government of Nawaz Sharif. Most notable in their endorsement of the general were his former colleagues from the CIA–Afghan jehad days and some scholars who had visited Pakistan numerous times during the same period. Reportedly, Milton Bearden, a CIA agent from that period, defended the general before the subcommittee of the Senate Foreign Relations Committee for South Asia, reminding its members that Pervez Musharraf had trained with US troops and that he had rendered valuable service in the Afghan war. His supporters in the former Clinton administration had later ensured that President Bill Clinton visited Pakistan as long as he visited India.

However, the most prominent example of Musharraf's backers was Gen. Anthony Zinni, the former Centcom chief. In his statement to the subcommittee of the American Congress soon after Musharraf's 12 October 1999 military coup, General Zinni said: 'Musharraf may be America's last hope in Pakistan, and if he fails, the fundamentalists would get hold of the Islamic bomb.' In the aftermath of the 9/11 attacks, US officials rallied around Musharraf. The basic idea of the 'last hope' was used to plead his case when doubts were raised in the US about Musharraf's ability to deliver in the war against terror. Stephen Paul Cohen of the Brookings Institute, and author of a book on the Pakistan Army, went to the extent of comparing Musharraf to the former American President Harry Truman: 'His situation is like that of Harry Truman, a man of average abilities but placed in opportune circumstances.'

This fondness for Musharraf is reportedly shared by segments of the Pentagon and some in the British defence establishment, primarily because he has done a higher training course in the UK and at least one secret training course at Fort Bragg in the US. Western observers and diplomats continue to feel that Western goodwill is at the core of General Musharraf's great gamble. They believe he is considered a moderate leader by their governments because he is willing to deal with the West since his military takeover.

MUSHARRAF'S REAL FACE

However, four years down the road since the 9/11, the outlook on General Musharraf's liberal credential is less than that of complete optimism. A March 2005 study carried out by the Washington-based Cato Institute, a leading American think tank, said, 'the Musharraf regime is unlikely to evolve into a long-term US ally in the war against terrorsim.' The institute was set up in 1977 to advise the American congress and the administration on key issues of international importance. The Cato Institute urged the Bush administration to vigorously pursue al-Qaeda and Taliban elements inside Pakistan's territory - preferably in cooperation with the Musharraf regime - mobilize international support to contain Pakistani nuclear proliferation, hold it accountable for allowing the export of nuclear technology, and focus on India as a potential long-term military and economic partner of the United States in the region.

According to the American think tank, the US policymakers should consider an alternate interpretation of Pakistan's behaviour. 'Since 9/11, General Musharraf has been opportunistic. He responded to political and military pressure from the United States by ending his country's alliance with the Taliban and other radical Islamic groups, taking steps to liberalize his country's political and economic system, and opening the road to an accord with India over Kashmir. But there are no signs that Musharraf and his political and military allies had made a strategic choice to ally themselves with the US long-term goals in the war on terrorism by destroying the political and military infrastructure of the radical and violent anti-American Islamic groups in Pakistan,' the study said.

The Cato Institute report goes on say: 'It is highly probable that Musharraf is not strong enough to do so. From that perspective, the partnership with the United States and Musharraf's willingness to negotiate with India over Kashmir are nothing more than short-term moves aimed at winning US assistance and preventing India from emerging as Washington's main ally in the region. If this alternate interpretation is correct, the current American relationship with Pakistan is, at best, a short-term alliance of necessity. Over the medium and long term, the US policymakers should distance themselves from

Musharraf's regime, seek out ways to cultivate liberal secular reforms in Pakistan, and engage in more constructive relations with India.'

A few months later, in August 2005, yet another study carried out by the Washington-based Stratfor, a leading intelligence and analysis firm, said that despite the current alliance between Pakistan and the US, a crisis in relations is brewing just beneath the surface. The study, which primarily looked at Pakistan-America relations in the light of the war on terror and Afghanistan, said, 'cooperation at the operational and tactical levels between the two countries is nearly nonexistent and calculated interference by Pakistani intelligence and security elements is hindering the American operations in the country.'

The report defines the relationship between Presidents General Musharraf and George Bush as one of 'cautious compromise', with Washington continuing to express confidence in Musharraf and offering increased military assistance to Islamabad. The reality, says the report, is different. 'There is professional rivalry between US and Pakistani security and intelligence agencies and the Pakistani security apparatus has also shown a dismal performance in containing the al-Qaeda threat.' The report mentioned that a few months ago, the CIA Director Porter Goss spoke of some 'weak links' — referring to Pakistan — which were hindering the capture of Osama Bin Laden and stressed that they needed to be strengthened. Goss's comment was clearly echoed by US intelligence and defense officials now active in Pakistan and working with Islamabad.

Pakistani security agencies, said the Stratfor report, have an 'ingrained distrust' of US and other foreign intelligence services and Pakistani officials do not like, 'the idea of US pressure against their government, while others dislike being told how to do their jobs'. Some also think that the U S is acting arrogantly and pursuing its own interests at Pakistan's expense. The report believed that Musharraf does not have tight control over its own intelligence and security services and that the military also wants to hide its past links with the militants. In some cases, said the report, the Musharraf administration has allegedly retained connections with Islamist groups and is said to view them as strategic assets that can be used at some point, a leverage it does not want to deny itself totally.

Given these factors – coupled with the potential for ineptitude and rivalries among the Pakistani and US security and intelligence agencies – there is a crisis that has brought the search for al-Qaeda leaders in Musharraf's present day Pakistan to a virtual halt. Analysts believe this situation cannot last indefinitely – the breaking point will come either with a misstep by Musharraf that destroys the political balance he has tried to maintain within Pakistan or a decision by the Bush administration that delay, obfuscation and overt obstructionism will no longer be tolerated and it will have to move on its own. According to the Stratfor study, 'Islamabad's response to the increasing US pressure is predicated on one unanswered question: Is Musharraf lying to the United States, or is he being lied to by his own people? In other words, is he in control of the obstructionism, or is he a victim of it? We believe the reality is somewhere in the middle. Nevertheless, the outlook is troubling.'

Bibliography

Abbas, Hassan, *Pakistan's Drift into Extremism, Allah, the Army and America's war on Terror*, M. E. Sharpe, New York, 2004.

Ali, Tariq, *The Clash of Fundamentalisms: Crusades, Jihads and Modernity*, Verso, London, 2003.

Bergen, Peter L. *Holy War Inc: Inside the Secret World of Osama Bin Laden*, Simon Schuster, New York, 2001.

Coll, Steve, *Ghost Wars: The Secret History of the CIA, Afghanistan, and Bin Laden, from the Soviet Invasion to 10 September 2001*, Penguin Press, 2004.

Edwards, David B., *Before Taliban: Genealogies of the Afghan*, University of California Press, Berkeley, 2002.

Firestone, Reuven, *Jihad: The Origins of Holy War in Islam*, Oxford University Press, New York, 1999.

Harinder Baweja (ed.), *Most Wanted Profiles of Terror*, Roli Books Pvt. Ltd., New Delhi, 2002.

Henri-Lévy, Bernard, *Qui a tue Daniel Pearl?*, Melville House Publishing, Hoboken NJ, 2003.

John, Wilson, *Karachi: A Terror Capital in the Making*, Rupa, New Delhi, 2003.

Katz, Samuel M., *Jihad: Islamic Fundamentalist Terrorism*, Terrorist Dossiers, Lerner Publishing Group, Minneapolish, 2003.

King, Gilbert, *The Most Dangerous Man in the World*, Chamberlain Brothers, New York, 2004.

Lapierre, Dominique and Larry Collins, *Is New York Burning?*, Pukalani HI, Full Circle, 2004).

Lewis, Bernard, *The Crisis of Islam: Holy War and Unholy Terror,* Modern Library, New York, 2003.

Lindsey, Hal *The Everlasting Hatred: The Roots of Jihad,* Oracle House Publishing, 2002.

Napoleoni, Loretta, *Modern Jihad: Tracing the Dollars Behind the Terror Networks,* Pluto Press, London, 2003.

Posner, Gerald *Why America Slept: The Failure to Prevent 9/11,* Random House, London, 2003.

Rana, Mohammad Amir, *A to Z of Jehadi Organizations,* Mashal Books, Lahore, 2004.

Rizvi, Hasan Askari , *Military, State and Society in Pakistan,* Sang-e-Meel Publications, Lahore, 2003).

Rizvi, Hasan Askari, *The Military and Politics in Pakistan,* Sang-e-Meel Publications, Lahore, 1986.

Sageman, Marc *Understanding Terror Networks,* University of Pennsylvania Press, Philadelphia, 2004.

Schwartz, Stephen, *The Two Faces of Islam: The House of Saud From Tradition to Terror,* Doubleday, New York, 2002.

Stern, Jessica, *Terror in the Name of God: Why Religious Militants Kill,* HarperCollins Publishers/Ecco, New York, 2003.

Wiktorowicz, Quintan, *Global Jihad: Understanding September 11,* The Middle East, Sound Room Pub., Falls Church, 2003.

Index

9/11 (Sep 11 terror attacks), XIV, XV, 6, 7, 9, 13, 23, 28, 38, 42, 43, 53, 73, 83, 97, 98, 99, 103, 105, 110, 115, 123, 128, 136, 141, 145, 157, 160, 162, 163, 165, 166, 168, 169, 171, 172, 173, 182, 196, 197, 201, 204, 205, 207, 209, 215-22, 223, 224, 232, 233-41, 243-50, 252, 254, 257, 258, 262, 293, 295, 296
9/11 National Commission, XV, 247
Abassi, Zaheerul Islam, 82
Abbas, Hassan, 62, 72n, 121, 122
Abbas, Maulvi, 285
Abbasi, Abdul Khalid, 27, 33
Abdul Rehman al-Dakhil, 71
Advani, L.K., 106
Afghani, Sajjad, 77
Afghanistan, IX, X, XV, 1-5, 7, 9, 12, 16, 18, 19, 28, 30, 31, 37, 38, 42, 43, 50, 52, 53, 55, 56, 57, 58, 61, 62, 64, 72, 75, 76, 78, 79, 80, 81, 82, 92, 93, 94, 98, 99, 102, 103, 109, 114, 115, 116, 118, 119, 123, 124, 127, 128, 129, 130, 131, 136, 139, 141, 143, 148, 149, 150, 153, 154, 155, 158, 159, 160, 162, 163, 165, 168, 169, 171, 173, 174, 177-86, 188, 189, 190, 191, 192, 194-96, 198, 199, 203-10, 212, 213, 217, 218, 220, 221, 222, 224, 228, 229, 233, 235, 237-41, 243, 244, 246-52, 255-57, 262, 263, 268, 273, 274, 275, 276, 277, 279, 280, 282-91, 293, 294, 297
Ahle Hadith, XI, 61, 72, 121, 147, 150
Ahmad, Mahmood, XIV, 233-41
Ahmad, Qazi Hussain, 88, 97
Ahmed, Danish, 71
Ahmed, Fayyaz, 86
Ahmed, Hussain, 97
Ahmed, Ikhlas, 36
Ahmed, Irshad, 75
Ahmed, Israr, 104
Ahmed, Khaled, XV
Ahmed, Khalique, 12, 16
Ahmed, Mohammad, 17

Ahmed, Mufti Rashid, 41, 272, 273, 274
Ahmed, Munir, 35
Ahmed, Mushtaq, 40
Ahmed, Rashid, 18, 33
Ahmed, Samina, 146
Ahmed, Shah, 136
Ahmed, Waqar, 267
Ajmal, Muhammad, 131
Akhtar, Qari Saifullah, 16, 21, 75, 78, 82
Akhtarabad, 275
Akora Khattak, 4, 149, 181
Al-Akhtar Trust, 271, 272, 274, 275-76
Alam, Noor, 287
Alam, Saeed, 35
Al-Badr, 92, 99
Albright, Madeleine, 77
Al-Faran, 77
Algeria, 67, 76, 161, 182, 190, 194, 195, 198
Al-Hazmi, Nawaf, 220
Al-Hamaza, 92
Al-Jazeera, 205, 216, 259, 282
Alkifah Refugee Center, 272
Alliance for Restoration of Democracy, 31
Al-Midhar, Khalid, 220
Al-Qaeda, XII, XIII, 8, 11, 12, 20, 23, 26, 27, 28, 33, 37, 38, 41, 44, 45, 46, 47, 51, 65, 73, 79, 81, 97, 98, 99, 106, 131, 132, 133, 140, 149, 157-75, 177, 178, 179, 183, 186, 188, 190, 193, 196, 197, 201, 204, 205, 215, 216, 217, 218, 219, 220, 221, 222, 223, 224, 225, 226, 227, 230, 231, 232, 237-38, 243, 244, 245, 247, 248, 249, 251, 252, 254, 255, 256, 258, 259, 262, 263, 271, 273, 275, 276, 277, 279, 280, 281, 282, 283, 287, 288, 289, 290, 291, 292, 293, 294, 296, 298
Al-Rashid Trust 41, 52, 271, 272, 273, 274
Al-Sayed, Medhat Mursi, 204
Al-Shibah, Ramzi bin, 169, 172, 216, 220, 244, 245, 252
Alvi, Masood, 75
Al-zarqawi, Abu Musab, 133
Al-Zawahiri, Aiman, XIII, XVI, XVII, 28, 160-63, 169, 172, 174, 175, 191-93, 198, 201-06, 258, 259, 282, 283, 288, 289
Al-Zumar, Aboud, 202
Anjuman Sipah-e-Sahaba, 117, 119
Anti-Ahmedi agitation, 120
Armed Islamic Group of Algeria (GIA), 161
Armitage, Richard, XIV, 8, 68, 90, 236, 237, 239, 241
Arshad, Mohammad, 273, 274
Aruchi, Mosabir, 132
Asadullah, Qari, 130
Ashrafkhel, Sher Zaman, 285
Atef, Mohammad, 192, 243
Atta, Mohammad, 42, 235
Attash, Waleed bin, 165, 172, 245, 252
Azad Kashmir, 8, 12, 13, 14, 16, 34, 62, 69, 91, 92, 95, 271, 274
Azhar, Masood, XIV, 6, 16, 18, 37, 38, 40, 43, 45-54, 56-57, 76-77, 89, 125, 272, 274, 275
Azhar, Yusuf, 59
Aziz, Abdul, 285
Aziz, Prince Ahmed bin Salman bin Abdul, 224, 225
Aziz, Prince Turki al-Faisal bin Abdul, 224
Aziz, Shaukat, 9, 167, 265
Azzam, Abdullah, 64, 65, 158, 159
Babar, Naseerullah Khan, 4

INDEX

Babar, Rehan, 17
Badawi, Atiya, 19
Badini, Dawood, 132
Bajwa, Saif-ul-Rehman, 87
Balli, Kaka, 122
Baluchistan, 4, 58, 98, 135, 136, 137, 138, 139, 229
Banat-ul-Islam, 91
Bangladesh, 58, 76, 168, 193
Bangroo, Mohammad Abdullah, 93
Barno, David, 284, 289, 290, 291
Basit, Abdul, 36, 230
Basra, Riaz, 125, 128, 130, 131, 132
Bayt-ul-Ansar, 65
Bergen, Peter, 65, 299
Bhai, Usman, 74, 91
Bharatiya Janata Party (BJP), 8, 151
Bhatti, Ghulam Sarwar, 36
Bhutto, Benazir, 29, 78, 82, 137
Bhutto, Zulfiqar Ali, 2, 29, 78, 82, 137
Billah, Imtiaz Ahmed, 29
Bin laden, Osama, XIV, XV, XVIn 2, 28, 42, 43, 48, 65, 66, 73, 78, 106, 108, 109, 149, 157, 158, 159, 160, 161, 162, 163, 165, 168, 169, 173, 178, 182, 183, 187-99, 201-06, 207, 209, 211, 212, 213, 216, 218, 219, 220, 221, 224, 225, 228, 230, 234, 237, 238, 240, 241, 243, 244, 245, 246, 247, 248, 249, 250n 1, 255, 274, 277, 279, 288, 293, 297
Binori, Mohammad Yousaf, 4
Blair, Tony, 175, 221
Britain, 161, 221, 234, 260
British India, 101
Bukhari, Naeem, 17
Burke, Jason, XVI, XVII
Bush administration, 73, 79, 143, 151, 154, 165, 168, 178, 233, 234, 237, 245, 254, 279, 296, 298
Bush, George W. 53, 58, 73, 79, 157, 164, 186, 196, 197, 235, 277, 297
Butt, Kamran, 17
Central Bureau of Investigation (CBI), 55, 56, 57, 58, 59, 110, 111
Central Intelligence Agency (CIA), XVn 2, 2, 3, 32, 65, 76, 78, 154, 157, 163, 187-99, 205, 219, 223, 224, 232, 234, 237, 238, 245, 246, 250n 1, 282, 286, 294, 297
Chamberlain, Wendy, 235, 239
Chechnya, 67, 68, 102, 104, 143, 194, 220, 248, 273
China, XI, 2
Clinton, Bill, 162, 196, 197, 239, 243, 246, 295
Cohen, Paul, 295
Cold War, 1, 180, 246
Coll, Steve, XIV-XV, 245, 246, 250n
Covert Action Division, 3
Dar es Salam, 198
Dar, Abdul Majid, 86, 88, 89, 92
Dar, Ahsan, 89, 92, 93
Dar, Ghulam Rasool, 86, 87, 88
Darul Uloom, 4, 54, 149, 181
Daura Aam, 63
Daura Khaas, 63
Deobandi, XI, 54, 71, 75, 76, 103, 117, 118, 121, 136, 147-50, 181, 210
Dewal Sharif, 71
Dogar, Zafar Iqbal, 35
Dostum, Abdul Rashid, 180
Dubai, 21, 56, 82, 83, 109, 110, 111, 193, 197, 198
Durand Line, XI, 184, 185
Echelon, 256
Eritrea, 68
Escobar, Pepe, XIV, 233, 241n1
Fahd, King, 189, 224
Fai, Ghulam Nabi, 91
Farooqi, Amjad Hussain, 166
Farooqi, Ziaur Rehman, 122, 123, 124

Fatwa, 193, 210, 244, 267-69
Federal Bureau of Investigation (FBI), 27, 41, 42, 46, 50, 55, 56, 57, 58, 73, 79, 81, 96, 97-99, 103, 108, 109, 110, 132, 163, 165, 169, 172, 177, 187, 198, 205, 216, 217, 218, 222, 223, 227, 230, 231, 232, 234, 236, 243, 244, 245, 251-56, 288
Ganji, Sadiq, 123, 132
Geelani, Syed Ali Shah, 87, 95
Ghaffar, Abdul, 27
Ghailani, Ahmed Khalfan, 165, 172, 252
Gilani, Mubarak Shah, 39
Gillani, Majid Raza, 122
Gillani, Syed Ali, 92
Guantanamo Bay, 44, 286, 287
Gujjar, Nawaz, 17
Gul, Hameed, 29, 102
Gunawan, Gun Gun, 170, 222
Hafeez, Abdul, 40
Hai, Abdul, 130
Hanif, Mohammad, 17, 74
Haq, Abdul, 4
Haq, Ehsanul, 218, 241
Haq, Ejazul, 29, 146
Haq, Zia ul, IX, X, XI, XV, XVII, 1, 2, 3, 24, 28, 29, 91, 92, 116, 148, 280
Harakat-e-Inquilab-e-Islami, 209
Harkat al-Jehad al-Islami (HuJI), 12, 16, 20, 75, 76, 77, 78, 79, 82, 83, 93, 102, 103, 166, 252, 265,
Harkatul Ansar, 34, 48, 76, 77, 111, 171
Harkatul Mujahideen al-Alami, 16, 17, 73-74, 75, 79, 265
Harkatul Mujahideen, XVIn 3, 3, 6, 8, 16, 47, 48, 54, 72, 73-83, 166, 194, 252, 265
Hashmi, Makhdoom Javed, 31, 33
Hashmi, Salim, 90

Hassan-al-Turabi, 93, 189
Hayat, Ahsan Saleem, 167, 170
Hekmatyar, Gulbuddin, X, 4, 98, 180, 181
Henri-Levy, Bernard, XIII, XIV, XVI, 57, 59, 235, 241, 299
Hindu, 28, 68, 91, 104, 110, 148, 151, 265
Hisham al-Wahid, 79
Hizb-e-Islami, 4, 75, 76, 89, 92, 98, 99, 180
Hizb-e-Wahdat, 180
Hizbul Mujahideen, 5, 6, 8, 85-95
Hizbul Tehrir, 47
Hyderabad, 26, 43
Ibrahim, Dawood, 39, 105-12, 171
Ibrahim, Mohammad, 275
IC-814, 46, 57-59, 166
Imran, Muhammad, 17, 74
India, XIV, XVIn 3, 3, 5, 6, 8, 9, 26, 28, 32, 33, 34, 39, 40, 43, 45, 46, 47, 48, 49, 54, 55-59, 61, 62, 63, 65, 66, 68, 70, 72, 75, 76, 77, 85, 86, 87, 88, 90, 92, 93, 94, 95,101, 105, 106, 107, 108, 109, 110, 111, 114, 125, 147, 150, 151, 155, 166, 171, 191, 210, 236, 248, 257, 264, 281, 294, 295, 296, 297
Indonesia, 70, 102, 161, 170, 218, 222
Intelligence Bureau (IB), XVn-XVIn, XVIIn 6, 39, 236, 256
Inter Services Intelligence (ISI), X, XII, XIII, XIV, XVn, XVI, XVIIn 6, 2, 3, 4, 5, 6, 7, 8, 9, 12, 14, 29, 30, 34, 37, 38, 39, 40, 42, 43, 45, 48, 49, 50, 57, 62, 65, 66, 70, 75, 89, 92, 93, 94, 98, 102, 108, 110, 111, 113, 122, 129, 153, 178, 181, 187, 216, 218, 225, 233, 234, 235, 236, 240, 241, 244, 245, 251, 252, 256, 258, 265
International Islamic Front for Jehad

INDEX

against the US and Israel, 66, 163, 244, 252
Interpol, 45, 46, 58, 107
Interservices Public Relations Department, 25, 33, 255, 283, 285, 290
Iqbal, Shaikh, 122
Iran, 14, 54, 67, 115, 116, 118, 121, 122, 123, 124, 125, 130, 132, 148, 180, 192, 209, 249
Ishaq, Malik, 131
Islam, Noor, 285
Islam, Rafeequl, 79
Islamabad, XVI, 2, 4, 6, 7, 8, 12, 13, 17, 18, 26, 30, 31, 35, 37, 38, 40, 43, 45, 46, 50, 55, 57, 58, 59, 61, 62, 63, 64, 66, 78, 79, 80, 81, 82, 85, 86, 87, 88, 90, 91, 106, 107, 109, 110, 115, 116, 119, 124, 130, 140, 153, 164, 177, 204, 229, 230, 232, 233, 234, 238, 239, 253, 256, 258, 263, 269, 273, 274, 284, 285, 288, 289, 290, 292, 297, 298
Islami Jamiat Talaba, 29
Islamic Salvation Foundation, 158
Islamic Society of North America, 104
Israel, 41, 65, 66, 68, 155, 161, 201, 202, 248, 273
J&K Liberation Front, 5
Jabbar, Abdul, 18, 50, 51, 52
Jaish-e-Mohammad (JeM), 6, 16, 17, 18, 37, 38, 41, 45-54, 57, 70, 71, 87, 125, 156, 161, 166, 171, 252, 260, 265, 267, 274
Jamaat-e-Islami Occupied Kashmir, 92
Jamaat-e-Islami, 5, 26, 29, 87, 91, 92, 93, 94, 95, 97-99, 136, 147, 156, 167
Jamaat-ul-Dawa, 47, 48, 61, 62, 63-64, 66, 67, 68, 69, 70, 71
Jamaat-ul-Furqa, 17, 18, 47, 48, 50, 51, 54
Jamiat Ulema-e-Islam, 4, 75, 76, 117, 119, 136, 143, 181
Jamiatul Mujahideen, 89, 99
Jamiat-ul-Ansar, 48
Jamil, Muhammad, 49
Jane's Intelligence Review, 161, 173
Javed-ul-Hasan, 32
Jehad-e-Kashmir, 63
Jhangvi, Haq Nawaz, 54, 117, 119, 121, 122, 123, 124, 125, 127
Jinnah, Mohammad Ali, 113
Jundullah, 167
Kabul, 2, 4, 13, 14, 55, 56, 59, 78, 81, 82, 155, 178, 179, 180, 181, 182, 183, 184, 186, 188, 208, 211, 221, 222, 244, 248, 274, 277, 287, 290
Kakar, Abdul Wahed, 82
Kamran, 74
Kandahar, X, 4, 48, 55, 56, 57, 59, 80, 83, 181, 183, 184, 186, 192, 194, 196, 197, 204, 209, 211, 212, 213, 220, 225, 240, 274, 276
Karachi, XIII, XVIn 2, XVIn 3, 4, 15, 17, 18, 26, 27, 34, 37, 38, 39, 40, 41, 42, 43, 46, 47, 48, 53, 54, 70, 73, 74, 79, 80, 82, 97, 104, 107, 108, 109, 110, 111, 112, 128, 130, 131, 132, 149, 167, 168-72, 175n 1, 216, 218, 219, 222, 226, 243, 244, 245, 252, 254, 256, 258, 272, 274, 275
Kargil, XI, 31, 32, 67, 294
Karmal, Babrak, 178, 179
Karzai, Hamid, 177, 183, 184
Kashani, Syed Nazir Ahmad, 87
Kashmir, IX, X, XI, XV, XVIn 3, 5, 6, 7, 8, 9, 10, 12, 13, 14, 16, 18, 19, 30, 33, 34, 37, 40, 43, 46, 48, 49, 51, 52, 55, 58, 61, 62, 63, 66, 67, 68, 69, 70, 71, 72, 75, 76, 77, 85, 87, 88, 89, 90,

91, 92, 93, 94, 95, 99, 108, 114, 115, 116, 125, 138, 139, 140, 142, 149, 150, 155, 156, 162, 166, 171, 186, 191, 194, 206, 235, 240, 248, 261, 262, 263, 264, 267, 268, 271, 272, 274, 275, 293, 296
Kashmiri, Abdul Wahid, 65, 66
Kaskar, Ibrahim, 105
Katyal, Rupin, 56
Khairun Naas, 69-70
Khalifa, Muhammad Jamal, 230
Khalil, Fazlur Rahman, 6, 73, 75, 76, 77, 78, 79, 80, 81, 82
Khan, Abdul Qadeer, 206
Khan, Masood, 109
Khan, Mohammad Anwar, 15
Khan, Mohammad Aziz, 14
Khan, Muhammad Siddique, 258, 259
Khan, Zahid Ahmed, 275
Khattak, Aslam, 35
Khattak, Nasruminallah, 35
Khilafat, 3, 78
Khokhar, Riaz, 8
Khudam-ul-Islam, 17, 45, 47, 48, 49, 50, 51, 54
King, Gilbert, 108
Kiyani, Ashfaq, 12, 19
Koran, 17, 27, 54, 101, 143, 147, 148, 152, 154, 155, 192, 210, 211, 284
Kosovo, 68, 273
Laghmanai, Abdullah, 213
Lashkar-e-Jhangvi, 16, 41, 79, 116, 117, 124, 125, 127-33, 166, 171, 252, 265
Lahore, 17, 32, 40, 49, 56, 63, 64, 65, 66, 98, 117, 122, 123, 125, 128, 145, 169, 235, 254, 256, 258, 268
Lahori, Akram, 16, 17, 131, 132
Lakhvi, Zakiur Rehman, 69
Lashkar-e-Toiba, 8, 16, 47, 49, 61-72,

87, 102, 103, 106, 108, 156, 252, 264, 267
Libbi, Abu Faraj Ali, 165, 166, 167, 172, 252, 288-89
Line of Control, 45, 62, 63, 87
London, XVIn 3, 174-75, 195, 197, 215, 216, 221, 257-69
Ludhianvi, Hafiz Yusuf, 76
Mahmood, Arshad, 35
Mahmood, Bashiruddin, 276, 277
Mahsud, Abdullah, 286-88
Majeed, Abdul, 277
Majid, Tariq, 15
Makki, Abdul Rehman, 70
Maktab-al-Khidamet, 158
Malik, Mohammad Abbas, 87
Markaz Dawa Wal Irshad, 61, 64, 65, 66, 69, 106
Markaz Dawa, Muridke, 68
Markaz Yarmuk, 68
Masood, Ahmad Shah, XIV, XVIIn 5, 13, 14, 181-182, 234
Mazhar, Abdullah Shah, 50
Mazhar, Mohammad, 276
Mecca, 188, 189
Medina, 188, 189
Mekhtabal-Khadamat, 64
Memon, Saud, 107-08, 275
Miandad, Javed, 111
Middle East, 3, 109, 163, 180, 190, 194, 201, 217, 248, 273
Military Intelligence (MI), XVn, XVIIn 6, 15, 19, 20, 241
Millat-e-Islamia Pakistan, 119, 124, 136
Milli Yakjeheti Council, 123
Ministry of Promotion of Virtue and Prevention of Vice, 182
Mir, Mushaf Ali, XIII, 223, 225, 226, 228
Mohammad, Khalid Sheikh, 26, 27,

41, 97, 132, 165, 169, 171, 172, 215-22, 226, 230, 231, 232, 252
Mohammad, Nek, 283, 284, 285, 287
Mohammad, Tufail, 91, 277
Moore, Jeanne, 46, 56
Moro Islamic Liberation Front, 103
Muaskar Abu Bashir camp, 71
Muaskar-e-Aqsa, 62
Muaskar-e-Toiba, 62
Mubarak, Hosni, 160, 190, 195
Mujahid, Sakhi Dad, 213
Muller, Robert, 255
Mumbai, 26, 38, 105, 109, 110, 111
Munir, Badar, 81
Murad, Abdul Hakim, 230, 231-32
Muridke, 63, 64, 65, 67, 68, 69
Murree, 17, 18, 50, 51, 53
Musharraf, Pervez, XI, XIII-XV, 6-21, 23-26, 28-29, 31-37, 39, 43, 45, 46, 49, 51, 53, 62, 63, 66, 68, 70, 73-75, 81, 82, 85, 95, 98, 108-10, 112-16, 119, 124, 130, 132, 136, 140-46, 150, 164, 166, 167, 170, 172, 177, 178, 186, 196, 197, 205, 206, 226, 233, 235, 237, 239, 240, 241, 249, 253-57, 260, 261, 265, 269, 280, 281, 285-89, 293-98
Muslim Brotherhood, 148, 201, 219
Muslim Mujahideen, 89
Muslim Youth of North America, 104
Mutmaen, Abdul Haj, 58
Muttahida Jehad Council, 85, 88, 94
Muttahida Majlis-e-Amal, 98, 135, 140, 152, 253, 284
Muttawakil, Wakil Ahmad, 56, 57, 58
Muzaffarabad, XVI, 62, 71, 86, 91, 95
Mylorie, Laurie, 230
Naeem, Mohammad, 12, 17
Naeemi, Sarfraz, 268
Najibullah, Mohammad, 4, 179, 180, 208

Naqshbandi, Yousaf Hussain, 50
Naseeruddin, Ghazi, 86
Nasir, Javed, 102
Naveed, Rana Muhammad, 36
Nawaz, Asif, XV, XVII
Nepal, 58
New Delhi, 6, 8, 43, 46, 49, 56, 57, 63, 65, 68, 86, 87, 91, 106, 107, 116, 147, 175n 1
Newsline, 43, 104, 110, 236
Nidal, Abu, 171
Noorani, Shah Ahmed, 136
North West Frontier Province, 26, 76, 98, 111, 135, 136, 137, 138, 139, 149, 288
Northern Alliance, 12, 13, 14, 56, 80, 129, 177, 178, 180, 181, 182, 183, 205, 234, 248
Nuss, Bela, 42
Omar, Mohammad, XIV, 82, 181, 184, 187, 188, 207-13, 247, 277
Pak Afghan Defence Council, 136
Pakistan, IX-XVI, XVII, 1-14, 16, 18-20, 23-40, 42-59, 61-73, 75, 76, 78-83, 85-95, 97-99
Pakistan Army, IX, XI, 11-14, 19, 23, 24, 26, 27, 29, 30-36, 67, 72, 78, 82, 139, 150, 183, 205, 206, 226, 227, 237, 283, 286, 287, 290-92, 295
Pakistan Muslim League (Quaid-e-Azam), 49, 137
Pakistan Peoples Party, 137
Palestine, 68, 192, 267, 268
Pearl, Daniel, XIII, XVIn 3, 20, 37-44, 46, 49, 56, 57, 59n, 108, 109, 131, 132, 169, 218, 235, 236, 241, 247, 260, 272, 275
Peshawar, XVIn 3, 38, 64, 65, 158, 159, 169, 188, 189, 191, 203, 218, 219, 241, 254, 281, 283, 284, 285, 289, 290, 291

Pickering, Thomas, 197, 239
Pir Panjal regiment, 91
Pir, Abdur Rasheed, 87
Posner, XII, 222, 224-25, 228
Powell, Colin, 107, 131, 237
Powell, Nancy, 47
Punjab, 35, 39, 48, 49, 53, 63, 67, 68, 71, 82, 120, 122, 128, 129, 130, 131, 132, 137, 138, 139, 140, 149, 167, 236
Qadoos, Abdul, 96
Qadoos, Ahmed Abdul, 97, 227
Qasoori, Saifullah, 70
Qazi, Javed Ashraf, 49, 153
Quddus, Adil, 26, 27, 226, 227
Quddus, Ahmed, 26, 227
Quetta, 38, 57, 58, 80, 197, 198, 213, 220, 254
Qureshi, Rashid, 98, 239
Rabbani, Burhanuddin, 5, 181
Raheem, Jamia Fathul, 258
Raheemi, Qari Ahlullah, 258
Rahim, Abdul, 43
Rahimi, Mohammad Ali, 123
Rahman, Fazlur, 4, 6, 73, 75, 76, 77, 78, 79, 136
Rahman, Zakiur, 71
Rana, Naseem, 102
Rauf, Mufti Abdul, 51, 57, 59
Rawalpindi, 9, 11, 12, 15, 17, 18, 20, 26, 27, 41, 45, 51, 59, 78, 81, 82, 90, 94, 97, 166, 169, 172, 216, 222, 223, 226, 227, 252, 254, 280, 288
Rehman, Abdul, 70, 71
Rehman, Attaur, 17, 167
Rehman, Fazlur, 80, 81, 181
Rehman, Habibur, 117
Rehman, Mufti Munibur, 268
Rehman, Saifur, 53, 266
Rehman, Zakiur, 69
Rehman, Ziaur 122, 123

Reid, Richard, 38, 39, 171, 217
Research and Analysis Wing (RAW), 26, 33, 77
Saad-ud-Din, 91
Sadat, Anwer, 163, 202
Saeed, Ahmed Omar, XIV, 37, 39, 44, 46, 56, 170, 218, 234, 235, 260
Saeed, Hafiz Mohammad, 47, 49, 61, 62, 66, 68, 69
Saeed, Hafiz, 6, 62, 63, 64, 65, 66, 68-71
Saifi, Saifur Rehman, 53, 266
Salahuddin, Syed, 6, 85, 86, 87, 88, 89, 90, 91, 93, 94, 95, 99
Saleem, Mohammad, 40
Sarfraz, Masood, 91, 94
Sarfraz, Mohammad, 17
Saudi Arabia, XV, 2, 64, 65, 68, 75, 76, 79, 83, 91, 102, 104, 115, 118, 121, 148, 149, 158, 159, 160, 161, 163, 164, 173, 178, 179, 180, 187, 189, 190, 191, 192, 196, 203, 212, 223, 224, 225, 238, 274
Sayyaf, Abdul Rasul, 180
Shah, Ejaz Hussain, 39
Shah, Miran, 76, 279
Shah, Mohammad Yusuf, 93
Shah, Shabbir Ali, 50
Shahabuddin, Ghazi, 87
Shahid, Sajjad, 76
Shamzai, Nizamuddin, 48, 50, 170
Sharif, Haji, 285
Sharif, Nawaz, XI, 11, 32, 102, 128, 137, 294
Sharif, Shahbag, 128, 129
Sheikh, Omar, XVIn 3, 38, 39, 40, 41, 42, 43, 46, 235, 236
Shia, 113, 115-24, 127, 129, 130, 147, 190, 262, 263, 266, 269
Shuhada Foundation, 34
Sial, Amanullah Khan, 122

INDEX

Siddiqi, Muhammed Islam, 34
Siddiqui, Abdul Islam, 34-35
Sikandar, Mohammad, 77
Sindh, 20, 26, 50, 69, 131, 132, 137, 138, 166
Singh, Jaswant, 57
Sipah-e-Mohammad Pakistan, 116, 117
Sipah-e-Sahaba Pakistan, 54, 79, 116, 117, 119-25, 127, 130, 229
Snow, John, 274
Sohail, Mohammad, 80, 81
South Asian Association for Regional Cooperation, 58
Soviet Union, XV, 1, 2, 3, 4, 5, 30, 61, 65, 76, 94, 115, 116, 138, 148, 149, 153, 154, 158, 159, 178, 179, 181, 188, 189, 192, 203, 207, 209, 246, 248, 249, 250n 1, 251, 280
Special Service Group (SSG), 2, 35, 40, 286
Spider Group, 251, 252, 254
Sudan, 67, 78, 93, 160, 168, 190, 191, 194, 195, 203, 248
Suddhan, Mohammad Jameel, 12, 14
Suhail, Ameer, 35
Sultan, Hazir, 12
Sultan, Shaukat, 25, 33, 255, 283, 290
Sunni Tehrik, 76, 116
Sunni, 4, 5, 35, 54, 75, 76, 103, 106, 113, 115, 116, 117, 118, 119, 120, 121, 122, 123, 124, 127, 129, 147, 190, 221, 229, 258, 266
Tableeghi Jamaat, 29, 75, 101-04
Taj, Nadeem, 15
Taliban, X, XIV, XV, 4, 5, 13, 14, 30, 39, 47, 50, 51, 53, 54, 55, 56, 58, 59, 76, 78, 79, 80, 83, 98, 103, 106, 109, 115, 119, 124, 129, 131, 135, 136, 138, 141, 149, 150, 152, 155, 156, 164, 169, 171, 173, 177-86, 187, 188, 191, 192, 193, 194, 196, 197, 207, 208, 209, 210, 211, 212, 213, 225, 228, 229, 234, 237, 238, 239, 240, 241, 246, 247, 248, 251, 252, 254, 256, 263, 273, 274, 275, 277, 279, 280, 283, 284, 285, 286, 287, 289
Tanweer, Shehzad, 258
Tanzeem-e-Islami of Pakistan, 104
Tariq, Azam, 119, 122, 124, 125
Taxila, 17, 18, 50, 51, 53
TECHINT, 282
Tehrik-e-Jafaria Pakistan, 116, 117
Tehrik-e-Nifaz-e-Fiqh-e-Jafaria, 117, 121, 122
Tehrik-e-Nifaz-e-Shariat Mohammadi, 116
Tehrik-ul-Mujahideen, 92
Tora Bora, 183, 192, 279, 282
Turkey, 3, 161
Turkey, Abdul Hameed, 77
Turrabi, Allam Rashid, 91, 94
Ullah, Shahadat, 76
Ummah Tameer-e-Nau, 271, 276
UN Security Council, 73, 218
United Arab Emirates, 42, 58, 108
United Kingdom, 58, 67, 70, 104, 109, 156, 160, 235, 257, 258, 295
United Nations, 180, 247
United States, XIII, XIV, XV, XVIn 2, 2, 3, 6, 7, 8, 9, 10, 11, 14, 16, 17, 18, 23, 31, 32, 33, 38, 39, 40, 41, 42, 43, 44, 46, 47, 48, 49, 50, 52, 56, 64, 65, 66, 67, 70, 72, 73, 74, 77, 78, 79, 80, 81, 82, 86, 90, 97, 98, 99, 102, 103, 104, 105, 106, 107, 108, 109, 110, 123, 124, 131, 136, 138, 139, 141, 143, 144, 145, 149, 150, 151, 155, 157, 158, 159, 160, 161, 162, 163, 164, 165, 166, 168, 169, 170, 171, 172, 173, 174, 177, 178, 179, 180,

182, 183, 184, 185, 186, 187, 188, 189, 190, 193, 194, 195, 196, 197, 198, 199, 201, 202, 204, 205, 206, 207, 208, 209, 212, 213, 215, 216, 217, 218, 219, 220, 221, 222, 223, 224, 227, 228, 229, 230, 231, 232, 233, 234, 235, 236, 237, 238, 239, 240, 241, 243, 244, 245, 246, 247, 248, 249, 250, 251, 252, 253, 254, 255, 256, 257, 262, 263, 268, 271, 272, 273, 274, 275, 276, 280, 281, 282, 283, 284, 285, 286, 287, 288, 289-92, 293, 294, 295, 296, 297, 298
US Consulate, Karachi, 74, 170
US Defence Intelligence Agency, 282, 283
US State Department, 51, 52, 65, 70, 77, 90, 97, 99, 105, 131, 193, 195
US Treasury Department, 72, 106, 107, 109, 272, 274, 275
USAID, 143
USS Cole, 159, 172, 217, 245
Vajpayee, Atal Bihari, 6, 40, 85, 109, 151

WAFA Humanitarian Organization, 277
Waliullah, Maulana, 50
Wana Operation, 280, 281, 282, 283, 285, 286
World Trade Center, XVIIn 5, 97, 157, 162, 171, 182, 194, 205, 217, 218, 219, 229-32, 235, 236, 243
Yazdani, Habibur Rehman, 117
Yemen, 67, 79, 103, 159, 161, 172, 187, 189, 216, 217, 220, 245
Younis, Mohammad, 35
Yusuf, Ramzi Ahmed, 162, 169, 171, 215, 217, 218, 219, 229-232,
Zaeef, Mullah, 39
Zaheer, Allama Ehsan Elahi, 117
Zakat and Ushr Ordinance of 1979, 116, 117
Zargar, Mushtaq Ahmed, 56
Zarrin, Qari, 17
Zia Tigers, 92
Zinni, Anthony, 295
Zubaydah, XIII, XVI, 165, 168, 169, 171, 172, 173, 222-25, 228, 245, 252